STAR WARS

ROGUE ONE

THE ULTIMATE VISUAL GUIDE

STAR WARS
ROGUE ONE™
THE ULTIMATE VISUAL GUIDE

WRITTEN BY **PABLO HIDALGO** • WITH ILLUSTRATIONS BY **KEMP REMILLARD**

CONTENTS

FOREWORD

I remember what a revelation *Star Wars* was when it first arrived. Before *Star Wars*, ambitious science fiction depicting alien worlds and creatures on a large canvas also came with a need to willingly suspend disbelief. Alien planets that were obviously inside a soundstage—with a painted backdrop, obvious miniature effects, or cheap "spacey" costumes—were the norm.

Then *Star Wars* came along with wild imagination, great design, and really high-quality execution. There was really nothing else like it, and I was the perfect age for it. *Star Wars* had changed everything. It changed the whole direction of my career plans. I pursued a career in entertainment because of *Star Wars*.

In developing the story idea for what would become *Rogue One: A Star Wars Story*, it was irresistible to revisit the era of *A New Hope* for a handful of familiar locations, characters, and vehicles. Nostalgia just for nostalgia's sake is not compelling, and we knew it was important to do something new and different. We tried to strike a balance of seeing new worlds and getting to know new characters—new imagery with just enough of the familiar that *Rogue One* could flow seamlessly into *A New Hope*.

The design challenge in doing that was immense, and I gained an increased respect for just how brilliant the design work for *A New Hope* was. So many perfect choices had been made back in the day, and much of it could not be significantly improved upon.

A large team of extremely talented designers has risen to the challenge of fitting into that design legacy. I'm extremely proud of the the work they have done over the last two years. The characters, sets, ships, costumes, and environments have succeeded in honoring that previous work. In looking through the following pages, I hope you will agree.

JOHN KNOLL
Executive Producer and
Visual Effects Supervisor on
Rogue One: A Star Wars Story

INTRODUCTION

The *Star Wars* galaxy is filled with stories. Beyond the ongoing saga of the Skywalkers and the Solos, there are countless tales to be told of everyday denizens facing unspeakable challenges. In a galaxy of conflict, heroes arise every day, and their names are not always recorded by history.

Now these hitherto untold tales are finally being given their spotlight on the silver screen, with an energy that promises to invigorate cinematic *Star Wars* storytelling and expand the horizons of what is possible in a *Star Wars* movie. These are new standalone adventures with contained events. Though the characters revealed in these stories may or may not have ongoing adventures beyond this chapter of their lives, they are nonetheless worthy of documentation and celebration.

This brings us to *Rogue One: A Star Wars Story*. Up until now, the tale of how a crack team of rebel commandos was able to steal the Death Star plans, paving the way to the battle station's historic defeat, has been the stuff of legend. The story of Jyn Erso, Cassian Andor, K-2SO, Baze Malbus, Chirrut Îmwe, and Bodhi Rook can finally be told.

And this book is your guide to that story.

OVERVIEW

FOR YEARS, the Galactic Empire has ruled the galaxy with an oppressive fist, curtailing freedoms in the name of increased security. Ever since the last embers of the Clone Wars cooled, scattered resistance movements have fanned the flames of rebellion, particularly in the galaxy's unruly Outer Rim.

An alliance has been forged between these rebel cells and sympathetic senators in the insulated Core Worlds who funnel them supplies and aid. Such acts of dissent have not gone unnoticed by the Emperor, who readies his ultimate solution for ensuring the galaxy bows down to his rule: a battle station capable of destroying entire worlds. The Empire develops this superweapon far from the prying eyes of the Senate.

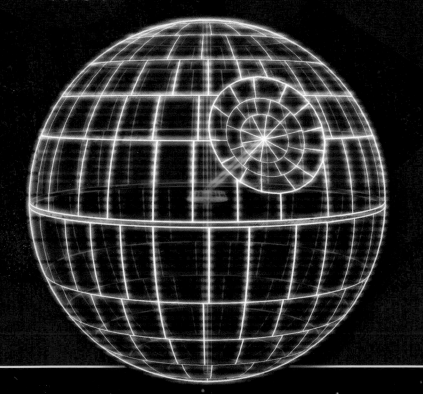

GALACTIC MAP

The territory ceded by the Separatists after their defeat in the Clone Wars spread the borders of Imperial space to limits far beyond the boundaries of the Galactic Republic. To police its expansive regions, the Empire instituted unprecedented military buildup. Much of the Imperial war machine is housed in the Outer Rim, home to the most lawless sectors and far from the Senate on Coruscant.

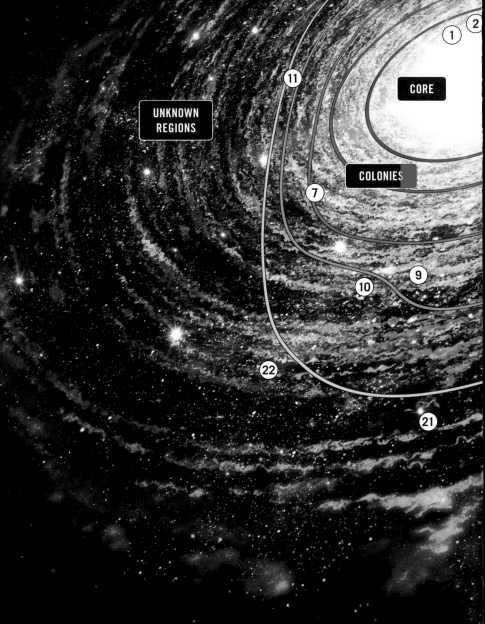

UNKNOWN REGIONS

CORE

COLONIES

COUNTDOWN TO WAR

The Empire ushered in nearly two decades of peace after the violent outburst of the Clone Wars. For a time, a beleaguered galaxy welcomed the sacrifices of freedoms in exchange for the promises of security. But gradually, more and more citizens are waking up to the truly awful nature of the New Order. Political dissent is transforming into open hostility. A period of civil war is inevitable.

BR1 = Years before Rogue One Mission

| Taxation dispute precipitates blockade of Naboo | Chancellery of Finis Valorum embroiled in scandal | A Separatist crisis escalates, threatening to split the Republic | Construction of Death Star begins over Geonosis |

30 BR1 .... **25** BR1 .... **20** BR1

| Popular Naboo Senator Palpatine elected Supreme Chancellor | Military Creation Act vote | Clone Wars erupt on Geonosis | Separatists' leadership escapes with preliminary Death Star plans |

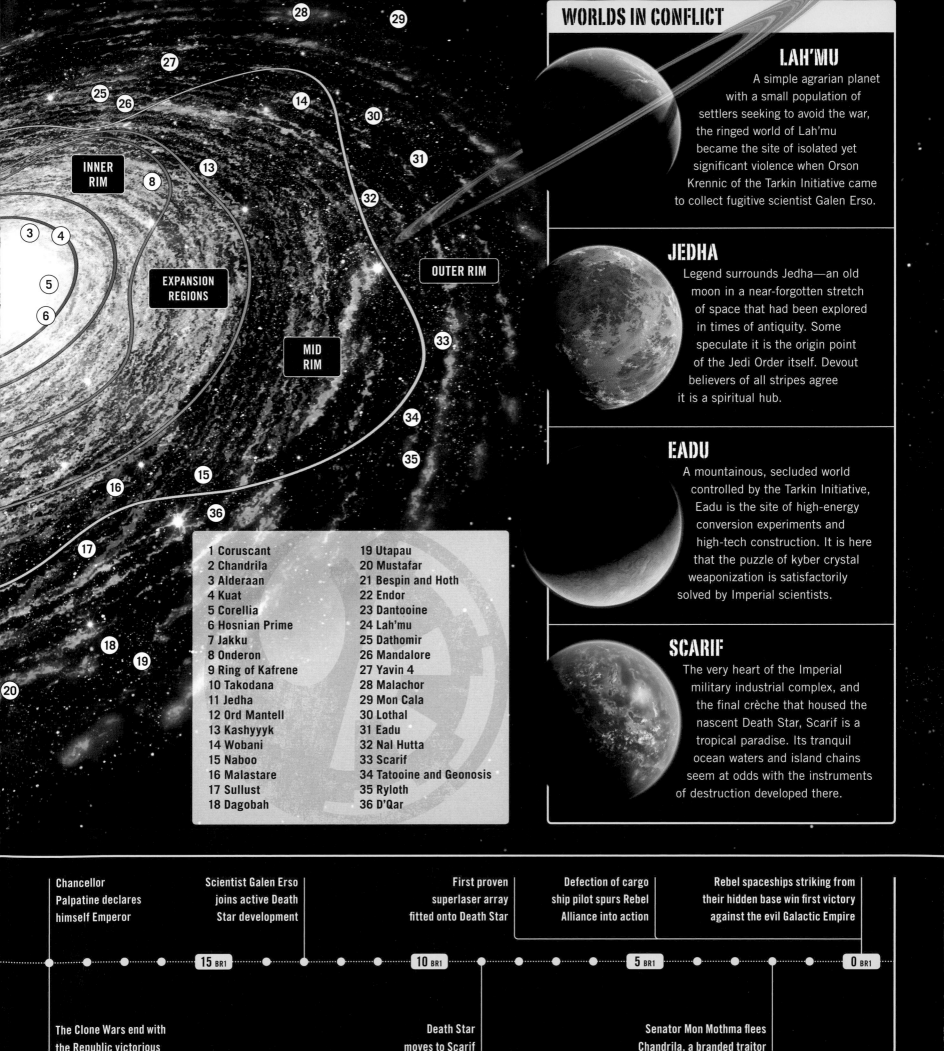

INNER RIM

EXPANSION REGIONS

MID RIM

OUTER RIM

WORLDS IN CONFLICT

LAH'MU

A simple agrarian planet with a small population of settlers seeking to avoid the war, the ringed world of Lah'mu became the site of isolated yet significant violence when Orson Krennic of the Tarkin Initiative came to collect fugitive scientist Galen Erso.

JEDHA

Legend surrounds Jedha—an old moon in a near-forgotten stretch of space that had been explored in times of antiquity. Some speculate it is the origin point of the Jedi Order itself. Devout believers of all stripes agree it is a spiritual hub.

EADU

A mountainous, secluded world controlled by the Tarkin Initiative, Eadu is the site of high-energy conversion experiments and high-tech construction. It is here that the puzzle of kyber crystal weaponization is satisfactorily solved by Imperial scientists.

SCARIF

The very heart of the Imperial military industrial complex, and the final crèche that housed the nascent Death Star, Scarif is a tropical paradise. Its tranquil ocean waters and island chains seem at odds with the instruments of destruction developed there.

1 Coruscant	19 Utapau
2 Chandrila	20 Mustafar
3 Alderaan	21 Bespin and Hoth
4 Kuat	22 Endor
5 Corellia	23 Dantooine
6 Hosnian Prime	24 Lah'mu
7 Jakku	25 Dathomir
8 Onderon	26 Mandalore
9 Ring of Kafrene	27 Yavin 4
10 Takodana	28 Malachor
11 Jedha	29 Mon Cala
12 Ord Mantell	30 Lothal
13 Kashyyyk	31 Eadu
14 Wobani	32 Nal Hutta
15 Naboo	33 Scarif
16 Malastare	34 Tatooine and Geonosis
17 Sullust	35 Ryloth
18 Dagobah	36 D'Qar

Chancellor Palpatine declares himself Emperor

Scientist Galen Erso joins active Death Star development

First proven superlaser array fitted onto Death Star

Defection of cargo ship pilot spurs Rebel Alliance into action

Rebel spaceships striking from their hidden base win first victory against the evil Galactic Empire

15 BR1   10 BR1   5 BR1   0 BR1

The Clone Wars end with the Republic victorious

Death Star moves to Scarif

Senator Mon Mothma flees Chandrila, a branded traitor

CHAPTER 1

A FRAGILE PEACE

It is six years since the end of the Clone Wars. The galaxy has healed from that conflict, embracing the promise of tranquility that comes with a strong, assured government. The banner of the Galactic Empire spreads peace and security, but some are wary of these changes. The vigilant seek escape—some for political reasons, others for reasons far more personal.

Planet's biosphere transforms iron into chlorophyll

Silica rings formed from remains of ancient pulverized moon

DATA FILE

REGION Outer Rim Territories

DIAMETER 12,618 km (7,840 miles)

TERRAIN Plateaus, mountain peaks, fertile lowlands, saline seas, black sand beaches, geysers, and volcanic areas

MOONS 1 (not including ring material)

POPULATION Not recorded; estimated less than 500

PEACEFUL SANCTUARY

LAH'MU

NAMED FROM A NEIMOIDIAN WORD meaning prosperity, Lah'mu is fertile, but its bounty is decidedly non-exotic. Its resources can be found on more accessible worlds, located closer to major hyperspace routes. As such, the planet is unremarkable to those driven by profit—making it a good place to hide. Sometime in Lah'mu's early geographic life, its crust split and split again, bringing minerals and soils to the surface, and setting it on its path to becoming a place of verdant, tranquil farmlands.

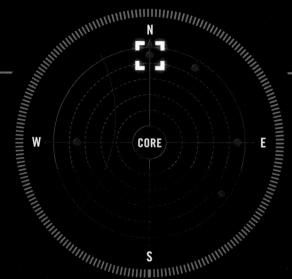

LIFE ON LAH'MU

FEW NEIGHBORS
Lah'mu is sparsely populated, with fewer than 500 settlers on the planet's western hemisphere. The Erso family did not relocate here to make friends.

SIMPLE LIVING
Scientist Galen Erso, hiding from the Empire on Lah'mu's less popular eastern side, grew crops to subsist and had no interest in outland trade.

ERSO HOMESTEAD
Consisting of 65 hectares, this homestead was purchased through several fronts, facilitated by Saw Gerrera, for the Ersos to hide on.

FILTRATION NEEDED
Tephra ejected by volcanoes during the formation of Lah'mu's rings contaminates its greenery. Lah'mu's soils need careful sifting.

Fill-status telemeter aerial

SE-2—general worker droid

Storage hopper cistern cap

PURIFICATION VAPORATORS

In worlds with minimal water, vaporators work to condense and filter moisture from the air. The Lah'mu hydrosphere is abundant, but the zinc, chlorine, iron, cobalt, nitrogen, and boron content of the soil makes the groundwater unpleasant to drink. The Ersos use hardy Pretormin Environmental GX-8 condenser units to distill water vapor from the air. The chemical content is condensed into a storage hopper, where Galen and his droids collect and reconstitute it to fill other needs.

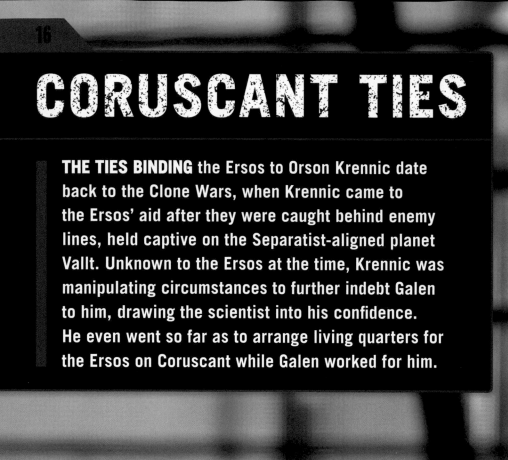

CORUSCANT TIES

THE TIES BINDING the Ersos to Orson Krennic date back to the Clone Wars, when Krennic came to the Ersos' aid after they were caught behind enemy lines, held captive on the Separatist-aligned planet Vallt. Unknown to the Ersos at the time, Krennic was manipulating circumstances to further indebt Galen to him, drawing the scientist into his confidence. He even went so far as to arrange living quarters for the Ersos on Coruscant while Galen worked for him.

YOUNG JYN ERSO

Four-year-old Jyn Erso is too young to know the intricacies of court intrigue or capital politics that pervade life on Coruscant. She is playful and content to be near her parents. Her health and happiness is what is most important to Galen.

LYRA'S MISGIVINGS

Though grateful to Krennic for their liberation from the Separatists, Lyra comes to realize that their life on Coruscant is just a different type of prison. She is eager to flee Krennic's observation, but security precautions established after the Clone Wars prohibit unapproved travel from the capital.

LYRA ERSO

MANY YEARS AGO, Lyra led a survey team on the planet Espinar that discovered and mapped an extensive cave system promising a bounty of rare crystalline deposits. She met Galen Erso and served as his guide as he led a field team that studied such minerals. Lyra was intrigued by this focused man and his obvious passion for science, and was amused by his tendency to lose himself so fully in his imagination and ruminations.

Lyra and Galen worked side by side for six months. While their expedition failed to uncover any kyber crystals—the area of Galen's expertise—it did ultimately prove fruitful in one major regard: Galen and Lyra left Espinar together and were married a year later.

Lyra moved on to live a pampered life on a secluded estate on Coruscant, while her husband Galen researched the deepest secrets of energy transformation. With Galen so intently focused on his work, it was Lyra who took notice of their Imperial benefactors and came to recognize a horrible truth: the Ersos were prisoners of the Imperial war machine, and Galen's knowledge would be transformed into destructive power beyond imagination.

Compressed sleeping roll inside canister

LYRA ERSO'S SURVIVAL BACKPACK

JYN'S KYBER PENDANT
This small stone—a fragment of kyber crystal from Galen Erso's research—caught Lyra's eye as the family fled Coruscant. She took it to be a good omen and passed it on to Jyn, who at the time didn't understand, but knew it was a gift nonetheless.

"TRUST THE FORCE."
– LYRA'S LAST WORDS TO HER DAUGHTER, JYN ERSO

BANEFUL INFLUENCE
Lyra never trusted Orson Krennic. She doubted the silver-tongued officer's words of patriotic encouragement, offered to Galen during his kyber crystal research.

SPIRITUAL CORE
Though Lyra never met a Jedi Knight, she studied their history and philosophies, even when the Galactic Empire frowned upon such research. It is not known if she ever made contact with the rumored Church of the Force movement reputed to be growing in the shadows of Coruscant, but she did at that time don the scarlet vestments of the sects native to Jedha—one of the last holy outposts of Force knowledge in the galaxy.

Having fled to secluded Lah'mu, Lyra found it hard to relax her vigil. Her family's safety remained at stake.

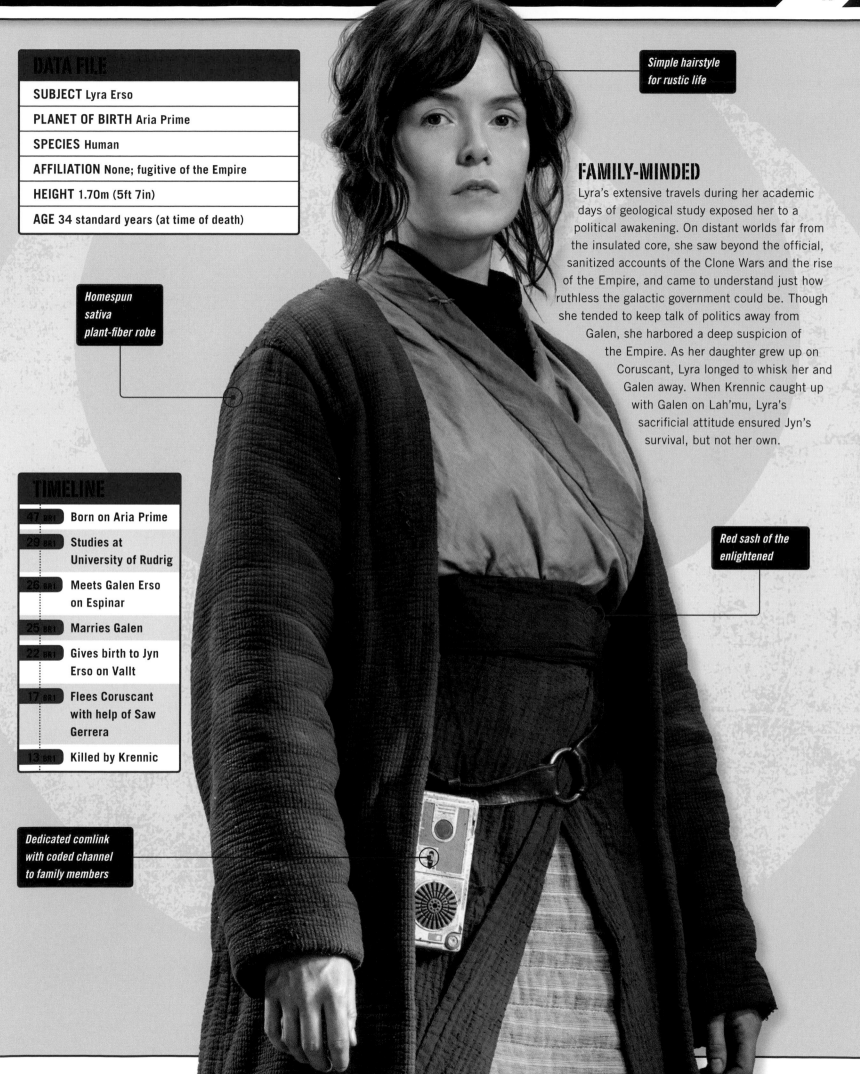

DATA FILE

SUBJECT	Lyra Erso
PLANET OF BIRTH	Aria Prime
SPECIES	Human
AFFILIATION	None; fugitive of the Empire
HEIGHT	1.70m (5ft 7in)
AGE	34 standard years (at time of death)

Simple hairstyle for rustic life

FAMILY-MINDED

Lyra's extensive travels during her academic days of geological study exposed her to a political awakening. On distant worlds far from the insulated core, she saw beyond the official, sanitized accounts of the Clone Wars and the rise of the Empire, and came to understand just how ruthless the galactic government could be. Though she tended to keep talk of politics away from Galen, she harbored a deep suspicion of the Empire. As her daughter grew up on Coruscant, Lyra longed to whisk her and Galen away. When Krennic caught up with Galen on Lah'mu, Lyra's sacrificial attitude ensured Jyn's survival, but not her own.

Homespun sativa plant-fiber robe

Red sash of the enlightened

TIMELINE

47 BR1	Born on Aria Prime
29 BR1	Studies at University of Rudrig
26 BR1	Meets Galen Erso on Espinar
25 BR1	Marries Galen
22 BR1	Gives birth to Jyn Erso on Vallt
17 BR1	Flees Coruscant with help of Saw Gerrera
13 BR1	Killed by Krennic

Dedicated comlink with coded channel to family members

*Recessed
sleeping bunk*

*Right: "Koodi," Jyn's
toy tooka doll; left:
"Stormie," toy trooper
doll (Koodi's best friend)*

*Environmental
control unit*

*Eight-year-old
Jyn packs up
her bedroom*

SERENE SANCTUM

ERSO HOMESTEAD

IN THE LAST DECADES of the Republic, the Ministry
of Economic Development encouraged citizens to
venture into the Outer Rim with incentives of land
parcels for homesteads. The mismanaged effort
fizzled, with many worlds only sparsely settled or
outright abandoned. The bust of past generations
became a boon for those like the Ersos, who sought
a world deemed to be safe but otherwise forgotten.

SUBTERRANEAN DWELLING

Most of the Erso's homestead extends beneath the soil, where shunts
plunging into geothermal vents provide power and heat. Galen built the
convertors to draw all the energy his family needs from the natural setting.

HOMESTEAD LIVING

SUPPLY TANKS
Galen Erso stores surplus energy from his geothermal tap in converted supply tanks. He keeps most for emergency use, but portions some out to power outlying moisture vaporators.

MASTER BEDROOM
Insulator drapes and chiller bars help regulate the temperature indoors and in close, stark quarters. Emergency contingencies called for personal effects to be abandoned.

FAMILY KITCHEN
The Ersos' modular kitchen features sturdy units to store dry goods and keep out vermin and insects. Home comforts go some way to offset the uncertainties of frontier living.

FAMILY BOARD GAME

GALEN ERSO'S WATER TESTING KIT AND BELT

Blissex-head duplex bit turner

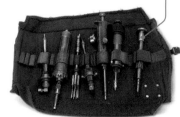

GALEN ERSO'S TOOL ROLL

Monocular photoreceptor with dual-imaging plane

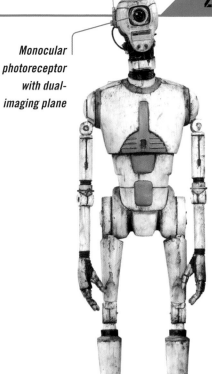

SE-2 "ESSIE" WORKER DROID
A utilitarian menial labor droid, Essie nonetheless has a very pronounced loyalty subroutine. He keeps an eye on the horizon for any intruders.

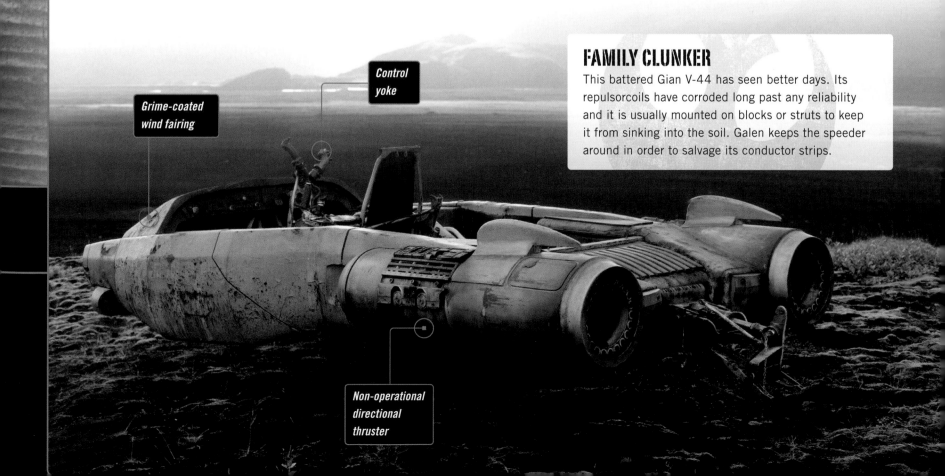

Grime-coated wind fairing

Control yoke

Non-operational directional thruster

FAMILY CLUNKER
This battered Gian V-44 has seen better days. Its repulsorcoils have corroded long past any reliability and it is usually mounted on blocks or struts to keep it from sinking into the soil. Galen keeps the speeder around in order to salvage its conductor strips.

JYN'S TOYS

THE GALAXY may be turning itself inside out with war and political upheaval, but children will always be children. Jyn Erso was born in the first year of the Clone Wars, when the Republic was wracked by the first full-scale war in a thousand years. She was spared the worst of the violence from the protective efforts of her parents, who made sure wartime shortages never affected their infant girl. As Jyn matured, her imagination grew as well. While her parents dealt with the grim adult matters of the growing Empire, young Jyn embarked upon flights of fancy fueled by a full toy box.

HOMEMADE ASTROMECH DROID

"LONGEE"

"ABOMMY THE GIG"

HOMEMADE ALDERAAN CRUISER

"STORMIE"

HOMEMADE TIE FIGHTER

HOMEMADE JEDI FIGHTER WITH HYPERSPACE RING

"OPEE OPEE"

"WUZZWORK"

"SNIKSNAK" THE SHAAK

HOMEMADE SEPARATIST
DREADNAUGHT

HOMEMADE IMPERIAL
STAR DESTROYER

"MR. IGGY"

"BAD MISTER GOOB"

"TINTA" THE
SNOW LIZARD

"STARRIE"
THE TOOKA

HOMEMADE
ARC-170 FIGHTER

"LUCKY HAZZ OBLOOBITT"

HOMEMADE JEDI CRUISER

"KOODIE" THE TOOKA

KRENNIC'S SHUTTLE

WITH ITS STARKLY GEOMETRIC hull shape and folding, batlike wings, an approaching *Delta*-class T-3c shuttle is an ominous sight. The sense of dread it inspires proves warranted when it lands and deploys its deadly passengers. The *Delta*-class did not see much use in the early days of the Empire, being outpaced in popularity by the more versatile *Lambda*-class. But Krennic's eye for bold architecture favored the design and he has kept one in active use for over a decade.

DATA FILE

MANUFACTURER Sienar Fleet Systems

MODEL *Delta*-class T-3c shuttle

AFFILIATION Galactic Empire

HEIGHT 25.1m (82ft 4in) with wings upright

LENGTH 14.39m (47ft 2in)

CREW 2, plus 15 passengers

ATMOSPHERIC SPEED 970kph (603mph)

WEAPONS 2 twin laser cannons; 3 wingtip laser cannons

TROOP CABIN
Unlike other long-range Imperial craft, Krennic's shuttle has few onboard amenities. The half-dozen death troopers typically transported as Krennic's personal guard are hardened soldiers. Simple crash seats and storage straps offer little, or no, comfort.

Forward navigational deflector grid and running lights

MULTIFUNCTIONAL WINGS
Like other vessels in the Sienar Fleet Systems and Cygnus shuttle program, the *Delta*-class features an articulated wing design. The folding lateral wings reduce the vessel's hangar and landing pad footprint when stowed, and add atmospheric stability and deflector shield transmission planes when deployed. To maintain contact with Imperial command during deep space flights, the huge wings contain HoloNet and subspace transmitter antennae, as well as power boosters. Each wingtip also features a defensive laser cannon and active sensor nodes.

Taim & Bak KX9 paired laser cannon

Starboard stabilizer foil

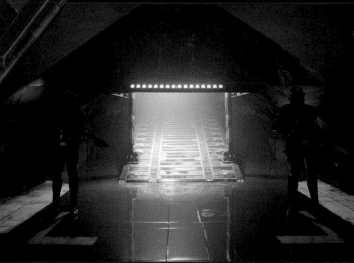

EXECUTIVE LANDING
Krennic's distinctive shuttle broadcasts security clearances that allows it entry at otherwise restricted landing ports. Krennic's pilots do not offer hailing signals, regardless of protocols or courtesy. Instead, the automated transponder passes along everything a listener would need to know: that shuttle ST 149 is on Tarkin Initiative business, with an Imperial advanced weapons director aboard.

LANDING CONFIGURATION

A quartet of landing gears deploys as the shuttle's wings fold up into stowed configuration. The central ramp hisses down, allowing access to the pyramidal primary hull. The compact shuttle has little interior space—much of its volume is taken up by fuel supply and power plant.

Sloped hull, skin composite, and engine configuration optimized for stealth operations

Central stabilizer foil

Primary sensor and communications transmission core

IMPERIAL MOMENTUM

Focused on the job at hand, Krennic and his aide, Captain Pterro, storm out of the angular craft, seemingly continuing the momentum of the ship's forward approach. A busy man on the eve of the Death Star's unveiling, Krennic is not one to dawdle.

DELTA-CLASS T-3C

ALTHOUGH THERE ARE better-appointed shuttle designs available, Director Krennic prefers the stark, unadorned simplicity of the *Delta*-class model. Sienar Fleet Systems, a longtime supplier of the Imperial military and the manufacturers of the ubiquitous TIE-series fighter, initially developed the T-3C as a side project, an exploratory canvas for its designers never intended for implementation. When Krennic saw the concept he became enamored with it, and Sienar advanced it into production.

TOUCHDOWN MODE

Republic Sienar Systems coaxed the design team from Cygnus Spaceworks to develop their Abecederian line of executive shuttles before the Empire came to power. Their output from their Mid Rim design studios shares many hallmark features—elegant lines, tri-foil symmetry, and articulated wings that fold during landing. The Cygnus design lead, Lamilla Tion, was a sculptor fascinated with paper-folding. She incorporated the variable geometry landing system into each of her designs at great expense, not only to compress each ship's docked footprint, but also as an artistic acknowledgment of her spiritual beliefs.

TALL WINGS

Imperial shuttlecraft typically maximize the space requirements of the primary hull by externalizing shield and communications systems into their sizable wing assemblies. The planar surfaces of the foils are ideal transmitters for energies related, but not limited, to hyperspatial signals, subspace radionics, and deflective mantles. The wing structures are also lined with heat dispersal systems. The ship's central computer manages these functions to prevent signal interferences.

Taim & Bak KX3 laser cannon

Multi-spectrum ranging laser

Repulsorlift field generator

Transmission quadruplexer processing bank

Radiator grill

Access ladder to troop cabin

Subspace and hypercomm antenna array

Service markings

Deflector shield generator

Aft deflector shield generator

SFS-215 ion engine thruster

Formation light

Landing strut (deployed)

Deflector shield generator

Flight deck access door

Diagnostics bay and refueling inlet

Lateral deflector shield transmission plane

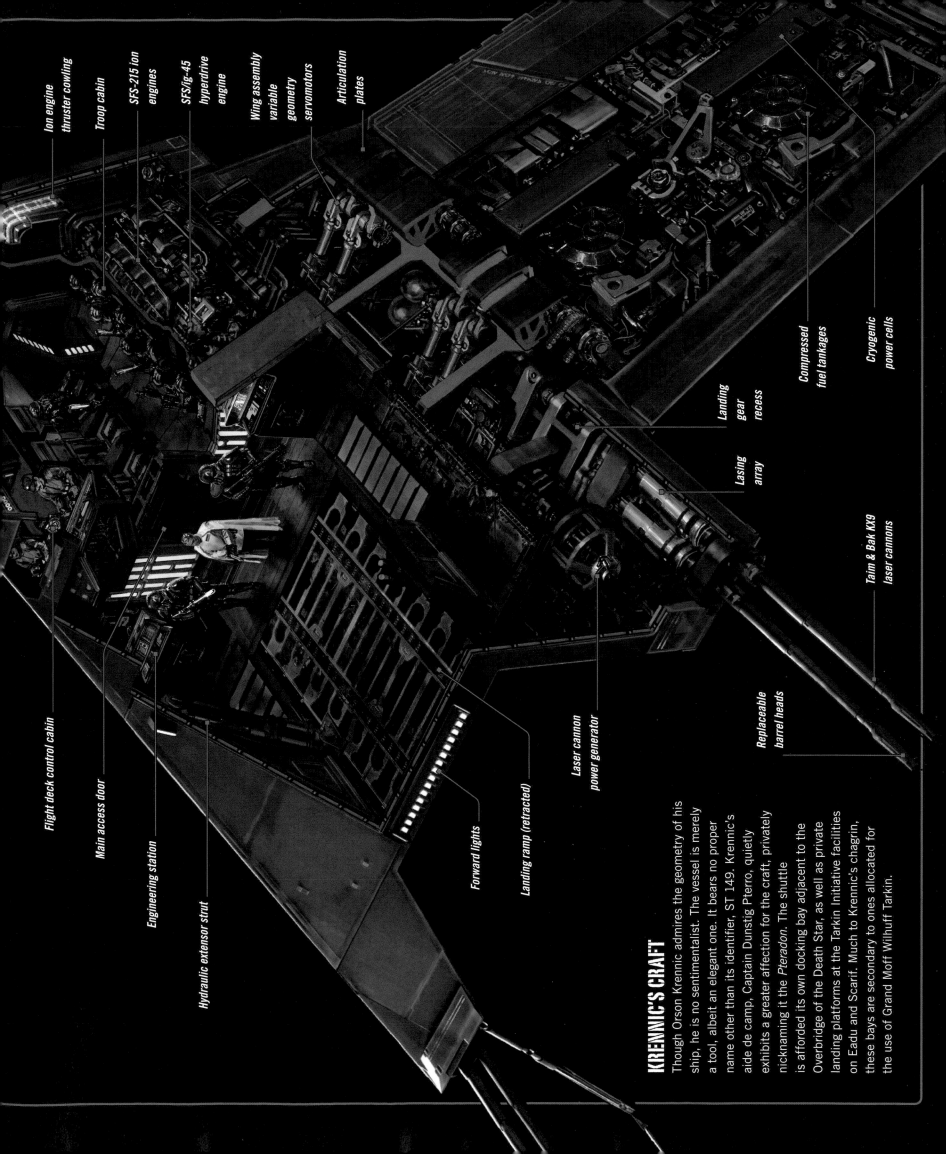

Ion engine
thruster cowling

Troop cabin

SFS-215 ion
engines

SFS/Ig-45
hyperdrive
engine

Wing assembly
variable
geometry
servomotors

Articulation
plates

Compressed
fuel tankages

Cryogenic
power cells

Landing
gear
recess

Lasing
array

Flight deck control cabin

Main access door

Engineering station

Hydraulic extensor strut

Forward lights

Landing ramp (retracted)

Laser cannon
power generator

Replaceable
barrel heads

Taim & Bak KX9
laser cannons

KRENNIC'S CRAFT

Though Orson Krennic admires the geometry of his
ship, he is no sentimentalist. The vessel is merely
a tool, albeit an elegant one. It bears no proper
name other than its identifier, ST 149. Krennic's
aide de camp, Captain Dunstig Pterro, quietly
exhibits a greater affection for the craft, privately
nicknaming it the *Pteradon*. The shuttle
is afforded its own docking bay adjacent to the
Overbridge of the Death Star, as well as private
landing platforms at the Tarkin Initiative facilities
on Eadu and Scarif. Much to Krennic's chagrin,
these bays are secondary to ones allocated for
the use of Grand Moff Wilhuff Tarkin.

DEATH TROOPERS

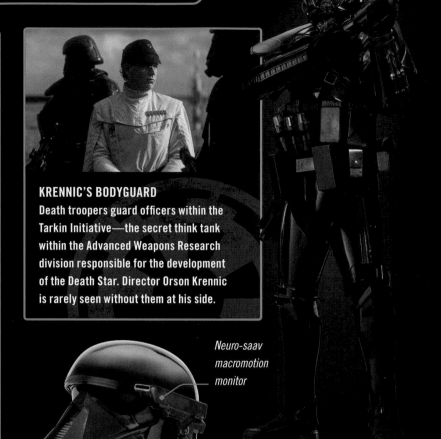

ENCASED IN SPECIALIZED stormtrooper armor that shines with an ominous gleam, the death troopers comprise an elite unit created to defend the most important operations and operatives within the Imperial military hierarchy. Recruited by Imperial Intelligence, these troopers form protection squadrons of bodyguards and enforcers for the leadership of the Tarkin Initiative and key fleet officials.

KRENNIC'S BODYGUARD
Death troopers guard officers within the Tarkin Initiative—the secret think tank within the Advanced Weapons Research division responsible for the development of the Death Star. Director Orson Krennic is rarely seen without them at his side.

Early on in his rule, the Emperor demonstrated a keen grasp of the importance of symbols—recasting ancient icons of strength and unity from the Republic and other cultures in a new and powerful Imperial light. As such, the name of the death trooper stems from a rumored project from the Advanced Weapons Research division, designed to animate necrotic flesh. Though the troopers do not appear to be derived from this scheme, the use of the name gives them a macabre reputation among the Imperial ranks. Their black armor makes their appearance all the more deathly.

Death troopers usually operate in small groups, exhibiting a great degree of cross-training and skill specialization.

Neuro-saav macromotion monitor

SENSORY SYSTEMS
Death trooper gear is an improvement on mass-produced stormtrooper kit. More sophisticated sensing apparatus keeps troopers in total situational awareness of combat arenas, allies, and enemies.

DRESSED TO KILL
Death trooper armor has a base of plastoid coated with a newly developed spray polymer called reflec, which warps the most common electromagnetic signals used in passive sensor arrays. This makes troopers harder to detect and well suited for stealth operations.

"IT'S THE TROOPER YOU DON'T SEE THAT WILL GET YOU."
— CASSIAN ANDOR

BLASTECH E-11D

Large-bore reinforced barrel

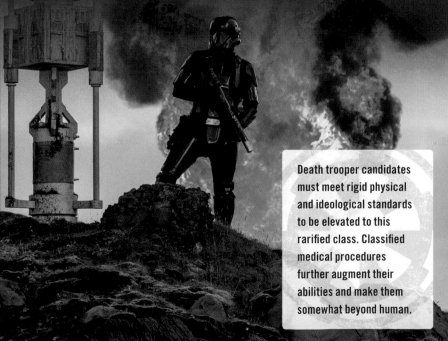

Death trooper candidates must meet rigid physical and ideological standards to be elevated to this rarified class. Classified medical procedures further augment their abilities and make them somewhat beyond human.

SCARIF DEFENSE
During the incursion of the Scarif Citadel, Krennic orders a contingent of his personal guard to clear the beach. The arrival of the elite death troopers on a specialized carrier craft escalates the intensity of the battle.

Integrated multi-frequency targeting and acquisition sensor system

THE BEST OF THE BEST

Select candidates that excel at stormtrooper training are reassigned to an advanced death trooper training camp on Scarif. Death trooper physical requirements include height and weight standards that exceed typical trooper averages. Rigorous training in exotic environs produces stronger, faster, and more resilient soldiers than the norm.

Image-intensifying active pulse emitters

IM-40 three-slot ammunition and tool pouch.

Featureless pauldron denotes specialist status when seen through trooper visor

MERR-SONN MUNITIONS FRAGMENTATION GRENADE
The C-25 fragmentation grenade consists of a sphere of baradium-impregnated detonite encased in a conductive shell. The shell itself is housed within a cylinder—activated with a twist.

Environmentally sealed bodysuit

BlasTech SE-14r light repeating blaster pistol

Compressed baradium thermal detonator

DATA FILE

SUBJECT DT-5537

HOMEWORLD Classified

SPECIES Human (with classified augmentations)

AFFILIATION Imperial Advance Weapon Development; Unit TI-23 "The Undying"

HEIGHT 1.96m (6ft 5in)

PROFICIENCIES Demolitions, improvised weaponry, guerilla tactics

PEACE DISRUPTED

THE TRANQUILITY of life on Lah'mu was not to last. Not even a brilliant man like Galen Erso can outrun a past tainted by the monstrous dreams of Orson Krennic. For years, Krennic has stood at the brink of success as his Death Star creeps ever closer to completion. However, the vital kyber crystal energy transformation sequence cannot be cracked by a lesser mind than Galen Erso's. Krennic needs the fugitive scientist and will not take no for an answer.

JYN'S HIDEOUT

At first sight of Krennic's approaching shuttle, Galen and Lyra urge young Jyn to hide. It is a well-practiced drill—Jyn is to run down the black gulch beyond the homestead's edge, into a cave where a well-disguised hatch rests beneath an artificial rock. In this shelter, she is to await help—help summoned by Lyra.

FORMER COLLEAGUES REUNITED

Krennic extends an invitation to Galen and his entire family—to return with him to Coruscant where they can continue the work they started. Krennic promises the Ersos glorious roles as heroes of the Empire, for he envisions the triumphant transformation of the galaxy through the realization of the Death Star. Galen refuses, but is made to return anyway, at great personal cost.

CHAPTER 2

REBEL ALLIANCE

A tempestuous union of star systems has declared itself opposed to Emperor Palpatine's New Order. This fragile Alliance has begun the great fight to restore the Galactic Republic, through whatever channels necessary. Outnumbered and not always aligned, these idealists need to come together in the growing darkness to cast a light of hope across the galaxy.

JYN ERSO

LIANA HALLIK. TANITH PONTA. KESTREL DAWN.
A cloud of aliases surrounds Jyn Erso, to the extent that hearing her true name for the first time in years gives her pause. She has spent half her life burying a past of grief and abandonment, paving it over with a steely resilience and recklessness. She has little purpose other than surviving. Doing so often puts the Empire on the receiving end of her violence, but her attacks are not political.

Alliance Intelligence has pieced together a hazy picture of Jyn's past, including a tenuous connection to Galen Erso, a renowned scientist who vanished under mysterious circumstances. When reports linking Galen to a secret Imperial weapons development program surface, the rebels launch a mission to recover Jyn from imprisonment in an Imperial labor camp on the planet Wobani. For Jyn, it's the swapping of one prison cell for another. She cares not for the cause of the Rebel Alliance, and being briefed by their command while still in binders does little to sway her. Until, that is, she hears about her father, a man she had decided had died years ago.

Life on the planet Lah'mu was simpler. Right and wrong were clearly defined under the guidance of Jyn's mother, Lyra.

CAUGHT UP IN CONFLICT
Jyn's icy attitude melts away upon witnessing the unthinkable plans of the Empire. She entreats the Alliance leadership for support but is met with frustrating skepticism and maddening indecision.

Cold weather survival gear features waterproof insulation

FROM REFUGEE TO SOLDIER
Born at the start of the Clone Wars, Jyn spent her early years on the move with her parents, Lyra and Galen, dodging galactic conflict. Her father's enlistment in Imperial scientific research transplanted the whole family to Coruscant, but his crisis of conscience led them to flee Imperial attention—an exit facilitated by Saw Gerrera. It was Saw who rescued Jyn when she was seemingly orphaned on rural Lah'mu, and she became a child soldier in his private war against the Empire.

"I'VE NEVER HAD THE LUXURY OF POLITICAL OPINIONS."
— JYN ERSO

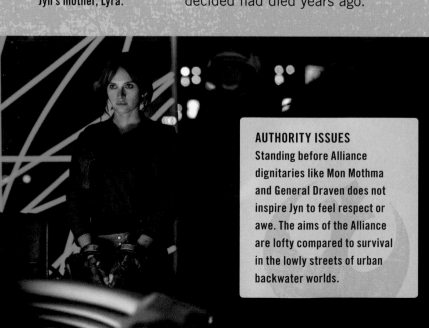

AUTHORITY ISSUES
Standing before Alliance dignitaries like Mon Mothma and General Draven does not inspire Jyn to feel respect or awe. The aims of the Alliance are lofty compared to survival in the lowly streets of urban backwater worlds.

REBEL ALLIANCE'S REPORT ON JYN ERSO

FENDING FOR HERSELF
Jyn Erso's time with Saw Gerrera's rebels taught her a range of survival skills. She became a tough hand-to-hand combatant, excelling with improvised weapons and favoring paired sturdy truncheons—effective even against stormtroopers.

DATA FILE

SUBJECT Jyn Erso

PLANET OF BIRTH Vallt

SPECIES Human

AFFILIATION Formerly part of Saw Gerrera's insurgents

HEIGHT 1.60m (5ft 3in)

AGE 21 standard years

HAND COMLINK
Jyn carries a battered but functional Crozo 2-MAL personal comlink—a cheap, simple, and effective communications device commonly used by the rebels.

SAW'S STUDENT

From the ages of eight to sixteen, Jyn remained a soldier in Saw Gerrera's roving band of insurgents—a group of rebels originating on Onderon who fought so dirty that their actions were disowned by the core Rebel Alliance leadership. Jyn found connection with the hardened warriors, but after a crippling setback suffered by the group, Saw abandoned Jyn, leaving the teenager on her own once again. These losses have left her with little capacity to trust anybody.

STOLEN BLASTER
Stripped of weaponry when imprisoned, resourceful Jyn wastes no time in lifting an unattended BlasTech A-180 to equip herself for the mission that lies ahead.

Simple style emphasizes utility

TIMELINE

22 BR1 Born on Vallt

19 BR1 Erso family move to Coruscant

17 BR1 Erso family escape to Lah'mu

13 BR1 Jyn rescued by Saw Gerrera

5 BR1 Jyn on her own: abandoned by Saw

0 BR1 Jyn freed from Wobani by rebels

Insulated mechanic's vest

Nondescript worker's tunic

CRIMES AGAINST THE EMPIRE

CLASS ONE INFRACTION
Aggravated assault against Imperial military personnel; escape from custody.

CLASS TWO INFRACTION
Possession of unsanctioned weapons; forgery of Imperial documents; resisting arrest.

JYN'S MISSION

THE RESURFACING OF GALEN ERSO'S NAME in connection to Imperial weapons development has sent Rebel Alliance Intelligence scrambling. An Imperial defector seeking out Saw Gerrera spoke of a "planet-killer" developed by Erso. Jyn is the thread connecting these fragments of alarming information. Though the Alliance leadership knows of Saw's whereabouts, relations between Mon Mothma's faction and Gerrera have been irreparably damaged by Saw's violent tactics. The Alliance looks to Jyn to help reach Saw.

PRISON TRANSFER

Jyn Erso's last brush with Imperial authorities landed her in a prison labor camp on the harsh, stony world of Wobani. A rebel SpecForce interception team ambushed a lone HCVw A9 turbo tank transporting a hold of prisoners to a work detail. Unshackled by Alliance Sergeant Ruescott Melshi, Jyn immediately bolted for freedom, to be finally stopped and taken into Alliance custody by the droid K-2SO.

DRAVEN'S DETERMINATION

As the leading Intelligence officer on Yavin 4, General Draven is responsible for piecing together the puzzle of Galen Erso. He fully believes the Empire capable of devising an unthinkable superweapon, and knows that now is not the time for hesitation. He grows impatient with Jyn Erso's impudence but trusts Cassian Andor to keep her in line and proceed with the mission—dubbed Operation Fracture by Draven—to find Galen Erso.

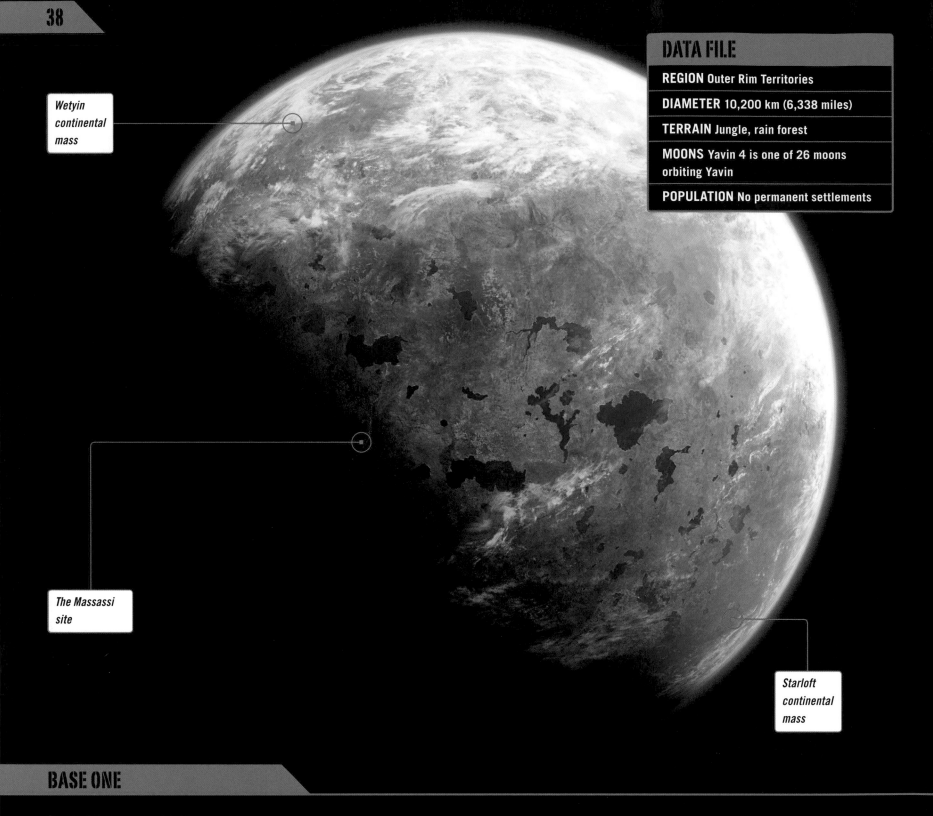

Wetyin continental mass

The Massassi site

Starloft continental mass

DATA FILE

REGION Outer Rim Territories

DIAMETER 10,200 km (6,338 miles)

TERRAIN Jungle, rain forest

MOONS Yavin 4 is one of 26 moons orbiting Yavin

POPULATION No permanent settlements

BASE ONE

YAVIN 4

AFTER REBEL ALLIANCE HIGH COMMAND abandoned its older base on Dantooine, it chose a jungle moon devoid of intelligent life for its next headquarters. Huge, crumbling edifices serve as evidence of past civilization. The Massassi site, a clustering of megalithic temples, houses the rebels under Mon Mothma, Bail Organa, and Jan Dodonna's command. It is from Yavin 4 that the rebels launch an assault that results in its first victory against the Empire in the Galactic Civil War.

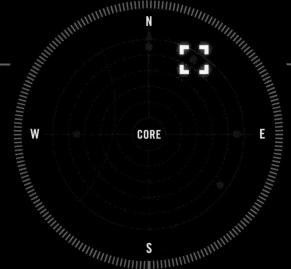

THE GREAT TEMPLE

The enormous Great Temple, the largest of the monuments in the Massassi site, houses the rebel base. Its sprawling interior has been transformed into a launch bay for the rebels' fleet of X-, Y-, and U-wing starfighters. Utility cables, plumbing, internal lighting, and other technology is roughly fastened in place to turn the ancient edifice into a workable—yet temporary—outpost.

Incom T-65 X-wing fighter receives technical attention

Rebel astromech droid R2-BHD on hand to assist in repair work

Rebel technician tests the weight distribution on landing gear

REBEL HEADQUARTERS

SQUADRON BASE
Active and reserve pilots from Gold, Blue, Green, and Red Squadron comprise the majority of the personnel at the Massassi outpost.

READY TO LAUNCH
The enormous entrance of the Great Temple allows for easy egress of starfighters from the deeper maintenance areas.

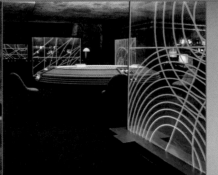

COMMAND CENTER
Banks of tactical and communications systems fill Base One's command center. From here, officers monitor and direct distant missions.

SENTRY POST
Most of Yavin 4 remains unexplored. Lonely rebel sentries on top of watchtowers keep vigil for any approaching dangers.

MON MOTHMA

MON MOTHMA was born into political life. Her father was an arbiter-general in the Galactic Republic, and her mother was a governor on their native Chandrila. When she was old enough, Mothma joined the Galactic Senate, becoming one of the youngest senators in the council to date. Her political ascendency accompanied the most trying times for the Republic—a Separatist crisis precipitating the outbreak of the Clone Wars.

VISION OF HOPE
Senators Mothma and Organa found ways to use the Senate to surreptitiously supply the burgeoning Rebellion. They had to tread carefully as the Senate was rife with spies from the Imperial Security Bureau. If discovered, their actions would lead to accusations of treason.

During the Clone Wars, Senator Mothma grew concerned with the amount of unchecked executive power Palpatine was accruing.

Mothma was a loyalist, adhering to the ideals of the Republic. But as the Clone Wars continued, she and other like-minded senators wondered what had become of the state.

To better manage the war effort, the Senate granted Supreme Chancellor Palpatine sweeping executive powers "for the remainder of the emergency." With this newfound authority, Palpatine sidelined many voices in the Senate. Conscientious politicians such as Bail Organa, Mon Mothma, and Padmé Amidala began to meet in private, to discuss ways to counter Palpatine's executive excesses within the framework of the Senate. When conversations turned to solutions outside of the Senate, the seeds of rebellion were planted.

"WE NEED TO STOP THIS WEAPON BEFORE IT'S FINISHED."
— MON MOTHMA, TO JYN ERSO

Mon Mothma directly recruits Jyn Erso to contact Saw Gerrera in the hope that the Rebellion can bring his evidence of Imperial superweapon development to the Senate.

GALAXY'S MOST WANTED
After escalating outrages committed by the Imperial military left her no choice, Mon Mothma spoke out publicly and directly addressed Emperor Palpatine as a "lying executioner" in a widely broadcast HoloNet proclamation. Such treason immediately rocketed Mothma to the top of the Empire's "Most Wanted" list, and she fled Coruscant—resigning her seat in the Imperial Senate. It was this declaration of rebellion that gave rise to the formal Alliance to Restore the Republic.

Senators Mothma and Bail Organa organized meetings at Cantham House on Bail's Coruscant estate to discuss the future structure of a rebellion.

SENATOR IN EXILE

As the Rebellion is both a political movement and a paramilitary force, Mon Mothma fills command roles in both capacities. She is the head of the Alliance Civil Government, with the title Chief of State. Well aware of the dangers of unchecked political power, she must act in accord with the rebel council leadership. Militarily, Mon Mothma is Commander-in-Chief of the Alliance Forces, encompassing ground troops, starfighter corps, and the Alliance fleet. Mothma prefers the title "senator," even though she is no longer part of that body.

Short Naylian-style haircut

DATA FILE

SUBJECT Mon Mothma

PLANET OF BIRTH Chandrila

SPECIES Human

AFFILIATION Leader of the Rebel Alliance

HEIGHT 1.73m (5ft 8in)

AGE 46 standard years

Draped fibercord livery collar

Chandrilan medal of freedom

Simple robe of office

ADMIRAL RADDUS

A DOUR AND GRUFF Mon Calamari of dark complexion and stern countenance, Raddus has the unenviable task of staring down the might of the Imperial Starfleet and not blinking. Raddus is in command of the fledgling Alliance fleet, an asset Mon Mothma has described as the most vital component of the growing rebel military. The rebel council predicts that if there is to be a decisive victory against the Empire, it will be won by warships in space.

As befits a hodgepodge organization like the Rebel Alliance, its fleet consists of a motley assortment of ships—Hammerhead corvettes, Dornean gunships, Alderaanian cruisers, and Gallofree resupply transports. However, in the remote Telaris star system, this fleet is in the process of acquiring a new and mighty spine. The Imperial occupation of the Mon Cala ocean-covered world triggered a massive exodus of Mon Calamari vessels. Enormous city-ships disappeared into hyperspace and are now being converted for war by rebels in deep-space facilities far from Imperial naval patrols. Raddus' flagship, the *Profundity*, is one of the first war-converted cruisers ready for combat.

MON CALAMARI ASSISTANCE
Raddus is well attended by a support staff of Mon Calamari aides—Caitken and Shollan—who snap to his orders with bustling efficiency.

MON CALA OF ACTION

Raddus is pragmatic—an outlook developed in the dark and cold depths of his home ocean. He leaves it to others to wax lyrical about freedom, justice, and other matters of philosophy that drive the Alliance to action. He is especially impatient with the dithering of the rebel council and considers any attempt at negotiation with the Empire to be a fool's dream.

"I SAY WE FIGHT!"
— ADMIRAL RADDUS

Raddus does not often set foot at the base on Yavin 4, as he is stationed with the ever-mobile fleet. Matters of major import to the rebel council, however, require his occasional presence.

STARFIGHTER SUPPORT
Although the Rebellion has primarily focused its resources on powerful starfighters, its capital warship fleet demands attention. Once ready, these carrier craft will bring fighters into action, increasing their operational range and reducing the risk of bases such as Yavin 4 being discovered.

Dense flesh acts as insulator to protect ocular circulation

FROM THE DEPTHS

Raddus and his school of Mon Calamari fleet officers hail from the depths of the colder polar regions of his watery homeworld. Theirs is a hardy breed whose blood is said to run thicker than that of their more colorful neighbors from the tropics. This is a reputation Raddus is only too happy to let spread—he is not one to pepper interactions with social pleasantries—for the Empire has made the grave error of underestimating the Mon Calamari and it would not do to have those on the rebel council repeat the same mistake.

Fleet flagship service uniform jerkin

Chromatosphoric skin aids camouflage

Sealed and coded datapad with mission orders

Civic crest marks past role in planetary defense

DATA FILE

SUBJECT Raddus

PLANET OF BIRTH Mon Cala

SPECIES Mon Calamari

STATUS Admiral of the Rebel Alliance Fleet

HEIGHT 1.90m (6ft 3in)

AGE 65 standard years

GENERAL DRAVEN

IT FALLS TO DAVITS DRAVEN to represent Alliance Intelligence on the rebel council and at the Yavin base, as General Airen Cracken is busy setting up spy networks in the Outer Rim. A veteran of the Clone Wars as well as a trusted field operative trained by Cracken, Draven has earned Mon Mothma's respect, though at times she finds him difficult. No-nonsense Draven has little doubt of the Empire's cruelty and the need to act now to counter it.

During the Clone Wars, Draven served in the Republic's military intelligence. Though he had no exposure to the Jedi generals in command of the clone army, he routinely worked with strategists, fleet commanders, and other high-ranking officers who would go on to form the core of the emergent Imperial military. This experience fuels Draven's authoritative views on Imperial psychology: he knows the men and women who built the military as well as the lengths they will go to ensure the Empire's dominance.

When Draven joined the Rebellion, it was with an urgent drive to stop the Empire before it became too powerful. Draven now feels that the rebels have squandered one too many opportunities to strike.

STRAINED TEAMWORK
General Merrick worries that Draven is too pragmatic and thus likely to forget the human variables when making his cold calculations. As an Intelligence chief, Draven does command a staff, but those who report directly to him are normally lone operators. In contrast, Merrick's squadrons of pilots commit themselves to cooperation and unit cohesion.

"THERE WILL BE NO EXTRACTION. YOU FIND HIM? YOU KILL HIM... THOSE ARE YOUR ORDERS."
– GENERAL DRAVEN TO CAPTAIN CASSIAN ANDOR

SILENT WARRIOR
In this era before open warfare, the Rebellion relies on surgical strikes that remain largely unseen. Sabotage, thefts, and assassinations yield unglamorous victories denied by both the rebels and the Empire. Draven knows the necessity of such missions and does not carry them out for recognition or praise but because he knows that he is capable.

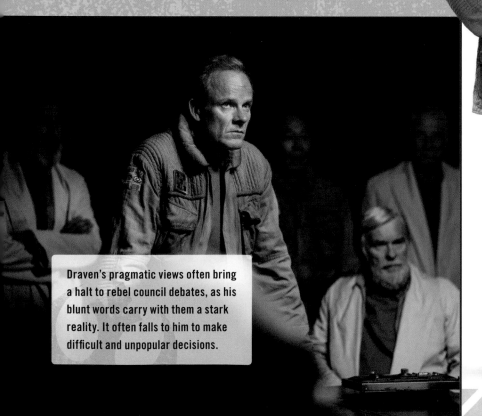

Draven's pragmatic views often bring a halt to rebel council debates, as his blunt words carry with them a stark reality. It often falls to him to make difficult and unpopular decisions.

DISASTROUS DISPATCH
Worried about Erso's destructive genius, Draven dispatches a squadron of starfighters to assassinate him on Eadu. Draven tries to recall the fighters when it is evident this puts at risk the rebel squad carrying out Operation Fracture, but by then it is too late.

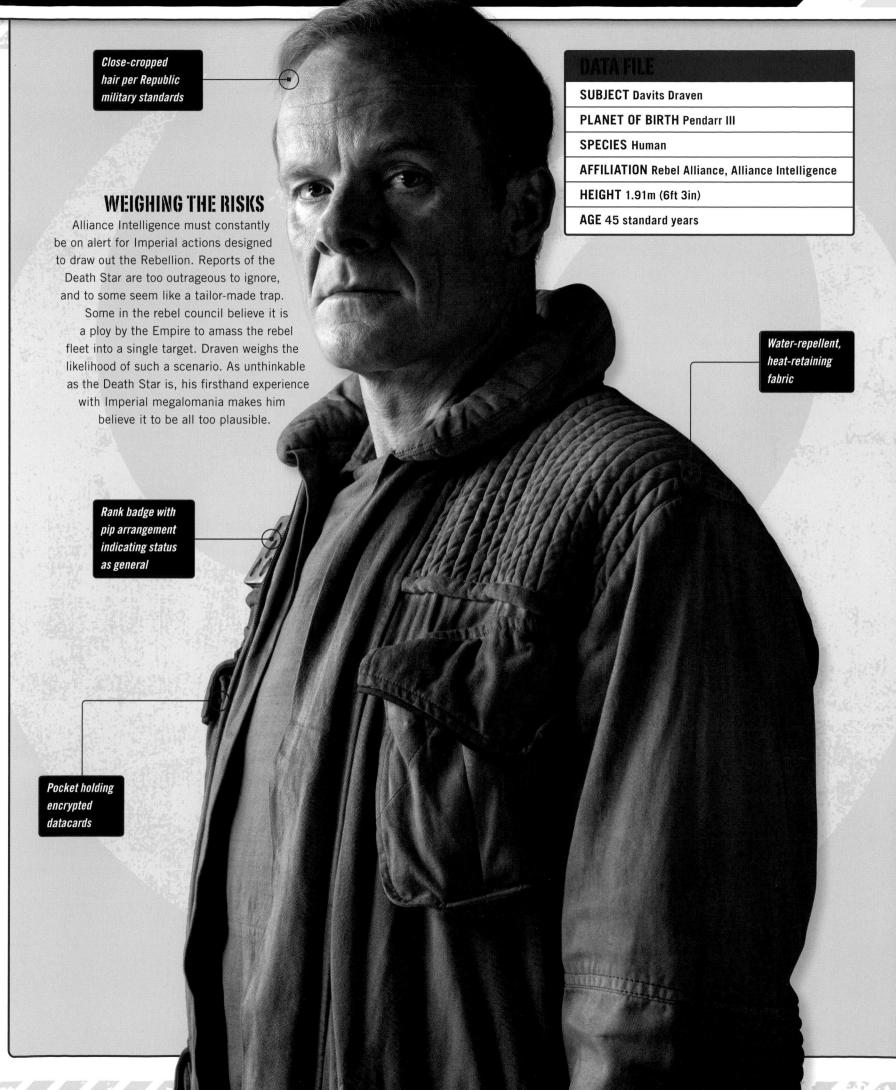

Close-cropped hair per Republic military standards

DATA FILE

SUBJECT Davits Draven	
PLANET OF BIRTH Pendarr III	
SPECIES Human	
AFFILIATION Rebel Alliance, Alliance Intelligence	
HEIGHT 1.91m (6ft 3in)	
AGE 45 standard years	

WEIGHING THE RISKS

Alliance Intelligence must constantly be on alert for Imperial actions designed to draw out the Rebellion. Reports of the Death Star are too outrageous to ignore, and to some seem like a tailor-made trap. Some in the rebel council believe it is a ploy by the Empire to amass the rebel fleet into a single target. Draven weighs the likelihood of such a scenario. As unthinkable as the Death Star is, his firsthand experience with Imperial megalomania makes him believe it to be all too plausible.

Water-repellent, heat-retaining fabric

Rank badge with pip arrangement indicating status as general

Pocket holding encrypted datacards

GENERAL MERRICK

STARFIGHTER COMMAND of the Yavin 4 rebel base falls to General Antoc Merrick. He has direct authority over the groupings of X-wing, Y-wing, and U-wing fighters assembled at the Massassi site on the jungle moon. He also flies as Blue Leader, the commander of Blue Squadron. Though he has logged hundreds of hours at the controls of a U-wing, when leading a squadron his preferred craft is *Blue One*, a T-65 X-wing fighter.

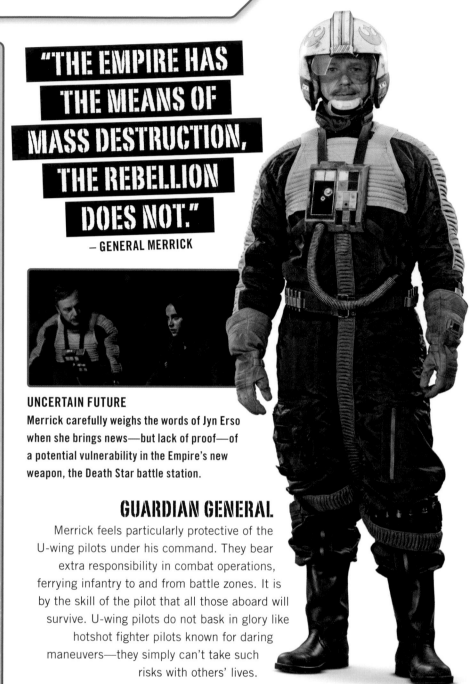

> ## "THE EMPIRE HAS THE MEANS OF MASS DESTRUCTION, THE REBELLION DOES NOT."
> — GENERAL MERRICK

UNCERTAIN FUTURE
Merrick carefully weighs the words of Jyn Erso when she brings news—but lack of proof—of a potential vulnerability in the Empire's new weapon, the Death Star battle station.

Merrick cares deeply for the fighter pilots under his command, and he will not risk their lives needlessly.

Merrick was once flight leader of a planetary defense force known as the Rarified Air Cavalry of Virujansi. When his home planet underwent political transformation with the installation of an Imperial governor that displaced the ruling Virujansi council, the local military forces loyal to the old regime were forced to disband. The pilots of the Air Cavalry were extended invitations to join the Imperial Navy, but Merrick saw the offer as hollow.

He and fellow pilot Garven Dries opted instead for early retirement, left the planet, and sought out membership in the Rebel Alliance, whose starfighter squadrons demonstrated greater unit coherence and piloting ability than the unimaginative TIE fighter forces of the Empire.

GUARDIAN GENERAL

Merrick feels particularly protective of the U-wing pilots under his command. They bear extra responsibility in combat operations, ferrying infantry to and from battle zones. It is by the skill of the pilot that all those aboard will survive. U-wing pilots do not bask in glory like hotshot fighter pilots known for daring maneuvers—they simply can't take such risks with others' lives.

As part of the rebel council, Merrick has a voice in the direction of the Rebellion in these pivotal days.

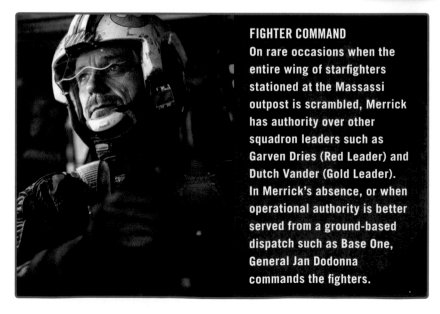

FIGHTER COMMAND
On rare occasions when the entire wing of starfighters stationed at the Massassi outpost is scrambled, Merrick has authority over other squadron leaders such as Garven Dries (Red Leader) and Dutch Vander (Gold Leader). In Merrick's absence, or when operational authority is better served from a ground-based dispatch such as Base One, General Jan Dodonna commands the fighters.

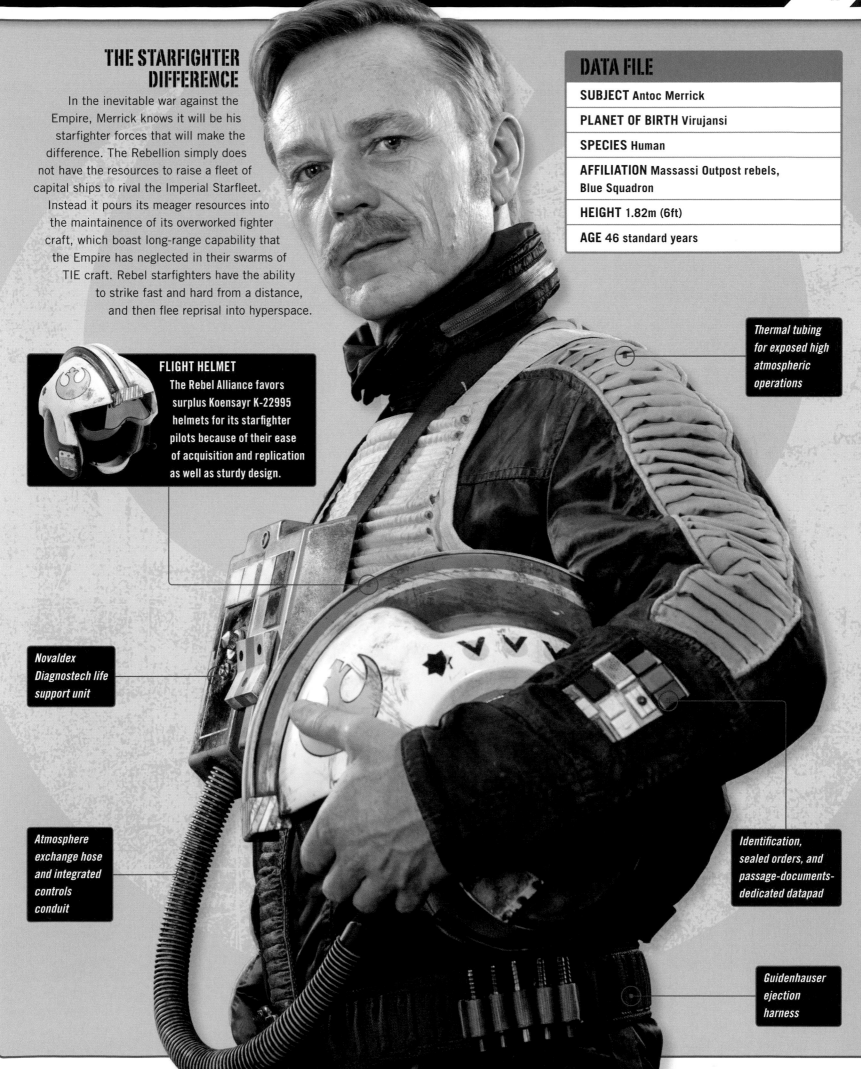

THE STARFIGHTER DIFFERENCE

In the inevitable war against the Empire, Merrick knows it will be his starfighter forces that will make the difference. The Rebellion simply does not have the resources to raise a fleet of capital ships to rival the Imperial Starfleet. Instead it pours its meager resources into the maintainence of its overworked fighter craft, which boast long-range capability that the Empire has neglected in their swarms of TIE craft. Rebel starfighters have the ability to strike fast and hard from a distance, and then flee reprisal into hyperspace.

DATA FILE

SUBJECT	Antoc Merrick
PLANET OF BIRTH	Virujansi
SPECIES	Human
AFFILIATION	Massassi Outpost rebels, Blue Squadron
HEIGHT	1.82m (6ft)
AGE	46 standard years

FLIGHT HELMET

The Rebel Alliance favors surplus Koensayr K-22995 helmets for its starfighter pilots because of their ease of acquisition and replication as well as sturdy design.

Thermal tubing for exposed high atmospheric operations

Novaldex Diagnostech life support unit

Atmosphere exchange hose and integrated controls conduit

Identification, sealed orders, and passage-documents-dedicated datapad

Guidenhauser ejection harness

ALLIANCE HIGH COMMAND

THE REBEL CELLS amassed in the Massassi outpost have combined to form the core of Alliance High Command. Despite Imperial claims to the contrary, the expanding Alliance masterminded by Mon Mothma and Bail Organa is in actuality quite structured. In addition to a civil government component, its military units conform to an established hierarchy. Some outlier rebel cells are more improvised than the Yavin group, but the Massassi outpost is a model of command efficiency.

Word of an Imperial superweapon project splits the rebel council over their next course of action.

The upper command staff of the Alliance military are known as the rebel council in common parlance and also include a civilian component of senators. Alliance High Command meetings can be intense, charged affairs, particularly in these testing times.

High-profile strikes against Imperial targets on Lothal, Garel, and Ord Biniir have emboldened the Alliance, but none of these actions have constituted a victory that proves to all the potency of their Rebellion. Some in the Alliance state firmly that their objective is a negotiated peace with the Empire, in which Palpatine would relinquish the wartime powers he accrued during the Clone Wars, and the Senate would be reinstated as the principal body of governance.

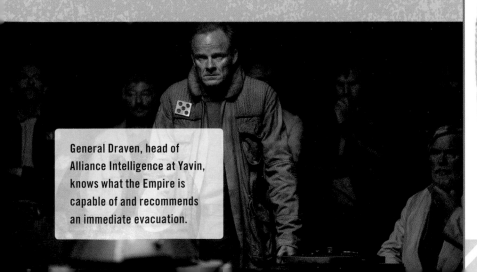

General Draven, head of Alliance Intelligence at Yavin, knows what the Empire is capable of and recommends an immediate evacuation.

REBEL INSIGNIA
The Alliance inherits the Alderaanian standard of five pips arranged on a brushed-metal backing to denote rank.

 General

 Colonel

 Commander

 Major

 Captain

 Lieutenant

GENERAL PITT ONORAN
Onoran heads up the Yavin 4 Special Forces division. He earned valuable experience as a logistics officer in the Republic army during the Clone Wars.

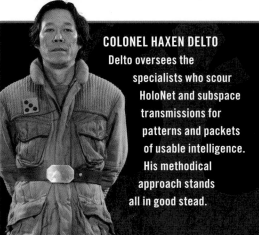

COLONEL HAXEN DELTO
Delto oversees the specialists who scour HoloNet and subspace transmissions for patterns and packets of usable intelligence. His methodical approach stands all in good stead.

COLONEL BANDWIN COR
While General Merrick oversees Alliance Starfighter Command, he defers to Colonel Cor for day-to-day decisions. Cor liaises closely with General Dodonna for the most efficient utilization of fighter resources in the Gordian Reach—the area of space that encompasses Yavin. By agreement with Merrick, Cor fills his role dispassionately, pragmatically treating the fighter resources as assets on a ledger.

Plate-style clasp buckle

Tan jacket is part of traditional Alderaanian military livery

COLONEL ANJ ZAVOR

The Yavin 4 liaison to Admiral Raddus, Colonel Anj Zavor works as part of Fleet Command. Zavor keeps a channel of communication open between the base and the ever-mobile admiral.

GENERAL BACCAM GRAFIS

Grafis heads up Ordnance and Supply—the procurement of essential materiel for the Rebellion. He pursues lines of supply for starship-grade fuel and weaponry.

GENERAL DUSTIL FORELL

Forell oversees Support Services, a division dedicated to the Alliance's anemic transportation network. On Yavin 4, this encompasses less than a dozen medium transports, and one military-converted light freighter.

MAJOR CAPIN HARINAR

Part of General Draven's Alliance Intelligence staff, materials analyst Harinar examines captured Imperial technology to assess the capabilities of the enemy and plan countermeasures.

GENERAL JAN DODONNA

As the Sector Command officer for the Yavin-based rebels, General Dodonna is an important voice on the rebel council. Now a veteran officer, Dodonna was a bridge officer aboard a *Venator*-class Star Destroyer in the Clone Wars. He continued his service into the earliest days of the Imperial Starfleet before disillusionment with the Empire led him to defect.

Wearing a tactician's overcoat is an Alderaanian custom

REBEL SENATORS

THE REBEL ALLIANCE HIERARCHY consists of two main bodies: the military and the civil government. The existence of a governmental apparatus within the Rebellion is indicative of its ultimate aim: to restore the Republic and the Galactic Senate as instruments of egalitarian and democratic rule. Arranged beneath Mon Mothma, the titular chief of state of the Alliance Civil Government, is the Cabinet—a collection of six allied ministers with specific areas of responsibility.

Bail Organa has been secretly orchestrating organized rebellion against the Empire for years. Alderaan is a major supporter of the cause.

The rebel council is a mix of military and civic government representatives. It is, by design, meant to encompass varied viewpoints. Debate and disagreement are both encouraged in the model of democratic governance. But in troubled times, such an open forum leads to deadlock. Mon Mothma is wary about wielding too much executive power, as that is the very embodiment of their sworn enemy, the Empire. Though no longer a member of the Senate, Mon Mothma remains in communication with her allies there, and sympathies for the Rebellion continue to grow. It is now the Rebellion's most crucial moment. If the Death Star menace is real, then the Alliance stands at the brink of destruction just as it is about to shine a light on the true evil that is the Galactic Empire.

Upon learning of the Death Star threat, Senator Vaspar recommends scattering the Alliance fleet and going into hiding.

SENATOR JEBEL

Senator Nower Jebel of Uyter is the Minister of Finance in the Alliance Cabinet. Jebel believes a negotiated peace settlement is possible, and the time for violence may be at an end. He has faith in the power of the Senate to be an instrument of diplomacy and is disdainful of the lean toward open hostility. He vividly remembers the violence unleashed by Saw Gerrera—strikes that claimed the lives of innocent bystanders. The path to peace cannot be stained by the blood of the innocent, he expounds, but he has offered little to prove his conviction that the Empire would be willing to compromise and risks becoming closed-minded to other points of view.

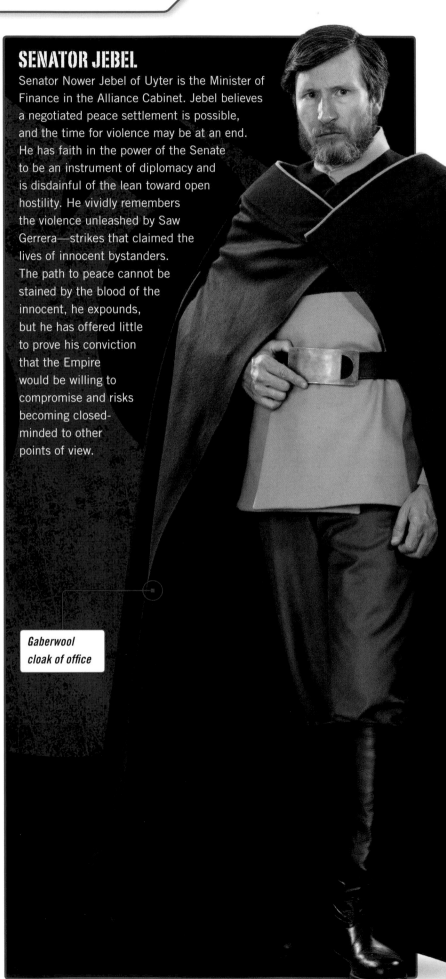

Gaberwool cloak of office

SENATOR VASPAR

Vasp Vaspar serves as senator of the Taldot sector and as the Alliance's Minister of Industry, overseeing the fledgling Rebellion's meager yet vital resources. This role leads him to be far more risk-averse than some of his fellow councillors, but, unlike Senator Jebel, he is not opposed to conflict. Vaspar believes hostility should be carefully rationed, and that a march to open warfare is unsustainable for a credit-strapped Rebellion. Vaspar does believe the Empire capable of creating a Death Star, but he agrees with Jebel that to attack it is unthinkable.

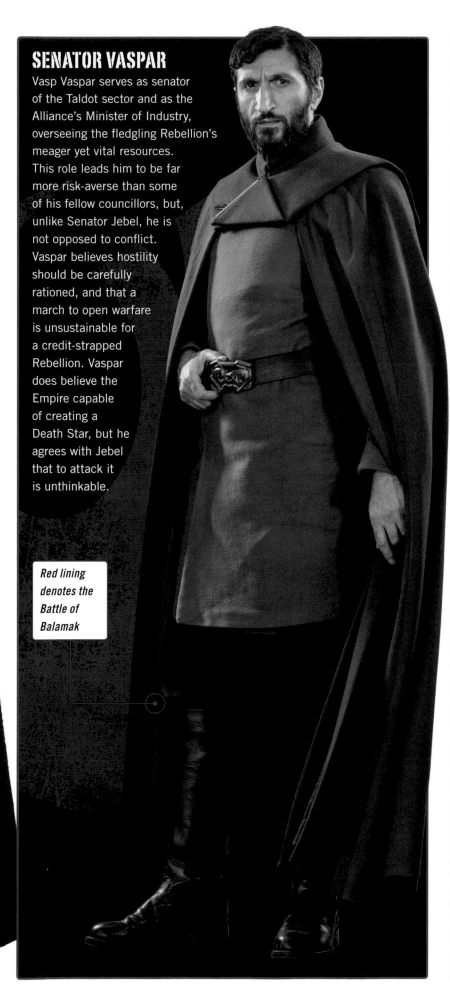

Red lining denotes the Battle of Balamak

BAIL ORGANA

Bail Organa of Alderaan has been wary of the executive power wielded by Palpatine since before the start of the Clone Wars. During that conflict, Organa—then senator of Alderaan—had been building a network of like-minded politicians and influencers who would meet at his estate on Coruscant. The resulting Delegation of the 2,000 formally objected to Palpatine's wartime overreach, but was met with the transformation of the Republic into the Empire at war's end. As the Senate's influence dwindled, Bail walked a razor's edge as he and then his successor, his daughter Leia Organa, continued to use Alderaan's popular voice to champion the downtrodden and investigate reports of Imperial abuse. In secret, Alderaan has funded, armed, and equipped the Rebellion at Bail's command.

SENATOR PAMLO

Senator Tynnra Pamlo of Taris is stirred by whispers of the Death Star. As Minister of Education, she liaises closely with Alliance Intelligence and has been exposed to evidence of the Empire's worst atrocities, including actions on Ghorman, Geonosis, and Lasan. Pamlo has no doubt the Death Star is real and that the Empire intends to use it, but she wishes to first consult with her people. She knows that to launch an attack against the Empire risks putting her homeworld in the crosshairs of a planet-killer.

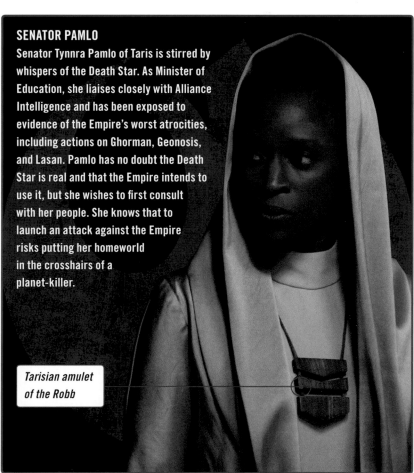

Tarisian amulet of the Robb

CASSIAN ANDoR

AN ACCOMPLISHED Alliance Intelligence officer with extensive undercover and combat field experience, Captain Cassian Andor is a disciplined operative with a deep respect for the chain of command and the carrying out of unquestioned orders. He earns respect from agents under his authority with his ability to keep a cool head and complete his missions with minimal resources.

SECURITY BYPASS
Cassian's years of law-bending have honed his escapology skills. With a compact security kit hidden in his boot, he cycles past the simple electronics of the locks in Saw Gerrera's underground prison on Jedha.

SECURITY KIT IN SENSOR-BAFFLING WALLET

Cassian believes the Empire capable of the worst crimes against civilization, so when whispers of a planet-killing superweapon reach him, he cannot dismiss them.

Now in his mid twenties, Andor grew up in the wilds of the Outer Rim and came of age fighting against the Republic during the tumultuous Clone Wars. His father was killed at the Carida military academy during a protest against the expansion of Republic militarism. Though not a formal Separatist, Andor became part of a Confederacy-backed insurrectionist cell at a young age, tossing rocks and bottles at Republic walkers and clone soldiers. He came to learn firsthand that even the most advanced combat machinery could be crippled with the right grit sprinkled in the right gears. In the time of the Empire, Andor was drawn into anarchist movements that continued to defy Imperial edicts. He was recruited by General Draven into the growing Rebellion.

"I'VE BEEN IN THIS FIGHT SINCE I WAS SIX YEARS OLD."
— CASSIAN ANDOR, TO JYN ERSO

ALLEY ALLIES
In the hivelike urban enclaves on the Ring of Kafrene, Captain Andor has a rendezvous with Tivik, an unscrupulous source of information the Rebel Alliance needs. The congested cityscape makes it easy for spies to disappear, but also hosts stormtrooper patrols.

Weatherproof directional fabric sheds water

BlasTech A280-CFE in sniper configuration

THE HARD CALLS
The fledgling Rebel Alliance relies heavily on covert operatives to stymie Imperial operations. These strikes are discreet and targeted. Acts of sabotage, espionage, and even assassinations fill Andor's casefile. Knowing from experience the efficacy of Imperial interrogation, Andor respects the need for secrets to be kept from field agents. He remains active to stave off the downtime that would plunge him into deeper reflection on some of his most extreme assignments.

Jyn Erso's defiant nature leads to prickly moments with Cassian when the two rebels pose as pilgrims visiting occupied Jedha.

INTELLIGENCE OPERATIVE

Cassian has spent most of his career in Alliance Intelligence working for the Operations department—a dangerous posting that places agents directly in contact with the Empire. Statistics place the odds of an agent surviving 20 field missions at 23 percent—roughly four-to-one odds against. Intelligence command has recently shifted Andor to the Retrieval department, where his mandate is to plan the operation to free Jyn Erso from prison and lead the search for Saw Gerrera and Galen Erso.

DATA FILE

SUBJECT	Cassian Jeron Andor
PLANET OF BIRTH	Fest
SPECIES	Human
AFFILIATION	Rebel Alliance, Massassi unit
HEIGHT	1.78m (5ft 10in)
AGE	26 standard years

Pips denote rank of Captain; color indicates Army service

Personal identifier transponder conceals "lullaby" suicide pill

OPERATIONAL ALIASES

WILLIX Government agent on Ord Mantell

AACH Senatorial contact on Darknell

JORETH SWARD Assistant to Imperial Admiral Grendreef

FULCRUM Recruitment agent in Albarrio sector

Corellian-cut field jacket

Compressed eleton blaster gas ampules

MULTIFUNCTIONAL WEAPON

Cassian's BlasTech A280-CFE (covert field edition) features modular construction that allows a core pistol to be reconfigured into a sniper or assault rifle.

Military fatigues

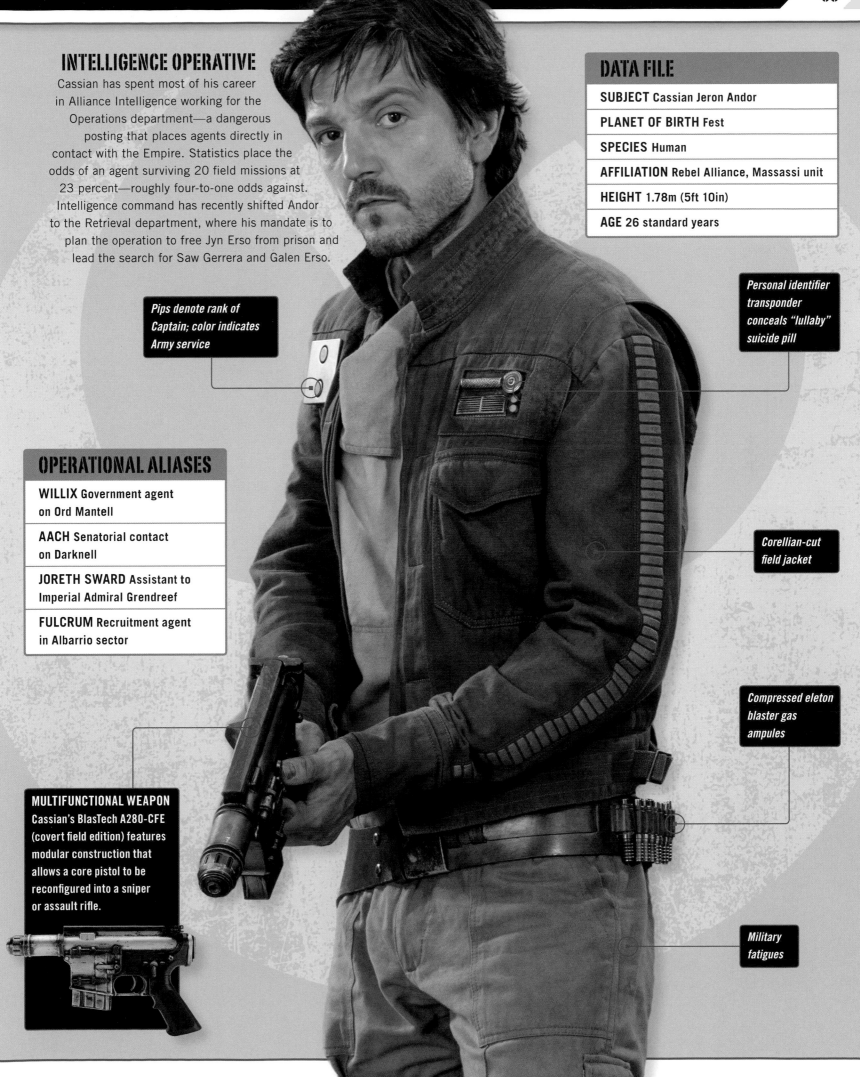

A NEW PARTNERSHIP

Cassian's spy experience makes him instinctively wary of Jyn and her checkered history. Meanwhile, years of surviving in the galaxy's toughest spots have made Jyn distrustful of everyone. For Operation Fracture to succeed, they'll need to overcome these self-built boundaries.

K-2SO

THOUGH NOW LOYAL to the Alliance, reprogrammed Imperial security droid K-2SO can be an alarming sight to fellow rebels when standing within their base on Yavin 4. Fear of combat droids—stoked by memories of the Clone Wars—runs deep, and the notion of such a droid operating uninhibitedly can unsettle many. However, the pragmatic K-2SO is an effective insertion agent, blending in perfectly at Imperial installations and outposts.

K-2SO is intimately familiar with the data architecture of Imperial computer networks and can navigate restricted pathways with ease.

When the Senate rolled out a mandate prohibiting the creation of battle droids, Arakyd Industries was able to curtail these restrictions by classifying the KX-series strictly as security droids. Their programming included built-in exceptions to the usual hard-coded restriction against harming organics, and defaults to recognize and defer to Imperial military personnel ranked lieutenant or higher.

It was Cassian Andor who undertook the difficult task of reformatting K-2SO's personality. His work has eliminated most of Arakyd Industries' presets, with one notable side effect: K-2SO is bluntly honest in all his assessments, even when such stark observations are not welcome.

Upon arriving on Jedha, Captain Andor orders K-2SO to stay out of sight for fear of drawing insurgent attention. K-2SO is less than impressed by this instruction.

SWIFT RESPONDER

Arakyd engineers pride themselves in the anatomical structure boasted by their KX-series. Although K-2SO's proportions are exaggerated beyond the human norm, his body and limbs are precision-engineered to give him the mobility of a human athlete. Complex gyro-balance systems keep him upright when running briskly and changing direction.

Articular ring joint and servo-driver

Comm package

"YOU ARE BEING RESCUED. PLEASE DO NOT RESIST."
— K-2SO, ON FIRST MEETING JYN ERSO

Recharge port

IMPERIAL CONNECTIONS

K-2SO has a built-in communications booster that allows him to scan and access standard Imperial communication frequencies. Depending on mission security requirements, Cassian may order K-2SO to avoid interfacing such networks. K-2SO's access may leave tell-tale "electronic footprints" that would divulge the presence of covert operatives.

PARTNERS IN CRIME
The relationship between Cassian and K-2SO is built on trust but still has its limits. While K-2SO pines for a blaster pistol in order to test his targeting accuracy, Cassian refuses to equip him with one.

DATA FILE

SUBJECT K-2SO, KX-series security droid

PLANET OF CONSTRUCTION Vulpter

MANUFACTURER Arakyd Industries

AFFILIATION Alliance Intelligence

HEIGHT 2.16m (7ft 1in)

AGE 12 standard years

Carboplast-composite shell encasing cognitive module

Vocodor assembly

TIRELESS VERSATILITY

K-2SO's versatility is representative of a disappearing design philosophy, as major droid manufacturers find greater profitability in selling specialist models rather than multifunctional models. With his humanoid shape and dexterous manipulators, K-2SO can operate a wide variety of tools and equipment, and carry gear tirelessly. His cognitive module is also programmed with specifications for more than 40 Imperial transport vessels, making him a capable pilot.

Faded Imperial cog insignia

Primary programming port access door

Concealed data spike in fist

Shock-absorbing femoral strut

REBEL SUPPORT

KEEPING THE REBELLION RUNNING requires an army of unsung technicians, mechanics, and droids. Unlike the Empire, with its seemingly bottomless well of resources to arm its military, the Rebellion must make do with the ships, weapons, and equipment it has. These finicky devices require constant upkeep and repair, as they are rushed from mission to mission with little downtime in between. While the soldiers in the field may draw the glory, it is the techs back at the base who make their exploits possible.

Astromechs trundle throughout the Massassi base. They are equipped to fine-tune almost any piece of rebel gear.

The necessities of an ever-mobile Rebel Alliance dictate that even this support staff be trained in combat skills. Some with a limited perspective may scoff that these rebels don't pull their weight in a firefight when the Empire attacks. The truth is that these technicians are too valuable to risk on the battlefield. Their expertise around machinery, computer systems, communications networks, and the administrative systems that keep the Alliance organized are vital to the success of the Rebellion.

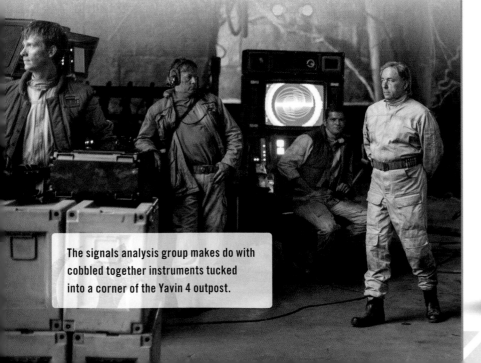

The signals analysis group makes do with cobbled together instruments tucked into a corner of the Yavin 4 outpost.

PRIVATE TENZIGO WEEMS

A vigilant Signals Intelligence technician in General Draven's command, Private Weems is part of an attentive team of analysts deciphering communications chatter from across the galaxy. An array of automated listening posts feed Base One's communications room, with a bewildering tangle of signals bouncing through a maze of repeaters to avoid giving the Empire a straight line to the rebel base. Weems tracks the progress of Operation Fracture from Jedha to Eadu, and breaks the news when the Rogue One team engages the Empire on Scarif.

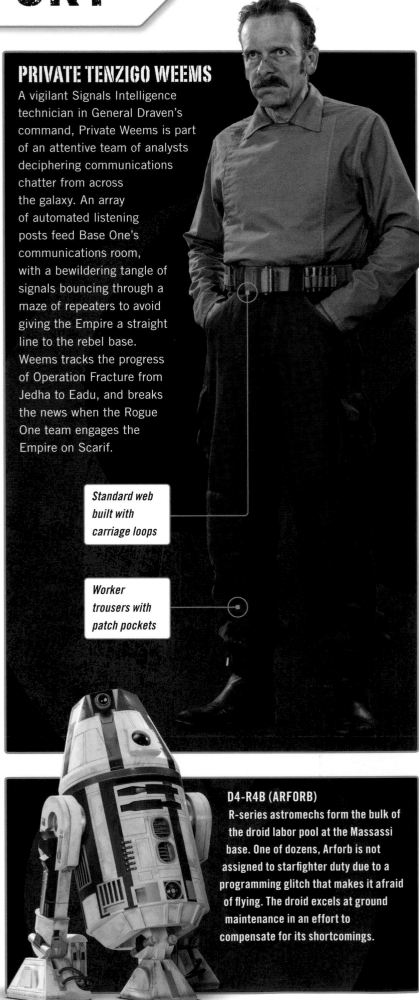

Standard web built with carriage loops

Worker trousers with patch pockets

D4-R4B (ARFORB)

R-series astromechs form the bulk of the droid labor pool at the Massassi base. One of dozens, Arforb is not assigned to starfighter duty due to a programming glitch that makes it afraid of flying. The droid excels at ground maintenance in an effort to compensate for its shortcomings.

Plastex dome

Holographic projector

Treaded feet

R3-S1 (THREECE)

With a clear dome that shows off her overclocked Intellex V processor, R3-S1 (or Threece) has picked up a decidedly vain programming flutter. Threece is not assigned to a specific starfighter; instead she is employed in the upkeep of technology throughout the Yavin base. Competitive to a fault, Threece does not work well with others, but she excels at organization, and has become the recognized chief of the astromech pool.

Service helmet with flash visor and integral comlink

Multi-pocketed spacer vest of Corellian cut

SERGEANT GALE TORG

Wearing the uniform of Alderaanian consular security, Gale Torg is assigned to guard and escort senators and dignitaries trusted to visit the secret rebel outpost on Yavin 4.

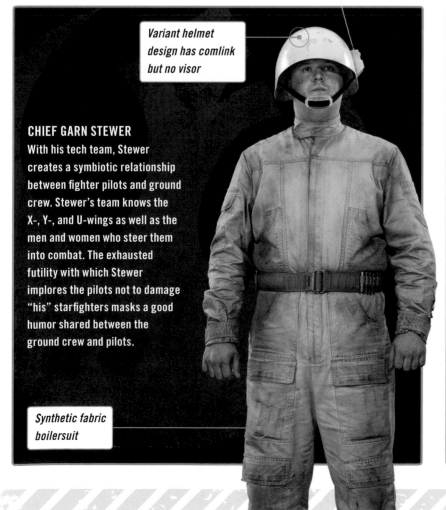

Variant helmet design has comlink but no visor

CHIEF GARN STEWER

With his tech team, Stewer creates a symbiotic relationship between fighter pilots and ground crew. Stewer's team knows the X-, Y-, and U-wings as well as the men and women who steer them into combat. The exhausted futility with which Stewer implores the pilots not to damage "his" starfighters masks a good humor shared between the ground crew and pilots.

Synthetic fabric boilersuit

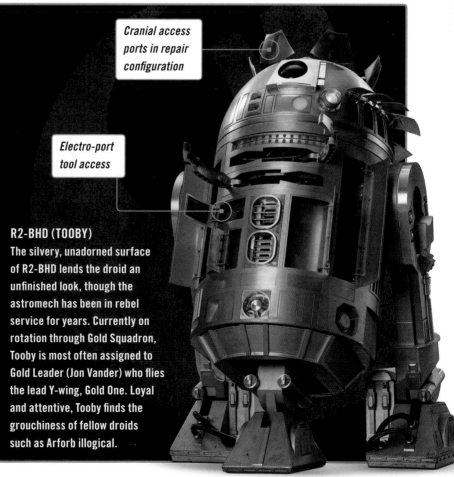

Cranial access ports in repair configuration

Electro-port tool access

R2-BHD (TOOBY)

The silvery, unadorned surface of R2-BHD lends the droid an unfinished look, though the astromech has been in rebel service for years. Currently on rotation through Gold Squadron, Tooby is most often assigned to Gold Leader (Jon Vander) who flies the lead Y-wing, Gold One. Loyal and attentive, Tooby finds the grouchiness of fellow droids such as Arforb illogical.

U-WING GUNSHIP

A STURDY TROOP TRANSPORT and gunship used by the Rebel Alliance, the U-wing starfighter is a well-armed swing-wing vessel that must penetrate heavy fire zones to deposit soldiers onto battlefields, then fly air support during dangerous missions against the Empire. Despite its informal "starfighter" moniker, the U-wing fills a support role that starfighters simply cannot. Fighters rely on their speed to keep them out of anti-aircraft range. U-wings, by necessity, must linger in areas filled with flak and enemy fire. The shielding and armor of a U-wing adds to an operational mass on top of a hold full of passengers. In short, a U-wing handles much more like a heavy repulsorcraft than a swift space superiority vessel.

DISPATCH FROM YAVIN

General Draven watches the departure of Cassian Andor, K-2SO, and Jyn Erso to Jedha. U-wings are the preferred vessel for extractions as the lack of passenger accommodation on regular starfighters makes them impractical for such missions. Operation Fracture's goal was to pick up one passenger—Galen Erso—but ends up leaving Jedha with three new recruits to the rebel cause: Bodhi Rook, Chirrut Îmwe, and Baze Malbus.

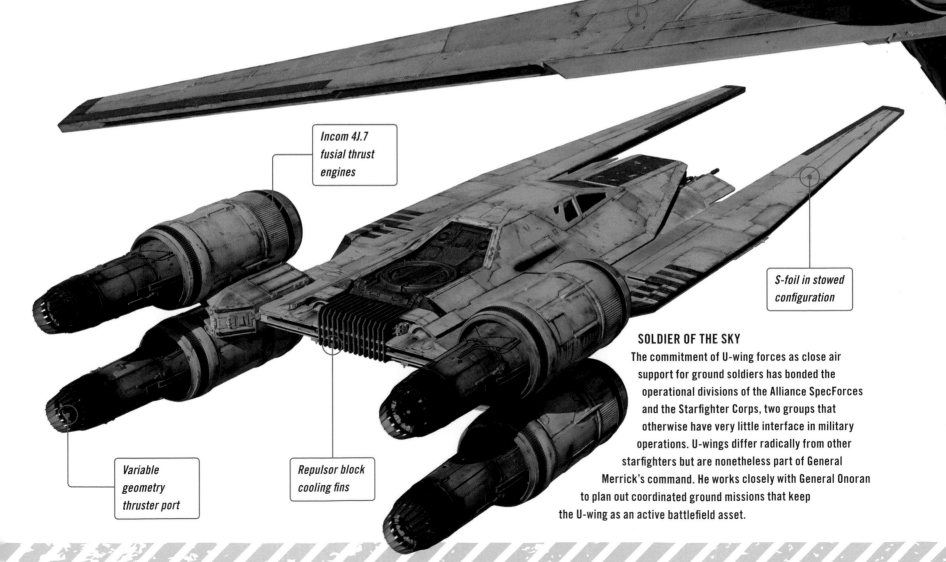

Defense configuration of S-foils increases deflector shield spread

Incom 4J.7 fusial thrust engines

S-foil in stowed configuration

Variable geometry thruster port

Repulsor block cooling fins

SOLDIER OF THE SKY

The commitment of U-wing forces as close air support for ground soldiers has bonded the operational divisions of the Alliance SpecForces and the Starfighter Corps, two groups that otherwise have very little interface in military operations. U-wings differ radically from other starfighters but are nonetheless part of General Merrick's command. He works closely with General Onoran to plan out coordinated ground missions that keep the U-wing as an active battlefield asset.

FLIGHT CONFIGURATION

Though not built for ship-to-ship dogfights, the U-wing does have a combat-ready flight configuration. Its S-foils, usually stowed in a forward sweep, swing outward and back, increasing the ship's wingspan. The foils help radiate excess heat from the engine cores, and also increase the coverage envelope of the ship's deflector shields. Atmospheric conditions may make wing deployment difficult, so this configuration is usually reserved for high altitude or interstellar operations.

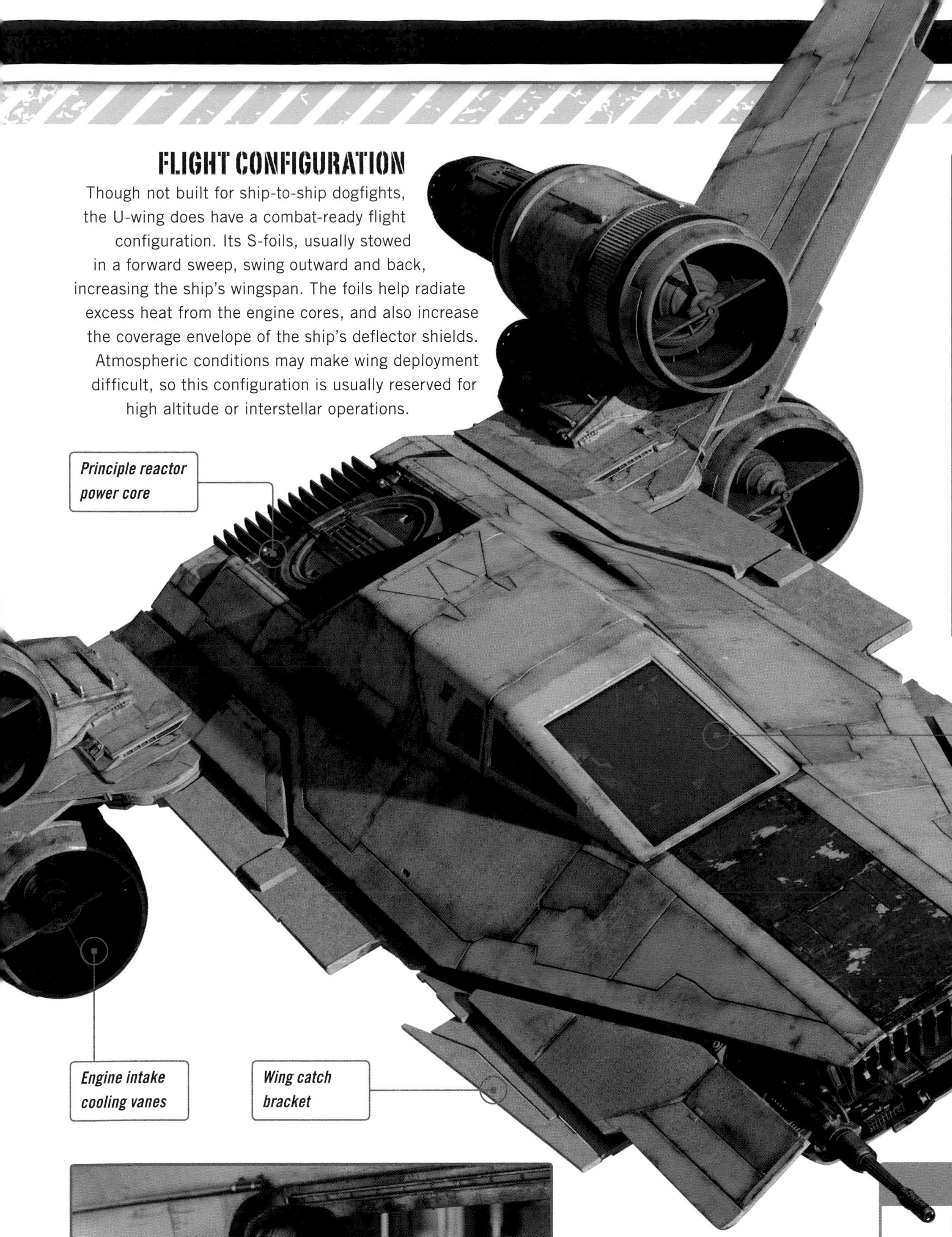

Principle reactor power core

COCKPIT CONTROL

Unlike most starfighters, the U-wing has a two-seater cockpit with tandem controls. A single pilot can operate the craft, but a flight team of two can better handle landing zone fire suppression and defense.

Engine intake cooling vanes

Wing catch bracket

Paired Taim & Bak KX7 laser cannons

CAPTAIN ANDOR

Cassian Andor and K-2SO are approved for solo or tandem flight aboard a U-wing fighter. As with many Incom designs, the U-wing features standardized controls that flatten the learning curve for new pilots already familiar with civilian aircraft from the manufacturer.

DATA FILE

MANUFACTURER Incom Corporation

MODEL UT-60D U-wing starfighter / support craft

AFFILIATION Rebel Alliance

HEIGHT 3.35m (11ft)

LENGTH 24.98m (82ft) with S-foils forward

CREW 2, plus 8 passengers

ATMOSPHERIC SPEED 950kph (590mph)

WEAPONS 2 laser cannons

UT-60D

VERSATILITY IS OF PRIME IMPORTANCE in Rebel Alliance weaponry and technology. Chronically underequipped, the Rebellion often presses its equipment into applications that were never conceived of by designers. In this way, the U-wing emerges as an ideal vehicle: troop transport, gunship, medevac lifter, courier ship, and shuttle are all roles the craft has been asked to play. That there are so few of them in the rebel ranks makes each one all the more valuable.

LIMITED RUN

One of the last designs to emerge from the Incom Corporation before it was entirely nationalized by the Empire, the UT-60D never enjoyed a full production run. The careful manipulation of Senate records by Bail Organa led to a rare shipment of U-wings being "lost" in transit to be found by the Rebellion. The U-wing's nearest cousin, the BT-45D civilian version of the craft—stripped of all its military offensive and defensive applications as well as its hyperdrive—can still be found on a few scattered worlds in the Mid Rim.

IMPROVISED GUNSHIP

The integrated weapons systems of the U-wing are focused on ship-to-ship combat. With fixed-position laser cannons, the primary weapons use the ship's orientation for targeting, limiting its application in ground support. The Rebel Alliance has not opted to refit the U-wing with side-firing modifications, but instead employs improvised weapon mounts to transform one or both of the loading doors into gunports. This is essential for covering landings and extractions. Any infantry-based heavy weapon could thus become part of the U-wing's loadout, providing the rebels can deploy a soldier willing to hang at the edge of the airframe in the thick of combat.

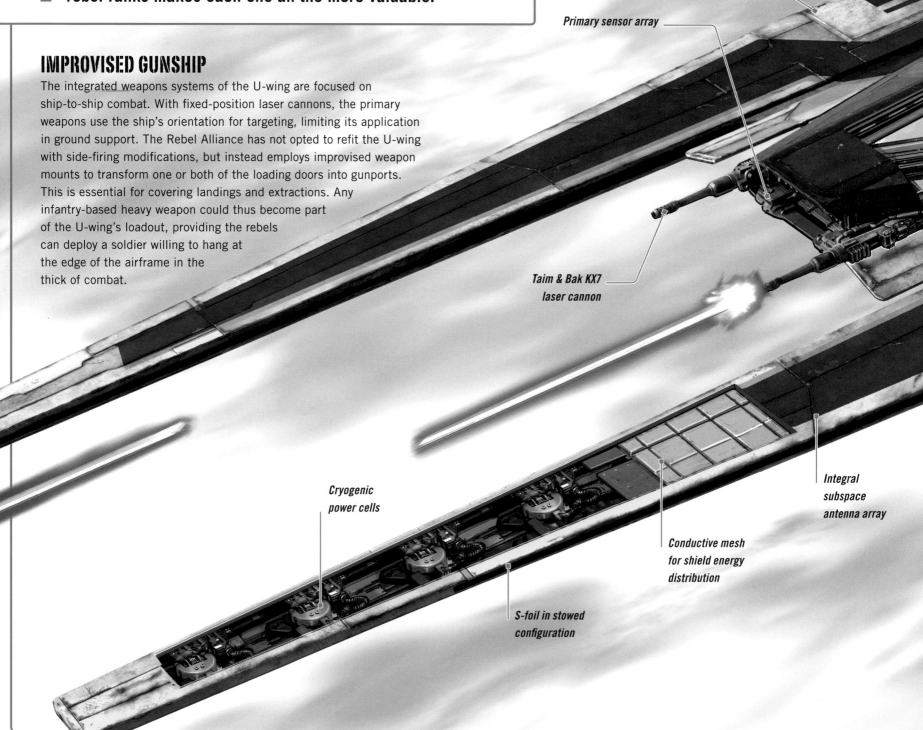

Deflector shield radiating plane

Primary sensor array

Taim & Bak KX7 laser cannon

Cryogenic power cells

S-foil in stowed configuration

Conductive mesh for shield energy distribution

Integral subspace antenna array

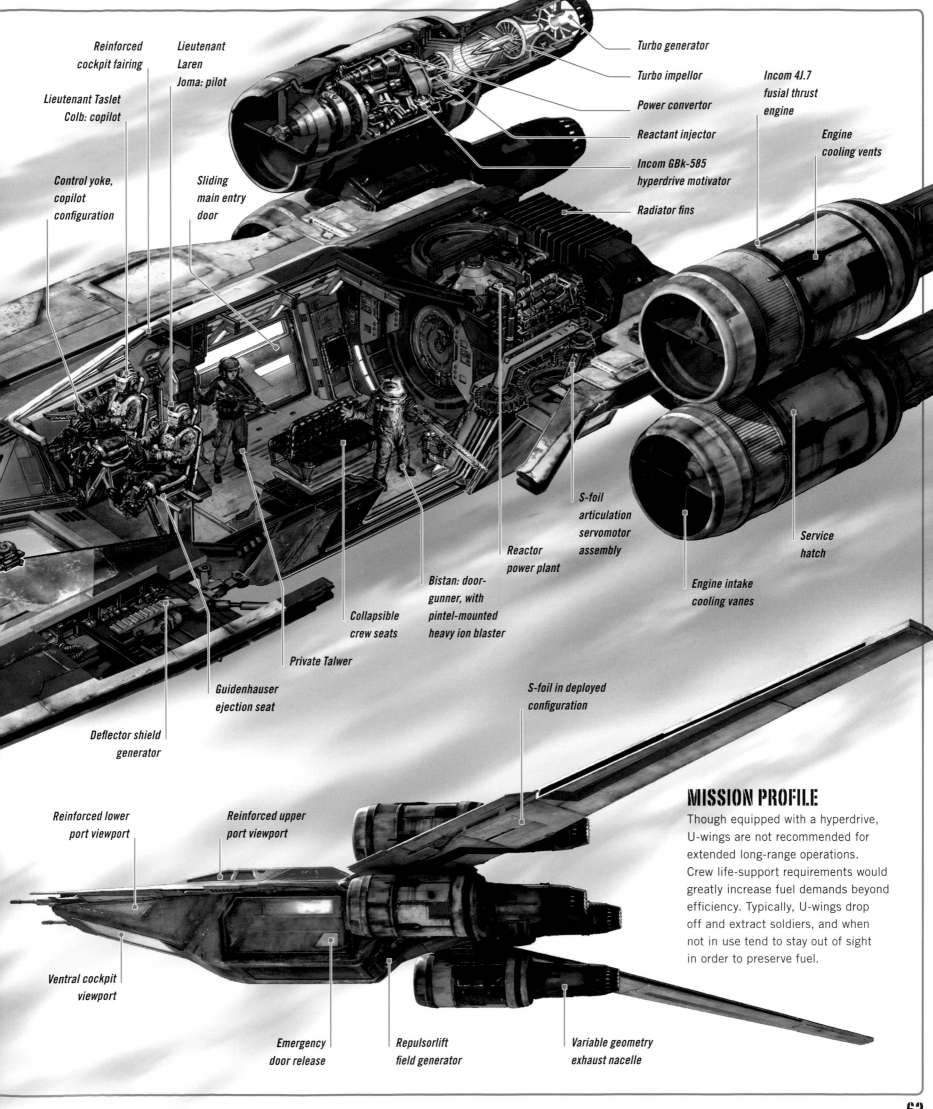

Reinforced
cockpit fairing

Lieutenant
Laren
Joma: pilot

Turbo generator

Turbo impellor

Incom 4J.7
fusial thrust
engine

Lieutenant Taslet
Colb: copilot

Power convertor

Engine
cooling vents

Control yoke,
copilot
configuration

Sliding
main entry
door

Reactant injector

Incom GBk-585
hyperdrive motivator

Radiator fins

S-foil
articulation
servomotor
assembly

Service
hatch

Reactor
power plant

Bistan: door-
gunner, with
pintel-mounted
heavy ion blaster

Engine intake
cooling vanes

Collapsible
crew seats

Private Talwer

Guidenhauser
ejection seat

S-foil in deployed
configuration

Deflector shield
generator

MISSION PROFILE

Though equipped with a hyperdrive,
U-wings are not recommended for
extended long-range operations.
Crew life-support requirements would
greatly increase fuel demands beyond
efficiency. Typically, U-wings drop
off and extract soldiers, and when
not in use tend to stay out of sight
in order to preserve fuel.

Reinforced lower
port viewport

Reinforced upper
port viewport

Ventral cockpit
viewport

Emergency
door release

Repulsorlift
field generator

Variable geometry
exhaust nacelle

X-WING FIGHTER

EMERGING ONTO the rapidly evolving stage of starfighter combat, the Incom T-65 has carved out its niche as the ultimate space superiority fighter—the measure against which all other fighter designs are compared. In this frame of reference, the T-65 has no major weaknesses. It is a swift, maneuverable, well-armed and well-armored combat vessel. There are examples of other craft that exceed the X-wing in these capacities, but all include a compromise that leaves an exploitable weakness.

Upper Taim & Bak KX9 laser cannon

DESIGN LINEAGE

Engineers closely examined the performance of preceding craft such as the ARC-170 and the Z-95 Headhunter flown in the Clone Wars. They produced a new fighter, which was poised to become a mainstay in the Imperial Starfleet when matters of politics and corporate rivalries sidelined the Incom Corporation in favor of Sienar Fleet Systems. The Incom designs would have gathered dust were it not for the resourceful engineers of the Rebellion who adapted and advanced them beyond initial specs to meet their needs.

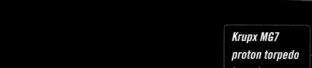

Krupx MG7 proton torpedo launcher

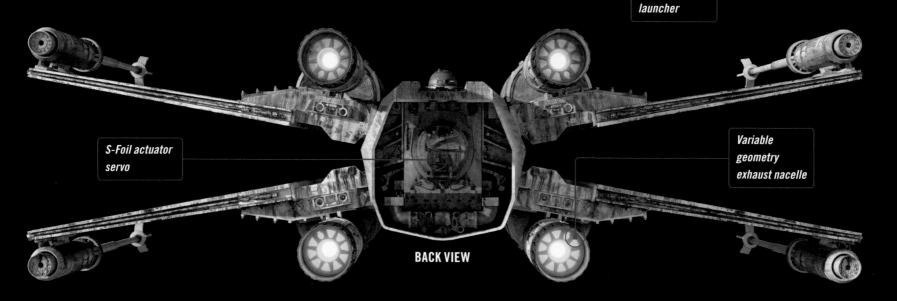

S-Foil actuator servo

Variable geometry exhaust nacelle

BACK VIEW

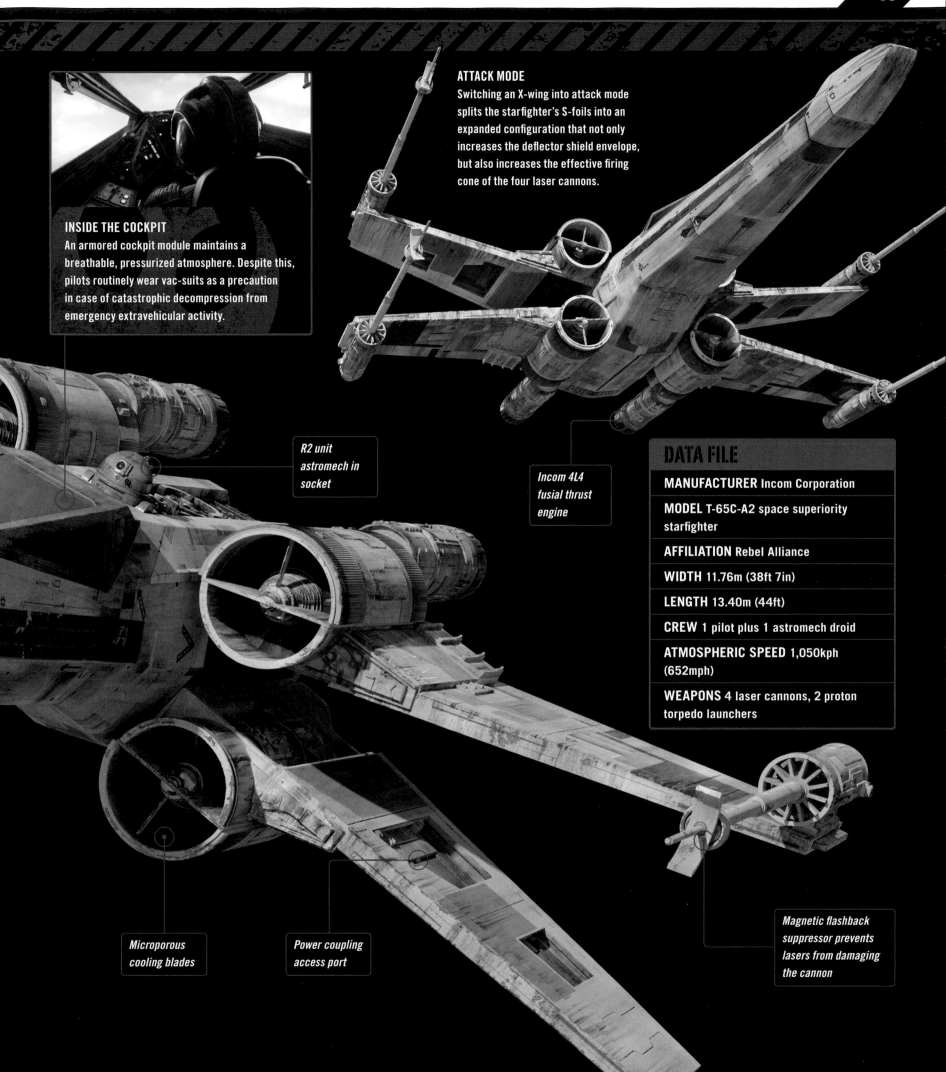

INSIDE THE COCKPIT
An armored cockpit module maintains a breathable, pressurized atmosphere. Despite this, pilots routinely wear vac-suits as a precaution in case of catastrophic decompression from emergency extravehicular activity.

ATTACK MODE
Switching an X-wing into attack mode splits the starfighter's S-foils into an expanded configuration that not only increases the deflector shield envelope, but also increases the effective firing cone of the four laser cannons.

R2 unit astromech in socket

Incom 4L4 fusial thrust engine

DATA FILE

MANUFACTURER Incom Corporation

MODEL T-65C-A2 space superiority starfighter

AFFILIATION Rebel Alliance

WIDTH 11.76m (38ft 7in)

LENGTH 13.40m (44ft)

CREW 1 pilot plus 1 astromech droid

ATMOSPHERIC SPEED 1,050kph (652mph)

WEAPONS 4 laser cannons, 2 proton torpedo launchers

Microporous cooling blades

Power coupling access port

Magnetic flashback suppressor prevents lasers from damaging the cannon

CHAPTER 3

OCCUPIED TERRITORY

The first destination in Operation Fracture is the cold desert moon of Jedha. It is here that Saw Gerrera's splinter group of rebels is ensconced, waging an ongoing insurrection against the Imperial occupation of the moon's Holy City. The Empire's forces are on high alert following the defection of an Imperial pilot. Jyn, Cassian, and K-2SO must watch their step as they make their way through the crowded city.

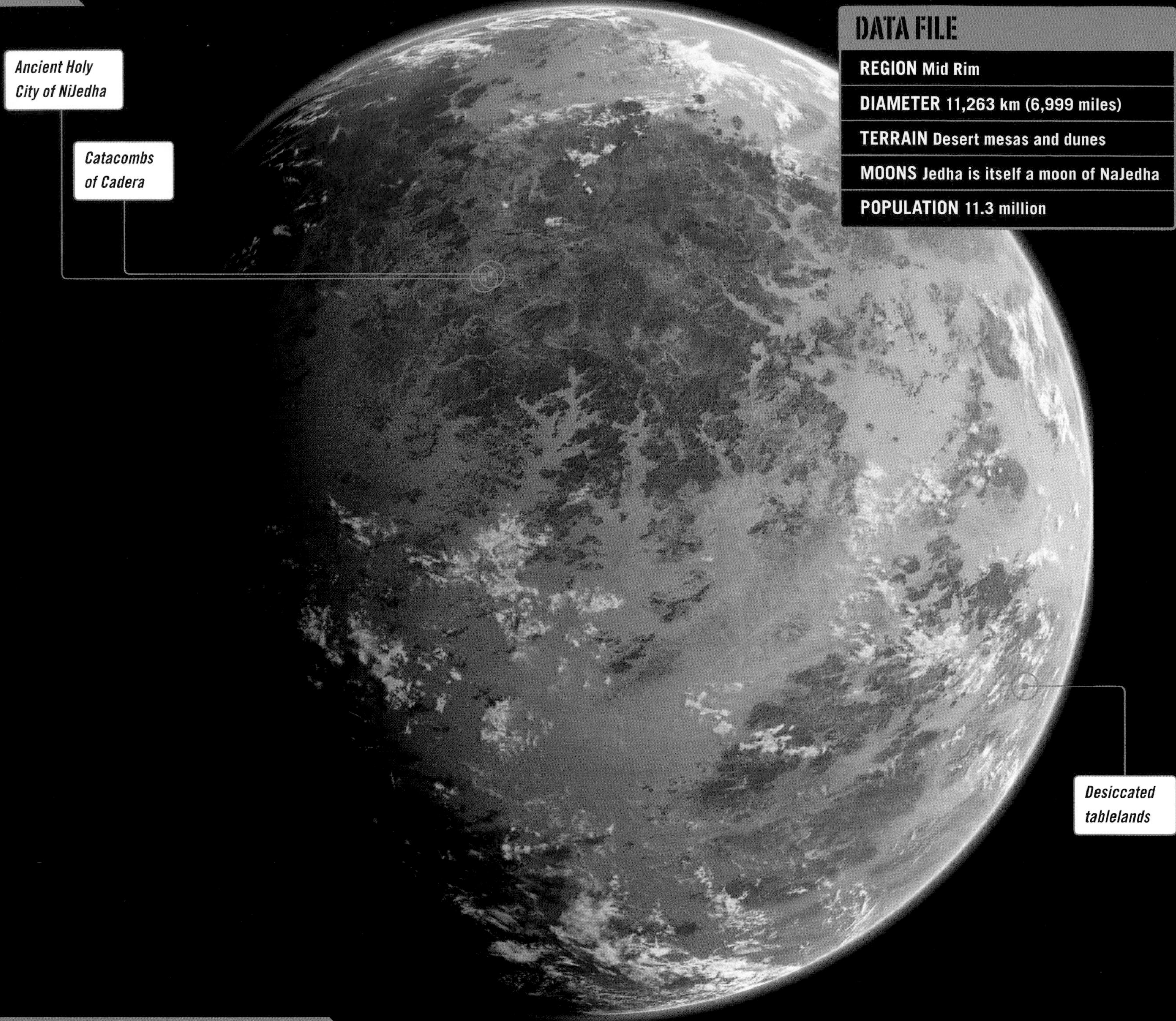

Ancient Holy
City of NiJedha

Catacombs
of Cadera

DATA FILE

REGION Mid Rim

DIAMETER 11,263 km (6,999 miles)

TERRAIN Desert mesas and dunes

MOONS Jedha is itself a moon of NaJedha

POPULATION 11.3 million

Desiccated
tablelands

ANCIENT SPIRITUALITY

JEDHA

AGING, WINDING HYPERSPACE ROUTES fell out of favor in
a growing galaxy, leading to once-popular Jedha becoming
an antiquated curiosity rather than a relevant destination.
Those who now seek Jedha are looking to be lost, or to find
a deeper purpose. Some insist that this sandy world of
ancient spirituality gave its name to the Jedi Order, though
most scholars believe it to be the other way around. All
agree the history of the Jedi and Jedha are intertwined.

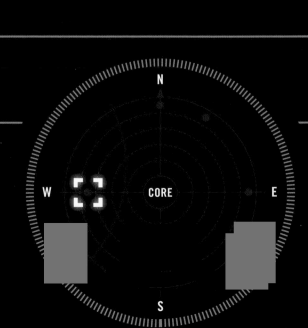

PATH OF ENLIGHTENMENT

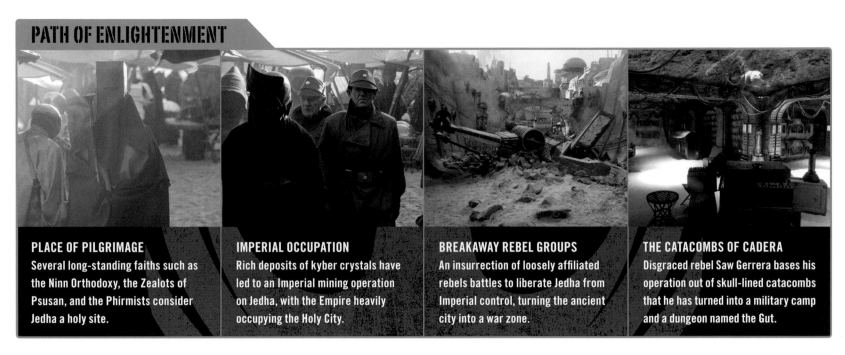

PLACE OF PILGRIMAGE
Several long-standing faiths such as the Ninn Orthodoxy, the Zealots of Psusan, and the Phirmists consider Jedha a holy site.

IMPERIAL OCCUPATION
Rich deposits of kyber crystals have led to an Imperial mining operation on Jedha, with the Empire heavily occupying the Holy City.

BREAKAWAY REBEL GROUPS
An insurrection of loosely affiliated rebels battles to liberate Jedha from Imperial control, turning the ancient city into a war zone.

THE CATACOMBS OF CADERA
Disgraced rebel Saw Gerrera bases his operation out of skull-lined catacombs that he has turned into a military camp and a dungeon named the Gut.

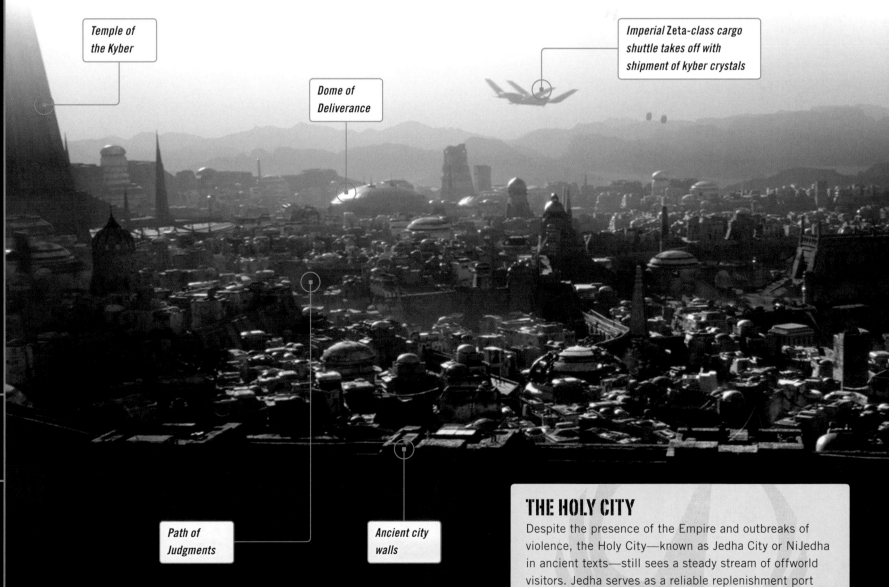

Temple of the Kyber

Dome of Deliverance

Imperial Zeta-class cargo shuttle takes off with shipment of kyber crystals

Path of Judgments

Ancient city walls

THE HOLY CITY

Despite the presence of the Empire and outbreaks of violence, the Holy City—known as Jedha City or NiJedha in ancient texts—still sees a steady stream of offworld visitors. Jedha serves as a reliable replenishment port compared to the uncharted systems that surround it, and the adventurous come here to escape the routine of the more populated inner systems.

POSING AS PILGRIMS

The crowded avenues of Jedha City make it easy to disappear, provided one is focused on maintaining a low profile. At first, Cassian orders K-2SO to stay behind with their ship, but having the droid as a tagalong proves fortuitous when he briefly attempts to convince a stormtrooper patrol that Cassian and Jyn are his prisoners.

JEDHA PILGRIMS

THE MOON OF JEDHA is soaked in history. Primordial structures—some of the earliest architecture known to exist in the galaxy—dot its desert horizons. Tantalizing clues etched into these withering sandstone edifices describe faded connections among dozens of ancient faiths, bringing the spiritually faithful to Jedha searching for answers to deep questions. These believers travel from across the galaxy hoping to find truths buried in the sands.

The Force has existed as a recorded concept in the galaxy for well over 25,000 years. The Jedi Order was its most well-known practitioner, but there are other schools of study and worship that have evolved in parallel on scattered planets. These cultures may not exhibit control and manipulation of the mystical energy field, but they do speak of its power and of its ability to shape and influence the destinies of individuals and history.

The crowded boulevards of the Holy City teem with adherents of many religions, with a wide range of orthodoxy and observances.

As the Empire has risen in power, it has become intolerant of such displays of spirituality and faith. Beginning with the extermination of the Jedi Order—done to prevent an attempted coup of the Republic—the Empire looks suspiciously on such supernatural beliefs.

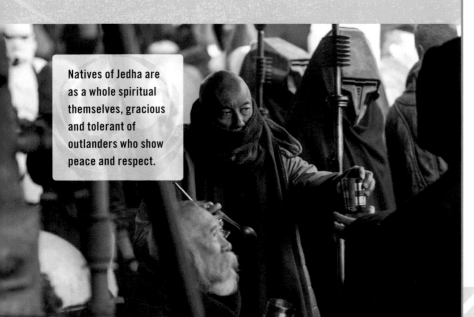

Natives of Jedha are as a whole spiritual themselves, gracious and tolerant of outlanders who show peace and respect.

Staff-mounted censer of Qatameric incense

TOSHDOR NI

A towering Lorrdian, Toshdor Ni cloaks his natural scent with the smoke of burning incense, which permeates the heavy fabric he wears. Swathed in the vermilion vestments of the Brotherhood of the Beatific Countenance, Ni and his fellow followers don concealing robes that act as a physical vow of silence—occluding the natural expressiveness of their stances and movements.

ANGBER TREL

The simple red robes of the Disciples of the Whills denote the oldest faith known to still be active on Jedha. While not as demonstrably active in their practices as the Guardians of the Whills, the Disciples can still be seen congregating at the Temple of the Kyber.

Walking stick made from salvaged power cells

THE HIGH PRIEST

A leader of a congregation of the Brotherhood of the Beatific Countenance, this robed individual has so taken to heart his faith's concealment of individuality that he has even stripped himself of a name. His followers refer to him only by a keening wail of specific pitch.

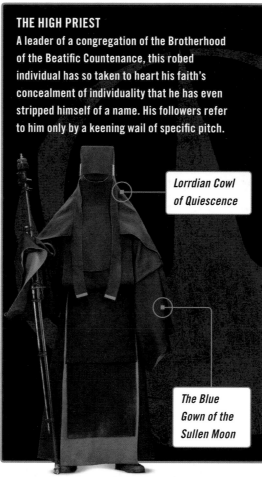

Lorrdian Cowl of Quiescence

The Blue Gown of the Sullen Moon

OMISHA JOYO

The Clan of the Toribota is a nomadic enclave native to Isde Naha, a world on the trailing edge of the Western Reaches. Astronomical conjecture pointed them to the moon of Jedha, believing the star in the system to have been the first one glimpsed by their early ancestors.

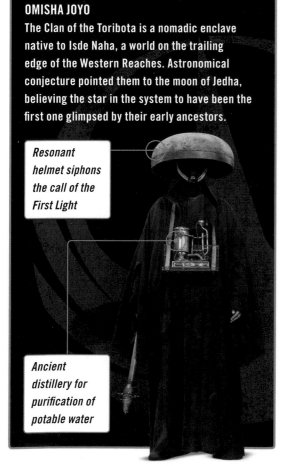

Resonant helmet siphons the call of the First Light

Ancient distillery for purification of potable water

KILLI GIMM

A Disciple of the Whills, Killi manages an orphanage in the shadow of the Kyber temple. She usually hides her human countenance—and her fear—behind a sand filtering mask.

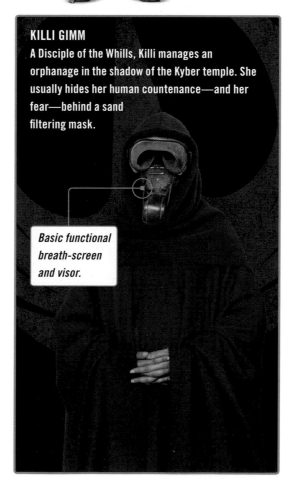

Basic functional breath-screen and visor.

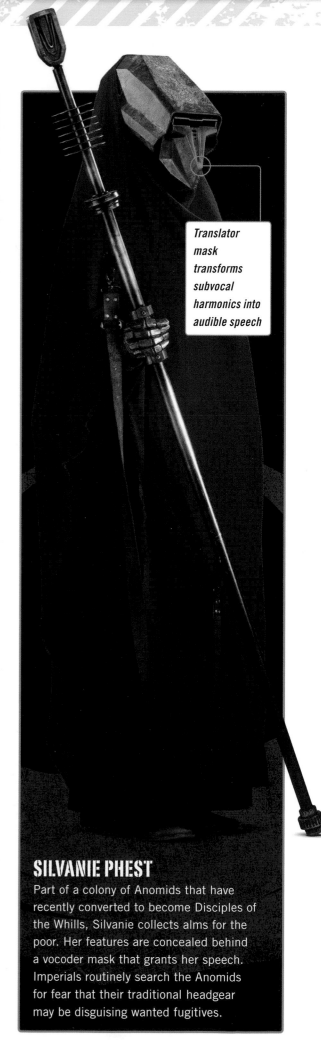

Translator mask transforms subvocal harmonics into audible speech

SILVANIE PHEST

Part of a colony of Anomids that have recently converted to become Disciples of the Whills, Silvanie collects alms for the poor. Her features are concealed behind a vocoder mask that grants her speech. Imperials routinely search the Anomids for fear that their traditional headgear may be disguising wanted fugitives.

JEDHA CIVILIANS

LIFE IN THE HOLY CITY continues despite the ongoing insurgency. The population, both settled and transient, has little choice. In a way, Jedha City is a portrait of what a galactic civil war portends: a costly and amorphous struggle between Empire and rebellion with civilians caught in between. With guerilla warfare tactics favored by the insurgents, every alleyway, building, or avenue could become an instant war zone.

Death-worshipping cultists of the Central Isopter frequent areas of violence, meditating on matters of mortality.

Despite the frequent violent flare-ups, life in Jedha goes on. Jedha's inhabitants try to adapt to the cruel realities of occupation and continue with their professions. Imperial prohibitions have fostered a growing black market. Local merchants have refocused their efforts on keeping the Imperial occupiers happy— offering goods both legal and illicit to unscrupulous officers to divert their attention away from any infractions. Cynical entrepreneurs look to make money off the struggles of the occupied and the needs of the spiritual. Transportation to and from the Holy City remains a lucrative business, as only specially licensed spacers are allowed direct access to the plateau ports. It is chaotic and unsustainable, but that is life on Jedha.

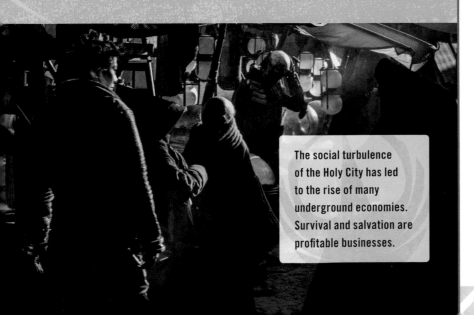

The social turbulence of the Holy City has led to the rise of many underground economies. Survival and salvation are profitable businesses.

THE DECRANIATED

Ghastly medical techniques perfected by a fugitive surgeon known to inhabit the Holy City have produced an order of servants known as the Decraniated. Wounded or incapacitated victims of the ongoing insurgency are transformed with cybernetic technology to become as subservient as droids. Disturbing rumors persist that those who undergo the surgery are in fact sold into unwilling servitude and stripped of their individuality by the medical procedure. The Decraniated servants of Gesh's Tapcafe keep boisterous off-duty Imperials content with tea and other libations.

Programmable neuro-box interface

Freshly brewed chav tea ready for serving

DOBIAS COLE-TRUTEN

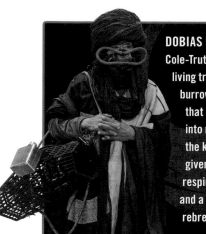

Cole-Truten makes a meager living trapping and selling burrowing silichordates that other vendors turn into meals. Digging near the kyber mines has given him a chronic respiratory condition and a need for a rebreather.

GAVRA UBRENTO

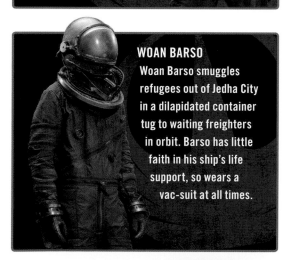

Part of a roving mechanic crew that offers repair services, Gavra Ubrento is skilled at keeping starship propulsion systems functional, despite a lack of access to state-of-the-art technical tools and facilities.

WOAN BARSO

Woan Barso smuggles refugees out of Jedha City in a dilapidated container tug to waiting freighters in orbit. Barso has little faith in his ship's life support, so wears a vac-suit at all times.

VALWID INED

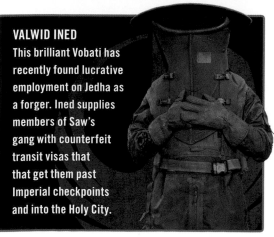

This brilliant Vobati has recently found lucrative employment on Jedha as a forger. Ined supplies members of Saw's gang with counterfeit transit visas that that get them past Imperial checkpoints and into the Holy City.

TAM POSLA

An interstellar lawman representing the Milvayne Authority (as marked on his helmet), Posla has voyaged well beyond his jurisdiction and become a bounty hunter. He is investigating claims of kidnapping, forced servitude, and surgical alteration of victims from the streets of Jedha. These reports resemble a rash of crimes on Milvayne, attributed to a pair of visiting spacers using the suspected aliases of Roofoo and Sawkee. Though Posla has been taken off the case by his superior officer, he is determined to bring these heinous criminals to justice.

Targeting array on articulated stalk

Portable scanner array in EM-proof pouch

Modified extended magazine BlasTech DL-17 blaster rifle

IPKC license in patch pocket

JEDHA CIVILIANS

Bottle marked with the name of the Roalj temple

GUCH YDROMA

Ydroma claims to have been touched by the god of his Phirmist beliefs during a desert pilgrimage, and gifted with the mystical ability to summon water. He has visited the many temples of the Holy City and brought forth water "as if from the air itself," sealing the liquid bounty into bottles marked with the temple name. He sells these bottles to believers and the thirsty alike.

K-OHN (KONE)

A manumitted L-1 tactical droid, K-OHN offers his programmed skills for hire in exchange for credits, spare parts, or direct power boosts. K-OHN's versatile language processors are often employed in the marketplace, where he is able to help travelers complete complex transactions, no questions asked. He has befriended a band of street urchins and shares a portion of his credits with them so they can eat. K-OHN is saving up for a processor upgrade so that he can begin to understand the nature of spirituality.

AA-1 VerboBrain processor

JEDHA CHILDREN

The tragedy of the Jedha insurgency is magnified when seen through the eyes of its most vulnerable. Orphans and castaway children are found throughout the Holy City, hungry and looking for protection. Many of the faiths within the city walls have taken the children as wards. Young Pendra Siliu is fortunate enough to still have a living mother, who is desperately seeking passage out of the war zone to somewhere—anywhere—safe.

Open cuff prone to dust contamination

FASSIO ABLUND

Fassio sought protection from the insurgency by selling secrets of their movements to the Empire. After getting caught stealing Imperial armor from a fallen trooper, he is declared a criminal, and now has no allies.

NESTA TERM

A self-proclaimed Lens of the Central Isopter, Nesta worships death itself. Her obsession with oblivion has brought her to dangerous places alongside her fellow cultists. On Jedha, they are said to study the harmonies of discord.

JALICE ANDIT

Gun-for-hire Jalice and her husband Joali are thrill seekers and profiteers who thrive in the chaos of the Holy City. They are loosely allied to Saw Gerrera's rebels, so long as credits keep flowing to them and they are allowed to participate in outbreaks of violence.

CAYSIN BOG

A high-gravity humanoid, Caysin Bog was blown apart in an insurgency strike and pieced together again by a mysterious man named Roofoo. The surgical work matches the work done on the Decraniated.

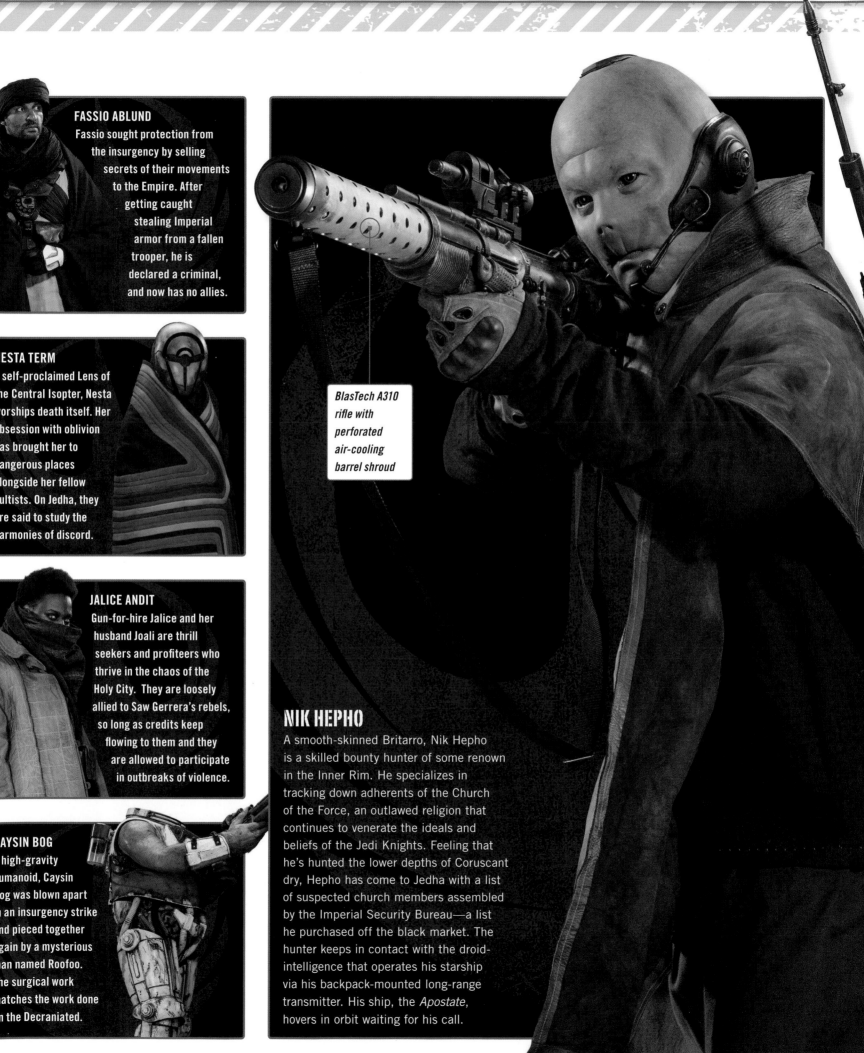

BlasTech A310 rifle with perforated air-cooling barrel shroud

NIK HEPHO

A smooth-skinned Britarro, Nik Hepho is a skilled bounty hunter of some renown in the Inner Rim. He specializes in tracking down adherents of the Church of the Force, an outlawed religion that continues to venerate the ideals and beliefs of the Jedi Knights. Feeling that he's hunted the lower depths of Coruscant dry, Hepho has come to Jedha with a list of suspected church members assembled by the Imperial Security Bureau—a list he purchased off the black market. The hunter keeps in contact with the droid-intelligence that operates his starship via his backpack-mounted long-range transmitter. His ship, the *Apostate*, hovers in orbit waiting for his call.

CULTURE CLASH

The ancient and the modern share uncomfortably close quarters in the tight corridors of the Holy City. Stormtroopers keep active patrols, confiscating sizable examples of kyber crystals, whether they be unrefined stones or already carved holy totems.

SAW GERRERA

EXTREMIST, MADMAN, AND TERRORIST are all labels that Saw Gerrera has been branded with—by sworn enemies and reluctant allies alike. Such slurs mean nothing to Saw. He has been waging war against the Empire since the very start of its reign, when the emergent power reneged on its promise of liberty for his homeworld of Onderon after the Clone Wars. Saw has lost so much in this fight that fighting is all he knows and has left.

A few years ago, before Saw's health began its downward spiral, moments of personable lucidity were more frequent.

During the Clone Wars, Onderon erupted in civil war as a revolt rejected a monarch installed by the Separatists. As the planet willingly joined the Confederacy of Independent Systems, the Republic could not wage open war there. Instead, Jedi Knights secretly trained and equipped the Onderonian rebels to battle the Separatists. Saw and his sister, Steela, were the young leaders of this insurgency. During this conflict, Saw was captured and tortured by agents of the Separatist king. This, coupled with the death of his sister, hardened Saw into a remorseless warrior. When the Empire annexed Onderon after the Clone Wars, Saw became a popular leader in a rebellion to repulse the offworlders. It is a bitter irony that the insurgent trained and armed as a proxy ally in one war would become the unscrupulous enemy in the next.

Saw became obsessed with stopping the Empire and discovering its secret plots, no matter what the cost to his humanity.

JEDHA REUNION
When Jyn Erso steps back into Saw's life, the warm man he once was reemerges. Saw saved Jyn as a child on Lah'mu and trained her to fight in his rebel cell. He was like a father to her, and he grew to view her as his daughter.

PARANOIA RUNS DEEP

As Saw has become increasingly battle-damaged and unstable, his paranoia has grown. He believes agents of both the Empire and the Rebellion are vying to assassinate him for his past crimes. This paranoia is the latest evolution of his conviction that the Empire is up to something monstrous.

"SAVE THE DREAM! SAVE THE REBELLION!"
— SAW GERRERA'S PARTING WORDS

CAPTURED KYBER CRYSTAL CONTAINER

Pressure suit cuff

Walking stick carved from dxunwood

PORTABLE NEGATIVE PRESSURE VENTILATOR

Cybernetic foot plate

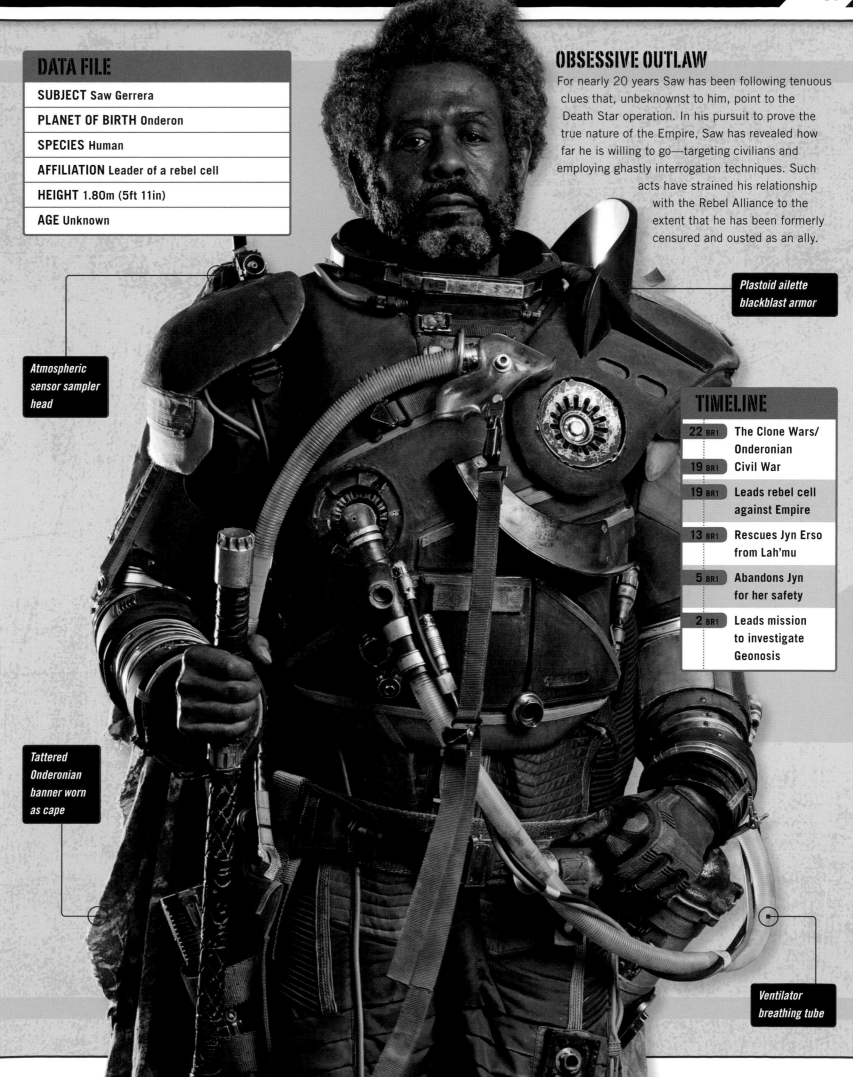

DATA FILE

SUBJECT Saw Gerrera

PLANET OF BIRTH Onderon

SPECIES Human

AFFILIATION Leader of a rebel cell

HEIGHT 1.80m (5ft 11in)

AGE Unknown

OBSESSIVE OUTLAW

For nearly 20 years Saw has been following tenuous clues that, unbeknownst to him, point to the Death Star operation. In his pursuit to prove the true nature of the Empire, Saw has revealed how far he is willing to go—targeting civilians and employing ghastly interrogation techniques. Such acts have strained his relationship with the Rebel Alliance to the extent that he has been formerly censured and ousted as an ally.

Atmospheric sensor sampler head

Plastoid ailette blackblast armor

Tattered Onderonian banner worn as cape

Ventilator breathing tube

TIMELINE

22 BR1	The Clone Wars/ Onderonian
19 BR1	Civil War
19 BR1	Leads rebel cell against Empire
13 BR1	Rescues Jyn Erso from Lah'mu
5 BR1	Abandons Jyn for her safety
2 BR1	Leads mission to investigate Geonosis

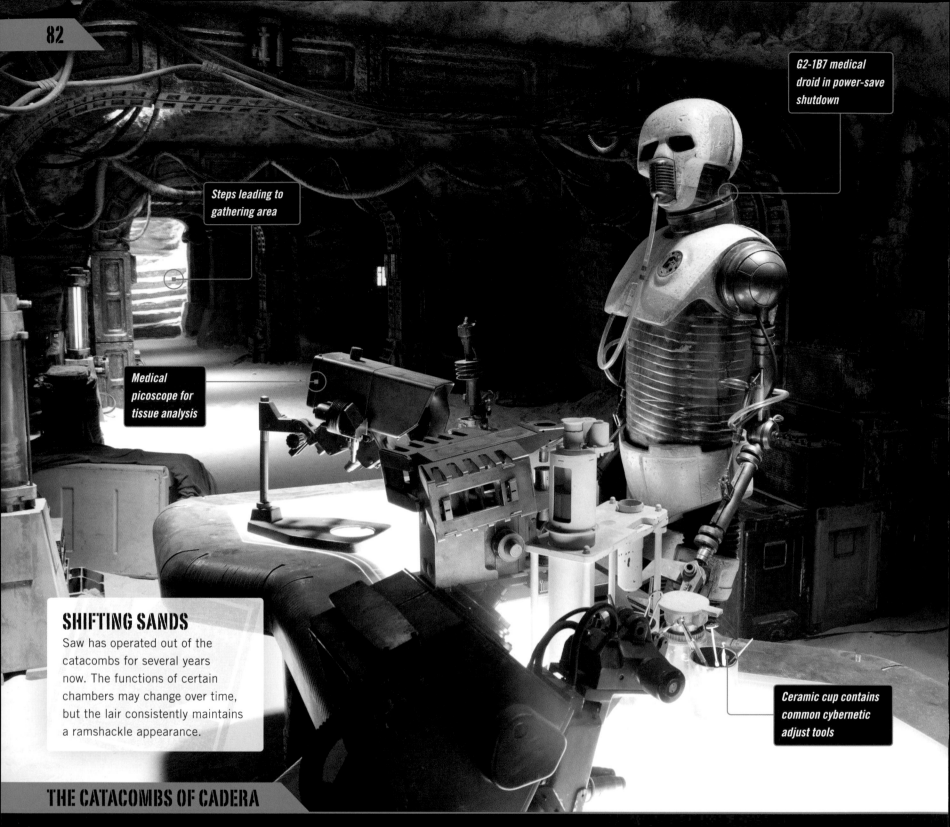

G2-1B7 medical
droid in power-save
shutdown

Steps leading to
gathering area

Medical
picoscope for
tissue analysis

SHIFTING SANDS

Saw has operated out of the
catacombs for several years
now. The functions of certain
chambers may change over time,
but the lair consistently maintains
a ramshackle appearance.

Ceramic cup contains
common cybernetic
adjust tools

THE CATACOMBS OF CADERA

SAW'S HIDEOUT

ACROSS THE DESERT from the butte that lifts the Holy City
above Jedha's flatland crater basin is a cluster of towering
wind-worn rocks. Known by locals as the Catacombs of Cadera,
this site contains the ancient remains of a people whose name
and history have been long forgotten. Statues that lined the
path to these rocks were toppled centuries ago. Locals give
the rocks a wide berth, believing them to be haunted. In a
sense they are, but by Saw—not by spirits of the departed.

VANTAGE POINT
The cave's latticed window is a more recent addition installed by the
Church of the Contained Crescent. It abandoned the catacombs prior
to Saw Gerrera's settlement on Jedha years earlier.

LIFE SUPPORT

Saw weathers poor health—driven beyond the limits of his broken body by his zeal to punish the Empire. The pressurized suit he relies upon to keep his shattered pulmonary system working requires constant upkeep. The time between Saw's diagnostic rests shrinks with each passing year.

Analysis computer tracks purging of Geonosian insecticide from reinforced lungs

Former flight chair refitted into diagnostics station

HIDDEN HEADQUARTERS

THE GUT
The dungeons of the catacombs are known as the Gut, for prisoners are known to stew here for long, listless stretches of time before being subjected to interrogation.

WEAPON RACKS
Saw launches his insurgency against the Jedha occupation from inside the catacombs. His soldiers repair and modify weapons here to keep them operational in harsh desert conditions.

POWERLESS PLAY
There are few amenities in the catacombs. Soldiers while away time playing dejarik in a hand-carved analog form, as they do not have access to a holographic game table.

G2-1B7

55VH Vocabulator

Saw's medical droid was modified to bypass some of the intrinsic programming that would ordinarily prevent a 2-1B unit from dispensing drugs at dangerous intervals. G2-1B7 is baffled that Saw is still alive. The droid is frequently deactivated to prevent it from building an ethical case to discontinue treatment.

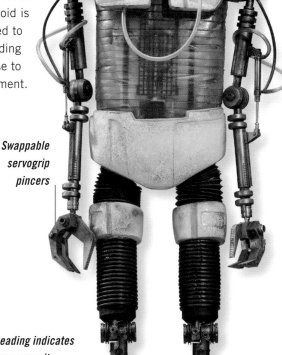

DEAD MAN'S BINSPO CARD GAME

Swappable servogrip pincers

Reading indicates lung capacity

IMPROVISED PLETHYSMOGRAPH

SAW'S MILITIA

SAW'S RAGTAG MOVEMENT has changed faces many times since its origin as an underground rebellion on Onderon during the Clone Wars. As Saw spread his activities far from his homeworld and began attacking scattered Imperial targets, he recruited like-minded warriors with a taste for conflict. This was the environment in which Jyn Erso was raised—surrounded by hardened soldiers whose idealism has been burned away by near misses and harsh losses.

Many question whether Saw is doing more harm than good on Jedha, as his militia's actions wound civilians just as often as they hurt the Empire. But Saw's zealotry knows few boundaries. He knows that the kyber deposits pulled out of Jedha are being used to create something unthinkable and, after years of investigating, finding the answers has become an obsession.

Some in Saw's ranks share his desire to expose the Empire. Others want to make the Empire hurt in revenge for past brutalities that have robbed them of a sense of belonging.

WEETEEF CYU-BEE

Kilo for kilo, Weeteef Cyu-Bee is one of the most destructive members of Saw's band of rebels. The diminutive Talpini can hide easily among the taller beings that congregate in the Holy City. A sharpshooter, Weeteef specializes in explosives. He custom-builds the sticky bombs used by the insurrectionists against the Imperial patrols of AT-ST walkers and tanks.

Tibanna-jacked DH-17/E-11 hybrid custom

MOROFF

Brawny Moroff seeks out combat zones across the galaxy, selling his firepower to anyone who might need it. Not interested in the details of the conflict between Empire and rebels, the mighty Gigoran mercenary figures there's money to be made for a towering gunner of great strength. He's found like-minded company in Gerrera's group and is part of the patrol that brings Bodhi Rook before Saw for questioning.

Vulk TAU-6-23 "Blastmill" rotary blaster cannon

Jyn Erso surprises the militia when she loudly proclaims herself to be the daughter of Galen Erso—the Imperial scientist mentioned in a message for Saw Gerrera.

KULLBEE SPERADO
Gunslinger Kullbee was recruited by Saw on Serralonis and is running from a past he refuses to talk about. Intensely private, Kullbee disappears for weeks on end, and has been spotted praying at the Temple of the Whills.

EUWOOD GOR
A former Rebel Alliance Pathfinder from Alderaan, Gor abandoned much when he "went native" fighting the Empire on Onderon and joining up with Saw's forces.

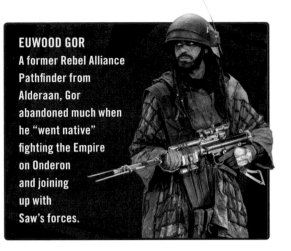

MAGVA YARRO
A survivor of the Ghorman Massacre, where Imperials slaughtered peaceful protesters, Magva believes Mon Mothma's rebels to be ineffective cowards. She is a forward spotter for Saw's Cavern Angels squadron.

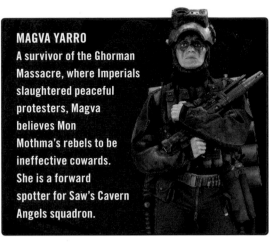

CYCYED OCK
The cyber-optic wired into Ock's brain grants him sharp vision. With this he analyzes kyber deposits and examines microcircuitry. He also has unerring aim when powerfully throwing his vibrorang weapon.

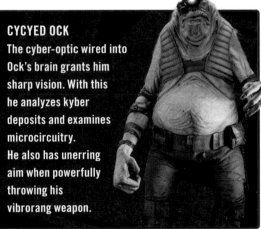

LEEVAN TENZA
A laconic Sabat who, until five years ago, was part of General Dodonna's team of rebels, Tenza faced court-martial for disobeying orders and preemptively engaging an Imperial target. The defiant toothpick-chomping Tenza didn't proclaim innocence. Instead he embraced his guilt and escaped rebel custody, aligning with Saw Gerrera.

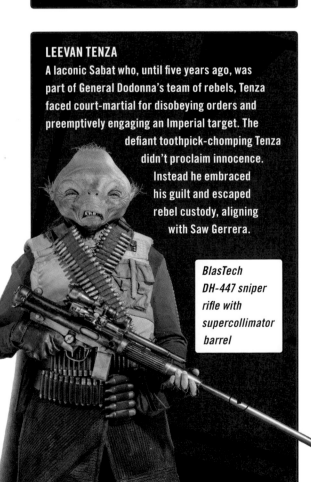

BlasTech DH-447 sniper rifle with supercollimator barrel

BEEZER FORTUNA
A cousin to Tatooine-based Bib Fortuna, Beezer resents his Twi'lek family's involvement in the criminal underworld and has always been the most politically-minded of his clan. During the Clone Wars he was inspired by the liberation efforts of Cham Syndulla's rebellion on their homeworld Ryloth. Beezer was captured by the Empire during a roundup of seditionists in the Twi'lek capital of Lessu but was freed in a raid launched by Saw Gerrera's troops. Now loyal to Saw, Beezer is one of Saw's chief strategists, mapping out activity both local, in the Holy City, and galactic, as he helps Saw carry out his private war against the Empire.

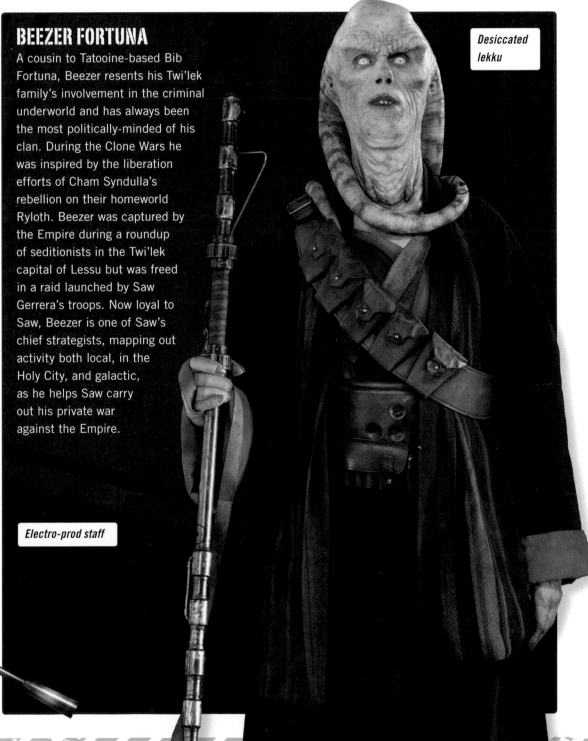

Desiccated lekku

Electro-prod staff

TWO TUBES

EDRIO AND BENTHIC are mercenary Tognaths who have signed up with Saw Gerrera's rebels and operate out of Jedha. They share the bluntly descriptive moniker of "Two Tubes" for the breathing apparatuses that allow them to operate in human-standard atmospheres. Their native world of Yar Togna was conquered and occupied by the Empire, forcing them to flee as refugees. With a desire to strike back at the Empire, Edrio and Benthic have no reservations about Gerrera's violent methods.

Benthic Two Tubes is a spotter and sniper who favors a monocular scope worn around his neck with a leather cord.

Evolutionarily ancient, members of the Tognath species have genetic markers indicating a distant relationship to the Kel Dor and Gand. Unusually, they combine both insectoid and mammalian traits, possessing endo- and exoskeletons. Their compound eyes require artificial lenses to better process the spectrum, and their hearing and sense of balance is better maintained with cybernetic enhancers fitted into recesses on their scalps. Though such devices look uncomfortable, Tognath have primitive nervous systems, making them immune to most pain. For this reason, Saw entrusts the Two Tubes duo with operational information, as he knows they cannot have such knowledge tortured from them.

Benthic prowls the narrow alleyways of the Holy City. Though he operates at the equivalent as a rebel lieutenant, he holds no formal rank.

EDRIO'S CAVERN ANGELS X-WING

CAVERN ANGELS

Saw maintains a small squadron of six X-wing fighters dubbed the Cavern Angels, which operates out of the caves near the Cadera Catacombs. The pilots swap parts between semifunctional fighters to make one or two reliable vessels. Limited supplies of astromechs and hyperdrive parts keep the Cavern Angels in usage.

"YOU STRUCK AT ONE OF US. YOU HAVE MADE MANY ENEMIES."
— EDRIO TWO TUBES

Edrio is the pilot while Benthic is the marksman of the Two Tubes eggmates, though both are skilled at ground combat.

LOST IN TRANSLATION

Benthic brought Imperial defector Bodhi Rook to Saw Gerrera, marching him blindfolded to the Catacombs from Jedha City. The term "defector" has no translation in Tognath, so it was fortunate Moroff was able to convey the concept to Two Tubes lest Bodhi not survive the encounter. Benthic would ordinarily not hesitate to kill an Imperial.

Pressure-tight corrugated metal breathing hose

BOND OF BROTHERS

The term "eggmate" is a translation of a Tognath phrase that is otherwise untranslatable into Basic. Most consider them brothers, but that is an imperfect comparison. On occasion, Tognath eggs graft together while in their suspension jelly. The emergent Tognath larvae share an unbreakable bond, exhibiting what appears to be rudimentary telepathy.

Canisters with improvised explosives (inert without detonators)

Black-market sniper blaster rifle

DATA FILE

SUBJECTS	Edrio and Benthic Two Tubes
PLANET OF BIRTH	Yar Togna
SPECIES	Tognath
AFFILIATION	Saw Gerrera's rebel faction
HEIGHT	1.90m (6ft 3in)
AGE	32 standard years

BODHI ROOK

A FORMER IMPERIAL, Bodhi has strong piloting and technical skills that he now puts to use for the Rebellion. Before defecting, Bodhi regularly flew cargo runs of kyber crystals from Jedha to a secret Imperial research facility on Eadu. Through this work, he came into contact with captive scientist Galen Erso. Erso impressed upon Rook the horrific nature of the Death Star under Imperial construction—a weapon whose existence Rook was facilitating with his flights.

Bodhi is cleared to pilot all manner of Imperial cargo vessels, from *Lambda*-class personnel carriers to the larger *Zeta*-class long-range shuttles.

A crisis of conscience led Rook to switch sides, but the Rebel Alliance is—by design—not easy to find. He surrendered to Saw Gerrera's forces, entrenched in occupied Jedha. As a captive of the ever-suspicious Gerrera, Rook was subjected to withering interrogation that tested his sanity, but he endured the questioning to pass on a crucial holographic recording to Gerrera—a recording that would draw Jyn Erso and the Rebel Alliance proper into his increasingly hectic life. Bodhi, a reluctant rebel, is nonetheless a far more reluctant Imperial and digs deep to find courage to fight the Empire. Ever practical, but anxious, he readily offers his skills and knowledge to help the rebels, even coining the team name "Rogue One."

Told to keep his engines hot and his eyes open during the infiltration of Scarif, Bodhi plays a crucial role in the eventual theft of the Death Star plans.

ASSESSING THE ODDS

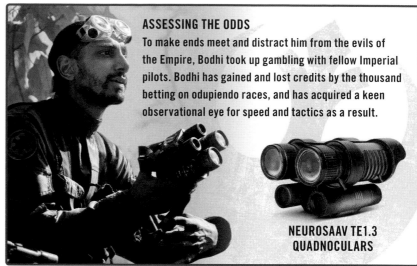

To make ends meet and distract him from the evils of the Empire, Bodhi took up gambling with fellow Imperial pilots. Bodhi has gained and lost credits by the thousand betting on odupiendo races, and has acquired a keen observational eye for speed and tactics as a result.

NEUROSAAV TE1.3 QUADNOCULARS

LOCAL PILOT

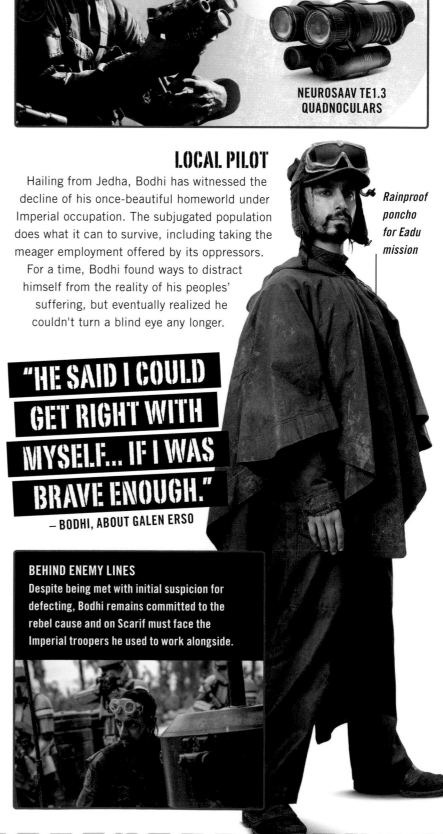

Hailing from Jedha, Bodhi has witnessed the decline of his once-beautiful homeworld under Imperial occupation. The subjugated population does what it can to survive, including taking the meager employment offered by its oppressors. For a time, Bodhi found ways to distract himself from the reality of his peoples' suffering, but eventually realized he couldn't turn a blind eye any longer.

Rainproof poncho for Eadu mission

"HE SAID I COULD GET RIGHT WITH MYSELF... IF I WAS BRAVE ENOUGH."
— BODHI, ABOUT GALEN ERSO

BEHIND ENEMY LINES

Despite being met with initial suspicion for defecting, Bodhi remains committed to the rebel cause and on Scarif must face the Imperial troopers he used to work alongside.

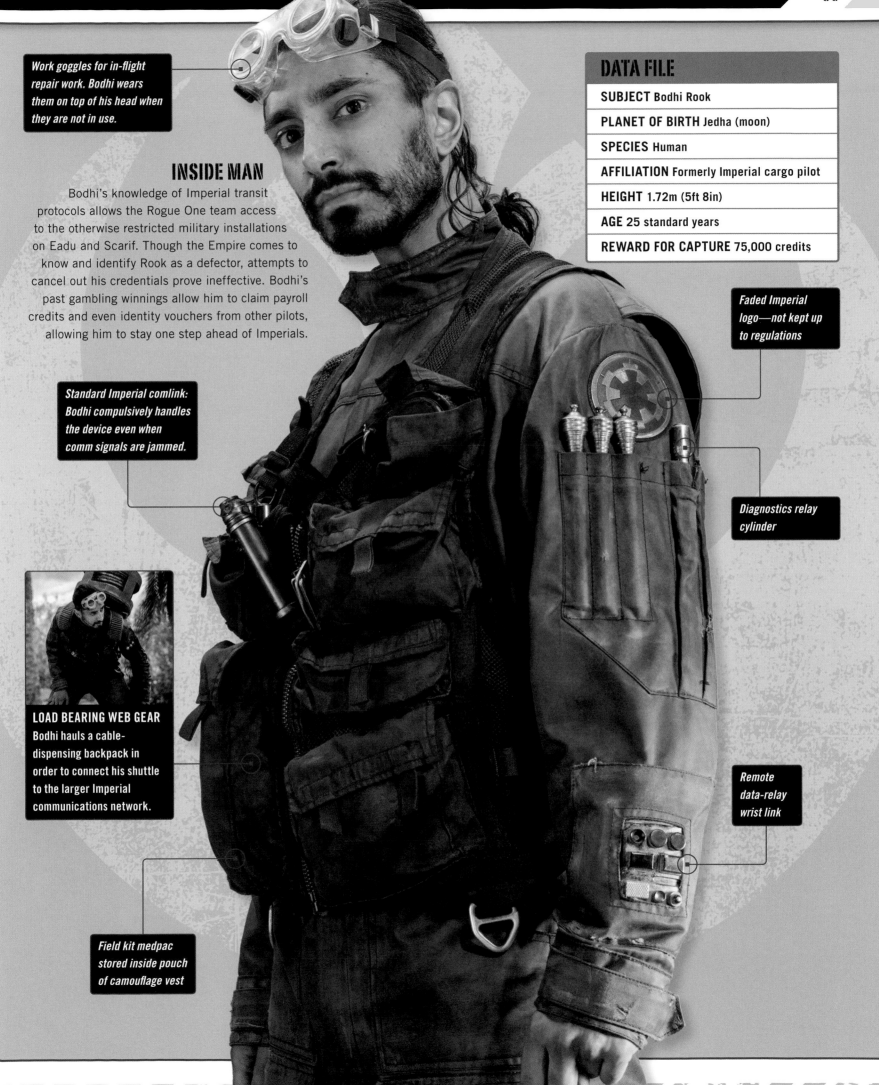

Work goggles for in-flight repair work. Bodhi wears them on top of his head when they are not in use.

DATA FILE

SUBJECT	Bodhi Rook
PLANET OF BIRTH	Jedha (moon)
SPECIES	Human
AFFILIATION	Formerly Imperial cargo pilot
HEIGHT	1.72m (5ft 8in)
AGE	25 standard years
REWARD FOR CAPTURE	75,000 credits

INSIDE MAN

Bodhi's knowledge of Imperial transit protocols allows the Rogue One team access to the otherwise restricted military installations on Eadu and Scarif. Though the Empire comes to know and identify Rook as a defector, attempts to cancel out his credentials prove ineffective. Bodhi's past gambling winnings allow him to claim payroll credits and even identity vouchers from other pilots, allowing him to stay one step ahead of Imperials.

Faded Imperial logo—not kept up to regulations

Standard Imperial comlink: Bodhi compulsively handles the device even when comm signals are jammed.

Diagnostics relay cylinder

LOAD BEARING WEB GEAR
Bodhi hauls a cable-dispensing backpack in order to connect his shuttle to the larger Imperial communications network.

Remote data-relay wrist link

Field kit medpac stored inside pouch of camouflage vest

CHIRRUT ÎMWE

DEEPLY SPIRITUAL CHIRRUT ÎMWE believes that all living things are connected through the Force. His sightless eyes do not prevent him from being a highly skilled warrior. Though he seemingly lacks Force abilities, this warrior monk has rigorously honed his body through intense physical and mental discipline.

Chirrut is from a near-extinct order, the Guardians of the Whills, which is devoted to protecting the Temple of the Kyber in the Holy City of Jedha. An ancient order, its origins are lost to time and inextricably woven into the legends of the Jedi Knights. Some believers insist the Jedi drew inspiration from the followers of Jedha, while historians surmise it is likely the opposite. Whatever the truth, it is all a matter of deepest faith to Chirrut.

Chirrut does not speak of how he came to be blinded, but due to the simplicity of Jedha medicine, the condition is real and irreversible. He has adapted to his new state well, with a mental discipline that filters the most crucial information from his remaining senses, and a keen control of body that allows him to move with pinpoint precision through his imagined surroundings.

OPPOSITES IN BALANCE
Chirrut Îmwe and Baze Malbus share a homeworld and a history, though they strike a compelling contrast. Baze is a hardened pragmatist, while Chirrut's faith flourishes even in trying times. They both claim to act as the protector of the other.

> **"THE FORCE IS WITH ME, AND I AM WITH THE FORCE. AND I FEAR NOTHING FOR ALL IS AS THE FORCE WILLS IT."**
> — CHIRRUT ÎMWE

FATEFUL BEACHHEAD
Chirrut accompanies the Rogue One mission to Scarif as part of the ground team offering vital cover for the infiltrators who penetrate the Citadel.

Handcrafted lightbow carried on back

Walking staff in defensive position

THE BLIND MASTER

Chirrut is a practitioner of zama-shiwo, a Jedha martial art also known as "the inward eye of the outward hand." The central pillar involves perfection of physical awareness—conscious accounting of a body's placement, contact, and internal functions. It is said that a master of these techniques can alter his heart rate, oxygen intake, and vital processes to produce seemingly supernatural effects. This is similar to Jedi physical exercises that emphasize bodily control—some believe due to a cultural connection with the ancient past.

Confronted by a patrol of occupying stormtroopers, Chirrut takes advantage of the enemy's tendency to underestimate his raw physical ability.

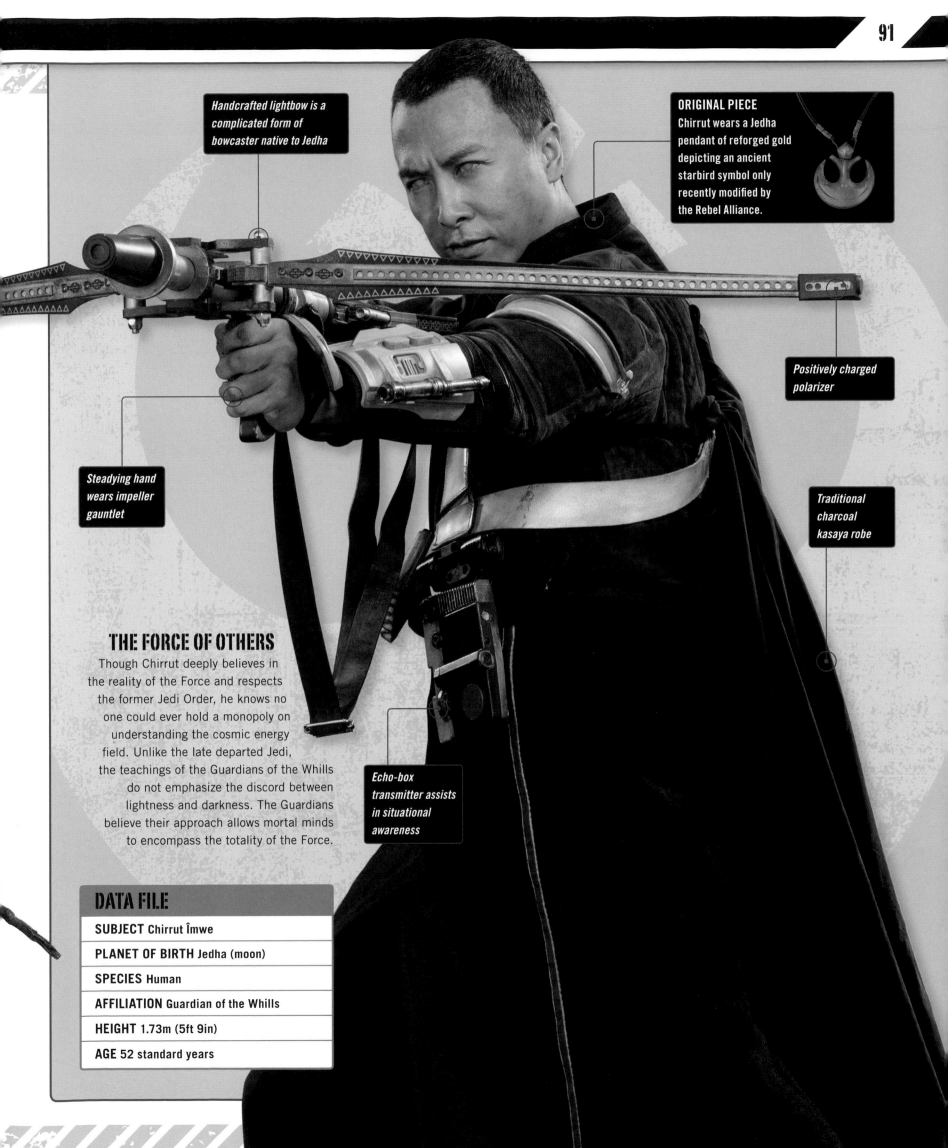

Handcrafted lightbow is a complicated form of bowcaster native to Jedha

ORIGINAL PIECE
Chirrut wears a Jedha pendant of reforged gold depicting an ancient starbird symbol only recently modified by the Rebel Alliance.

Positively charged polarizer

Steadying hand wears impeller gauntlet

Traditional charcoal kasaya robe

THE FORCE OF OTHERS

Though Chirrut deeply believes in the reality of the Force and respects the former Jedi Order, he knows no one could ever hold a monopoly on understanding the cosmic energy field. Unlike the late departed Jedi, the teachings of the Guardians of the Whills do not emphasize the discord between lightness and darkness. The Guardians believe their approach allows mortal minds to encompass the totality of the Force.

Echo-box transmitter assists in situational awareness

DATA FILE

SUBJECT	Chirrut Îmwe
PLANET OF BIRTH	Jedha (moon)
SPECIES	Human
AFFILIATION	Guardian of the Whills
HEIGHT	1.73m (5ft 9in)
AGE	52 standard years

BATTLE ON JEDHA

SENSING A GOOD SOUL in Jyn Erso, Chirrut Îmwe comes to her assistance by standing up to a squad of stormtroopers. The incredulous—and unimaginative—Imperials cannot believe the gall of this local. In attempting to apprehend Îmwe, however, the stormtroopers get an unforgettable lesson that looks can be deceiving. Chirrut dodges their attempts to apprehend or blast him, sidesteps their attacks, and delivers powerful blows with his walking stick.

SURROUNDED

While Jyn tries to battle past the stormtroopers they come up against in Jedha's streets, and K-2SO tries to bluff his way past them with faked Imperial authority, it is Chirrut's fast moves and Baze's firepower, that eventually save the Operation Fracture team from immediate and early failure.

STREET FIGHTING

A heavily armed tank becomes the object of insurgent attack, as Saw Gerrera's militia take advantage of the tank's decreased mobility in the congested city streets. A well-thrown sticky bomb transforms the vehicle into a smoldering roadblock, and rebels strike from the overhead parapets with blasters and grenades. Unaware that they are allies, the insurgents nearly take out Jyn Erso and Cassian Andor in the attack.

BAZE MALBUS

FORMER GUARDIAN OF THE WHILLS Baze Malbus has found a more concrete cause in fighting the Empire. A combat-hardened veteran of countless skirmishes on embattled Jedha and elsewhere, Baze has a bravado that provides a marked contrast to the spiritual centeredness of his best friend and moral compass, Chirrut Îmwe. Baze's faith has seemingly evaporated in the fires of Jedha, and the weight of his world's subjugation has crushed his soul to a compressed core of anger. But his gruff demeanor is also marked with gallows humor and constant exasperation at his best friend's mantras.

Baze Malbus eyes newcomers to Jedha with a seasoned wariness, and his finger is never far from a very responsive trigger.

Baze used to have little regard for the Rebel Alliance, lumping Mon Mothma's freedom fighters in with Saw Gerrera's extremists in his mind. Provided everyone was firing in the same direction—toward the Empire—he cared little for individual politics. But when the threat of the Death Star forever changes Jedha, the Rebellion becomes intensely personal for Baze.

Baze kneels on the beaches of Scarif, ready for the fight against the Empire to intensify.

ON SCARIF
Amid the blazing wreckage of a downed U-wing, Baze opens a spray of return fire at incoming death trooper reinforcements.

Modified and highly illegal repeating blaster

"THEY DESTROYED OUR HOME. I WILL KILL THEM."

— BAZE MALBUS

HEAVY GUNNER

Baze has done away with the vestments of the Guardians of the Whills, exchanging them for combat armor and a flight suit delivered by an offworld visitor to Jedha. When Baze defends his occupied city, the elegance and discipline of the Guardians is forgotten. Baze's heavy repeating blaster gives him a sense of retribution, which, like the ammunition cells that power his cannon, requires constant replenishment.

HANDIWORK
Baze prefers heavy firepower, such as this launcher, which he fires against an AT-ACT walker, but he hasn't forgotten his hand-to-hand combat skills. While on Scarif he silently incapacitates many enemies—thus aiding the Rogue One infiltration mission.

REPEAT AFTER ME

Baze's repeating cannons use an internal cycling lasing array to increase the operational lifespan of the internal componentry. The equivalent of five laser rifles' worth of destructive output streams through the weapon. To better fit this amount of technology into a compact frame, much of the hardware is externalized, distributed through a flexible belt and backpack-carried cooling and power cell. Baze's weapon is clearly illegal for civilian use, but laws on Jedha have become meaningless in times of survival and insurgency.

Baze has let his hair grow past what is customary for Guardians

Exhaust vent for generator

Dust and weather shroud

Quad-folded plastoid polymer armor

High-density power cells in carriage frame

Galven-circuitry flexible charge belt

Static-grounded cannon muzzle

DATA FILE

SUBJECT	Baze Malbus
PLANET OF BIRTH	Jedha (moon)
SPECIES	Human
AFFILIATION	Former Guardian of the Whills
HEIGHT	1.80m (5ft 11in)
AGE	53 standard years

GUARDIAN WEAPONS

THOUGH BOTH ARE GUARDIANS OF THE WHILLS, Baze and Chirrut could not be more different in their approach to combat. Traditionalist Chirrut still carries weapons associated with the ancient order, while Baze adopts an implement of modern warfare. Their methods suit them individually, and both are effective extensions of their distinctive personalities. Though Baze may chide Chirrut for his antiques, and Chirrut may decry Baze's reliance on soulless tools, they trust each other's defenses to such weapons.

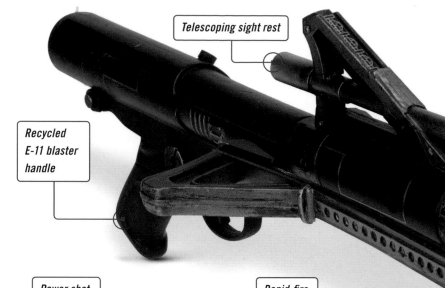

Telescoping sight rest

Recycled E-11 blaster handle

Electroscope

Power shot barrel

Rapid-fire barrel

ROCKET ATTACK
Non-traditional Baze has no problem using whatever weapon is at hand, including the SpecForces HH-12 rocket launcher that he appropriates on Scarif.

Carry bar

Galven-circuitry charge belt

Exhaust vent

DATA FILE

MANUFACTURER	Morellian Weapons Conglomerate
WEAPON SYSTEM	MWC-35c "Staccato Lightning" repeating cannon
MASS	30kg (4st 10lbs)
POWER SYSTEM	Condensed K-grade conductor cells
COOLING SYSTEM	Tankage of R717 refrigerant
AMMUNITION YIELD	35,000 rounds when fully charged

MULTI-FIRE, MULTI-TARGETS

Baze's repeating cannon has two fire modes. The standard mode fires at a rapid rate that allows Baze to spray a wide field of targets. The fitted electroscope has a smart targeting array that takes into account Baze's position and facing, and groups shots into bursts that maximize hits on specified targets. The secondary mode is a single-fire power shot. The lower barrel collects energy into these shots primed by a pump-action foreguard. Both modes draw from the same power source, but yield different levels of destructive output.

DATA FILE

MANUFACTURER Chirrut Îmwe	
WEAPON SYSTEM Traditional Guardian of the Whills lightbow	
MASS 8kg (1st 4lbs)	
POWER SYSTEM Diatium power cell	
COOLING SYSTEM Air-cooled	
AMMUNITION YIELD With standard blaster power cell, 50 rounds	

LIGHTBOW DEPLOYED
Stabilizing the long-barreled lightbow with an impeller-gauntlet-fitted hand, Chirrut pulls back on the handle deploying the opposing polarizer limbs. The impeller helps keep the flight of the bolt true and provides Chirrut with a sense of feedback.

Serving barrel

Polarizer limb (stowed)

Articulated riser gear teeth

Flashback suppressor rim

CHIRRUT'S LIGHTBOW

A lightbow is the traditional handcrafted weapon built by a Guardian of the Whills upon completion of the seventh duan—marking the Guardian's progression to physical perfection. The bow is largely analogous to the bowcaster weapons built by the Wookiees of Kashyyyk. The limbs of the bow extend on articulated risers, and each is tipped with a polarizer array that draws a charged particle round from the serving barrel. The released blast is more powerful than a heavy rifle.

Stabilizing handle

Case-hardened emitter barrel

CHIRRUT'S STAFF

Chirrut carries a flame-hardened uneti-wood staff to help guide his path as he walks through the streets of Jedha. The top is capped with a metal lamp that contains a kyber sliver. Designed as a symbolic source of inner illumination, it also allows Chirrut to better gauge where the end of the staff is, as he can hear both the battery and crystal harmonic.

Crystal containment lamp

Sanded uneti wood

Central grip

COMBAT ASSAULT TANK

THE EMPIRE HAS EXPENDED great effort to evolve its ground-based army beyond the already impressive capabilities inherited after the Clone Wars. The Empire has a vast amount of land to control, and as impressive as its starfleet is, control of a world requires planet-side presence. The growing arsenal of ground assault vehicles (GAVs), including heavy combat assault tanks, is seeing increasing deployment on worlds occupied by the Empire.

DATA FILE

MANUFACTURER	Rothana Heavy Engineering
MODEL	TX-225 GAVw "Occupier" combat assault tank
AFFILIATION	Galactic Empire
HEIGHT 1.82m (6ft)	LENGTH 7.30m (24ft)
CREW	3 (commander, driver, gunner)
SPEED	72kph (45mph) on road; 45kph (28mph) offroad
WEAPONS	2 elevating medium double laser cannons, 1 forward medium double laser cannon

PRECIOUS CARGO

The Empire confiscates kyber crystals from local mines and from the possession of the Jedha faithful, and stores them in armored cargo modules coded an orange hue. The tanks form an essential link in carrying these modules to waiting shuttle craft for transport to offworld Tarkin Initiative scientists.

Kyber crystal armored transport containers

Sealed hatch on commander station

Elevating gun-laying servo assembly

Magnetically secured modules

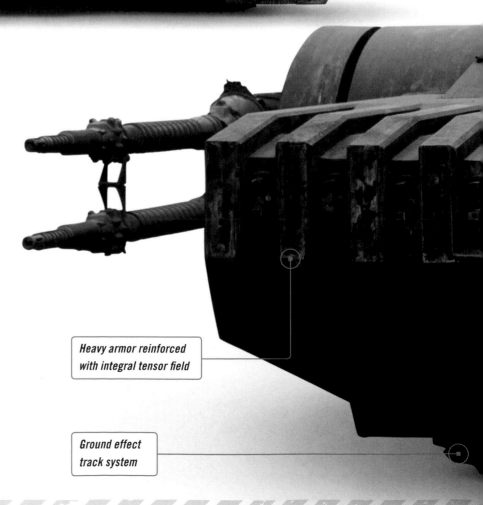

Heavy armor reinforced with integral tensor field

Ground effect track system

INSURGENT AMBUSH

As the tank turns onto Jedha City's Tythoni Square, it enters a perfect ambush site. Insurgents hidden in the parapets and on rooftops open fire, throwing explosives at the tank's propulsion system. A well-placed bomb disables the tank's treads, turning it into an even more exposed target.

Commander HC-4120 (First Sergeant Jimmon Arbmab)

ORDERS FROM THE TOP

The tank commander issues orders from the topmost hatch of the TX-225 "Occupier" combat assault tank, coordinating the actions of his crew. When deployed with accompanying infantry, the tank commander also leads those units as well, as the soldiers must defer to the needs and actions of the heavy armored vehicle. The commander's helmet systems are synced with the tank's combat computer, keeping up to date on rapidly evolving situations.

INFANTRY SUPPORT

Despite its heavy armor and armament, tanks may still be vulnerable to infantry assault. The close urban environment and elevated vantage points can be exploited by trained guerillas to trap and target tanks. To counter such attacks, an escort of standard stormtroopers accompanies the tank's slow progress through Jedha City.

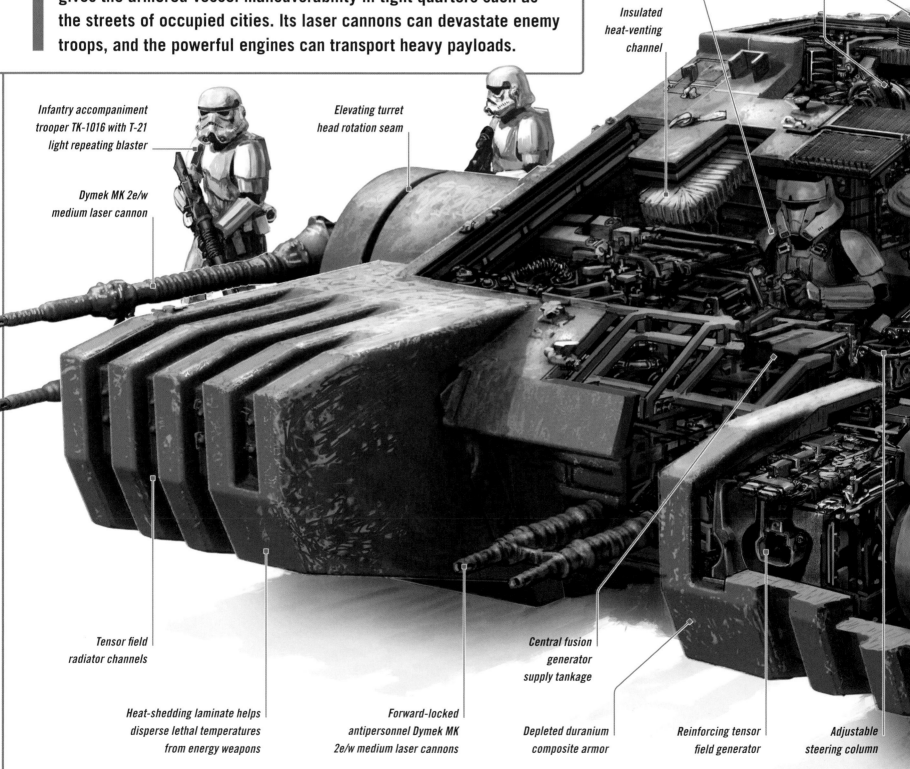

TX-225 OCCUPIER

ROTHANA HEAVY ENGINEERING has a long history of supplying armor to the Empire, including producing the first walkers deployed in the Clone Wars. Now a shadow of its former robust self, Rothana specializes in ground effect and repulsorlift armored vehicles. Its Imperial TX-225 assault tank rumbles along segmented tracks, which gives the armored vessel maneuverability in tight quarters such as the streets of occupied cities. Its laser cannons can devastate enemy troops, and the powerful engines can transport heavy payloads.

ARMOR STRUCTURE

Ground vehicles rarely boast shields, as air friction undercuts their performance and overworks deflector shield generators. Instead, the TX-225 has a composite laminate armor that balances weight with durability. A matrix of quadanium-enriched titanium interspersed with ceramic plates and phase-bonded onto an elastic lattice gives the armor remarkable resilience and toughness without overtaxing the vehicle's propulsion systems with excess weight.

Gunner/technician

Rothana Heavy Engineering ADGT-1500 engine block

Radiator cap

Insulated heat-venting channel

Infantry accompaniment trooper TK-1016 with T-21 light repeating blaster

Elevating turret head rotation seam

Dymek MK 2e/w medium laser cannon

Tensor field radiator channels

Heat-shedding laminate helps disperse lethal temperatures from energy weapons

Forward-locked antipersonnel Dymek MK 2e/w medium laser cannons

Central fusion generator supply tankage

Depleted duranium composite armor

Reinforcing tensor field generator

Adjustable steering column

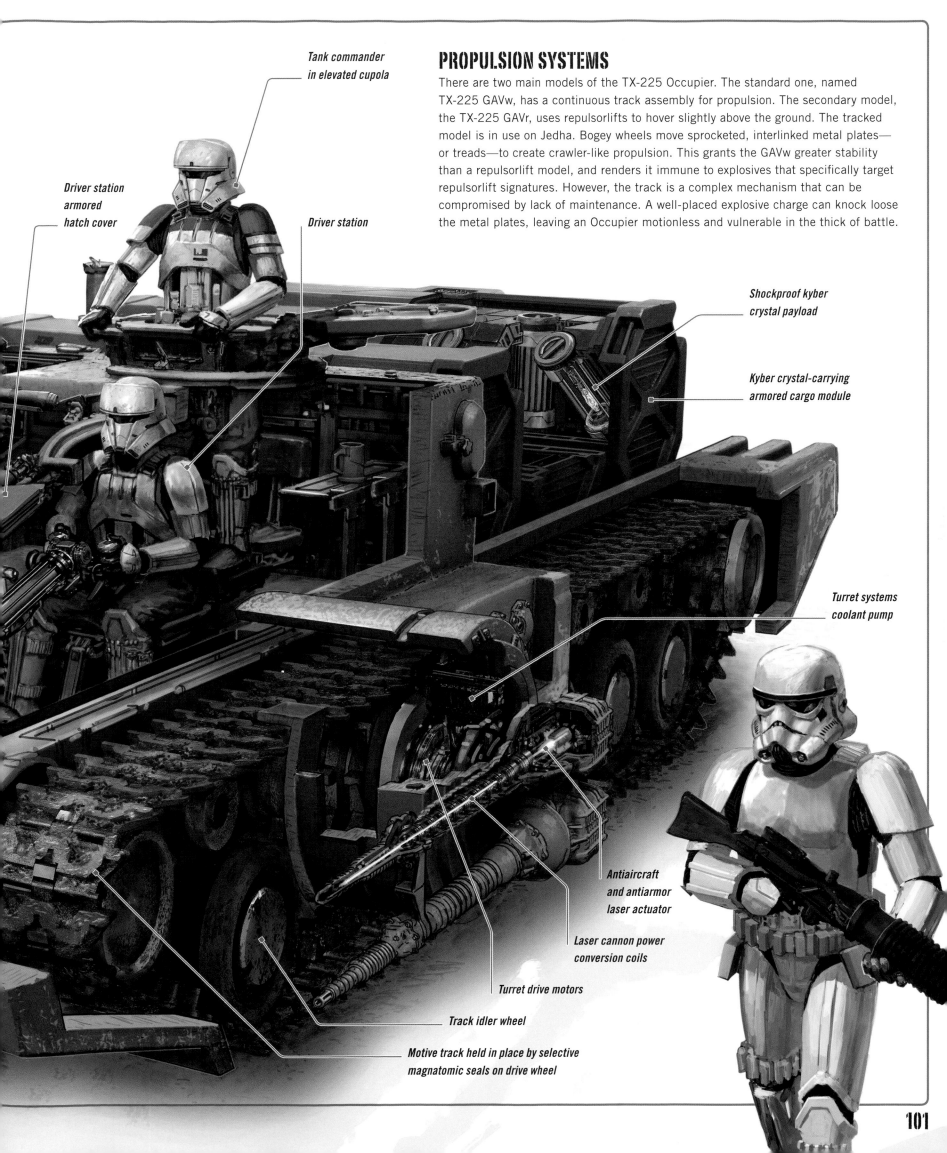

Tank commander
in elevated cupola

Driver station
armored
hatch cover

Driver station

PROPULSION SYSTEMS

There are two main models of the TX-225 Occupier. The standard one, named TX-225 GAVw, has a continuous track assembly for propulsion. The secondary model, the TX-225 GAVr, uses repulsorlifts to hover slightly above the ground. The tracked model is in use on Jedha. Bogey wheels move sprocketed, interlinked metal plates—or treads—to create crawler-like propulsion. This grants the GAVw greater stability than a repulsorlift model, and renders it immune to explosives that specifically target repulsorlift signatures. However, the track is a complex mechanism that can be compromised by lack of maintenance. A well-placed explosive charge can knock loose the metal plates, leaving an Occupier motionless and vulnerable in the thick of battle.

Shockproof kyber
crystal payload

Kyber crystal-carrying
armored cargo module

Turret systems
coolant pump

Antiaircraft
and antiarmor
laser actuator

Laser cannon power
conversion coils

Turret drive motors

Track idler wheel

Motive track held in place by selective
magnatomic seals on drive wheel

TANK DRIVERS

IMPERIAL COMBAT DRIVERS operate the Empire's ground assault vehicles (GAVs)—driving everything from troop transports to heavily armed combat assault tanks. Combat drivers are lightly armored, relying on the thick skin of their vehicles to protect them in battle. On Jedha, combat drivers steer the mighty TX-225 combat assault tanks through the narrow avenues of the Holy City, demonstrating their superior firepower and escorting the kyber shipments being extracted from the planet.

Perched on top of the vehicle's armored hull, a tank commander has a vantage point that allows him to make immediate decisions during combat operations.

The TX-225 has a minimum crew requirement of three: a tank commander, a driver, and a gunner. The commander, with gray markings on his armor, coordinates all actions on the tank, as well as any accompanying vehicles or infantry that form part of the patrol. The gunner and driver wear identical armor. The driver operates the tank and is responsible for mechanical upkeep of the track drive and powertrain systems. The gunner fires the mounted weaponry, and maintains its combat readiness.

JEDHA PATROL
Grenades, mines, and resistance snipers are a recurring threat to Imperial patrols. The TX-225 is an intimidating presence but also presents a tempting target.

Gray markings denote commander status

LIGHTWEIGHT ARMOR
The Imperial combat driver uniform design has changed several times during the Empire's reign, reflecting improvements in versatility and further specialization of the vehicle operator ranks. Its latest incarnation is a partial suit of plastoid plate that provides protection but also permits the flexibility required to sit in the cramped quarters of an armored vehicle, such as a tank.

"ROLL FORWARD. CRUSH EVERYTHING AHEAD OF US."
— HC-4120, IMPERIAL HAMMERS ELITE ARMOR UNIT

Flexible greave plates allow for a secure fit

The congested avenues of Jedha's Holy City necessitate a slow advance. Accompanying infantry keep an eye out for insurgents.

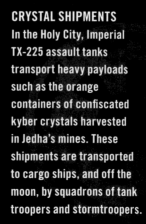

CRYSTAL SHIPMENTS
In the Holy City, Imperial TX-225 assault tanks transport heavy payloads such as the orange containers of confiscated kyber crystals harvested in Jedha's mines. These shipments are transported to cargo ships, and off the moon, by squadrons of tank troopers and stormtroopers.

Wireless telemetry receiver for tank system interfaces

COORDINATED CONQUEST

Imperial GAV crews rely on coordinated actions with multiple unit types for maximum effectiveness. Army doctrine stipulates that GAVs should not operate without adequate air or orbital cover, and whenever possible should work in tandem with infantry. While tank crews belittle foot soldiers with terms such as "tiny tanks" or "lightfoots," infantry refer to tanks as "fire magnets." Given the rarity of Rebel Alliance armor units, counterattacks on Imperial tanks typically come in the form of mines or improvised explosives.

Plastoid rerebrace

Breathmask filter screen

Utility belt with compact repair and diagnostic kits

DATA FILE

SUBJECT HH-4413 (Sergeant Warda Gojun)

PLANET OF BIRTH Saleucami

SPECIES Human

AFFILIATION 71st GAV battalion

HEIGHT 1.81m (5ft 11in)

AGE 22 standard years

AT-ST

INSURGENTS OFTEN UNDERESTIMATE

the potency of the All Terrain Scout Transport (AT-ST, or scout walker). Its deceptively rickety gait belies a potent patrol vehicle. The Empire usually deploys AT-STs on open battlefields for swift reconnaissance and troop support. In the cramped quarters of Jedha City, the AT-ST's firepower is magnified, and it becomes a deadly threat against ill-equipped street-fighting rebels. Small arms fire bounces harmlessly off its armor, though improvised explosives can unsettle it.

ARMORED COCKPIT

Reinforced armor plate envelops their control cabin, protecting the two-person crew. From this elevated perch, the driver and gunner have a commanding view. The walker's "head" rests on top of a turret, increasing the field of fire of three primary weapon points. The walker's "chin" houses recoiling twin laser cannons preset into a syncopated firing pattern; its "temples" each mount a modular weapon pod; and its "face" includes two opening viewports deliberately set to give any viewer the unsettling sensation of staring into the face of a soulless beast or oversized combat droid.

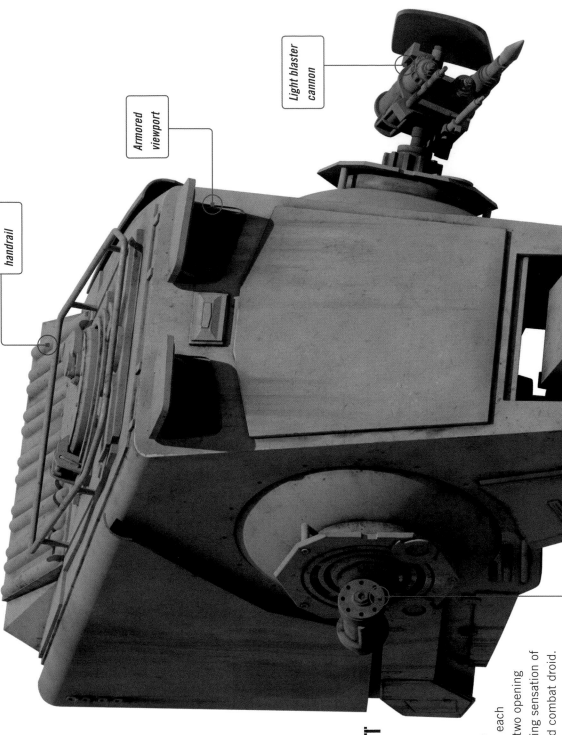

Light blaster cannon

Armored viewport

Entry hatch handrail

Armored joint shield

Concussion grenade launcher

Telemetry receiver unit

AT-ST PILOT'S HELMET

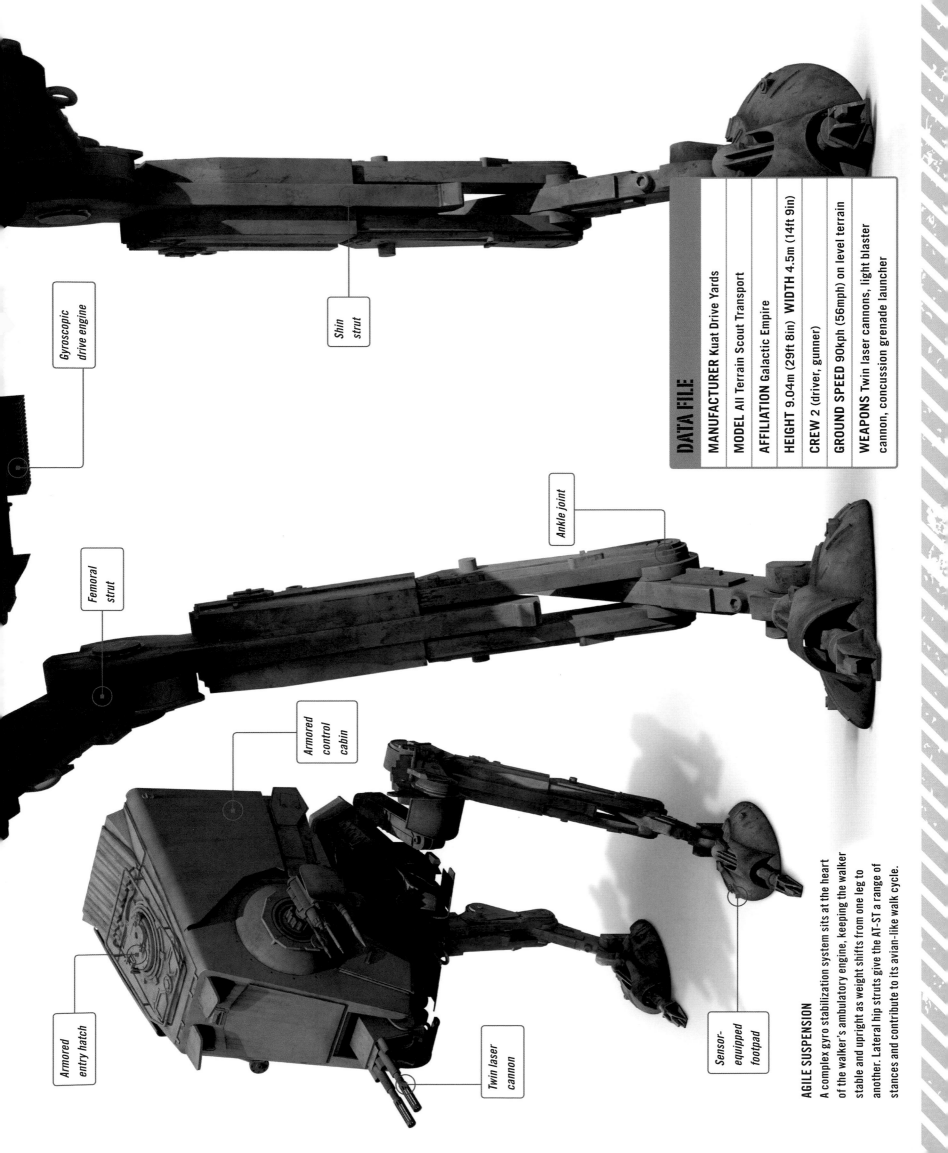

Gyroscopic drive engine

Shin strut

Femoral strut

Ankle joint

DATA FILE

MANUFACTURER Kuat Drive Yards

MODEL All Terrain Scout Transport

AFFILIATION Galactic Empire

HEIGHT 9.04m (29ft 8in) **WIDTH** 4.5m (14ft 9in)

CREW 2 (driver, gunner)

GROUND SPEED 90kph (56mph) on level terrain

WEAPONS Twin laser cannons, light blaster cannon, concussion grenade launcher

Armored control cabin

Armored entry hatch

Sensor-equipped footpad

Twin laser cannon

AGILE SUSPENSION

A complex gyro stabilization system sits at the heart of the walker's ambulatory engine, keeping the walker stable and upright as weight shifts from one leg to another. Lateral hip struts give the AT-ST a range of stances and contribute to its avian-like walk cycle.

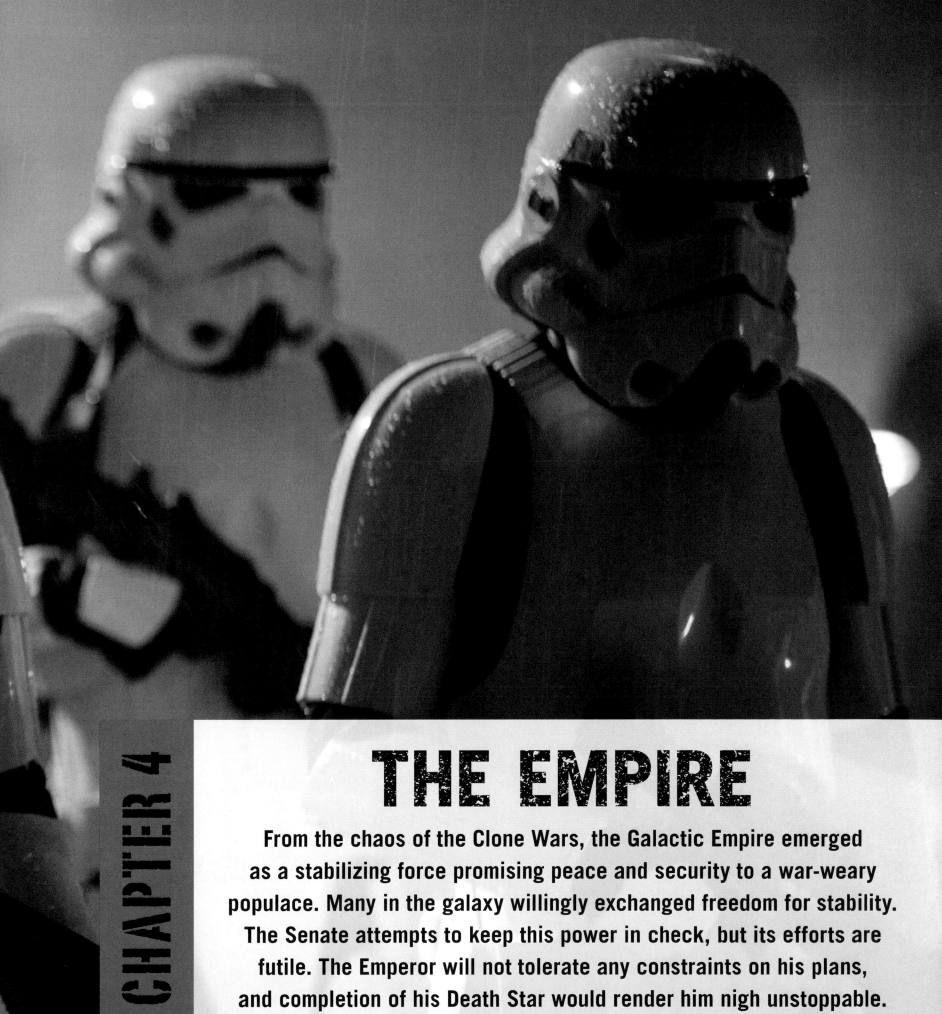

CHAPTER 4

THE EMPIRE

From the chaos of the Clone Wars, the Galactic Empire emerged as a stabilizing force promising peace and security to a war-weary populace. Many in the galaxy willingly exchanged freedom for stability. The Senate attempts to keep this power in check, but its efforts are futile. The Emperor will not tolerate any constraints on his plans, and completion of his Death Star would render him nigh unstoppable.

ORSON KRENNIC

AS DIRECTOR of Advanced Weapons Research for the Imperial Security Bureau, Orson Krennic is obsessed with the completion of the long-delayed Death Star project. A cruel but brilliant man, Krennic has staked his reputation on the delivery of the functional battle station to the Emperor. Having lived through the violence of the Clone Wars, Krennic knows the need for a strong hand to steer the future of galactic civilization. Long convinced of his own genius, he believes himself to be that strong hand.

When Krennic was a young man, his brilliance earned him a place in the Brentaal Futures Program, an educational institute meant to incubate developing prodigies. Young Orson's listed area of excellence was architecture. However, many of his counselors would state that his ability to manipulate people was as effective as his talent for building.

During the Clone Wars, it was Krennic who oversaw the transformation of municipal grounds on Coruscant into military command centers. His designs replaced the sweeping lines of Republic architecture with the bold brutalist face of what would become the Imperial aesthetic. As the Death Star evolves from concept to terrifying reality, Krennic's personal star continues to rise.

Chronic delays of the Death Star operation weigh heavily on Krennic. His reputation rests on the delivery of a working superweapon.

ON THE HUNT
After landing a lofty appointment in Imperial Intelligence, Krennic used every tool at his disposal to track down the fugitive Galen Erso. Orson manipulated and deceived his longtime colleague Galen into carrying out research vital to the Death Star's completion. With pressure mounting to complete the weapon, ruthless Krennic disposed of any displays of friendship.

DEATH APPROACHES
On Lah'mu, Krennic and his cadre of death troopers marched on the Erso farm. Krennic believes he gave Galen every opportunity to comply and see things his way. That Galen cannot is an intolerable flaw in his character.

"WE WERE ON THE VERGE OF GREATNESS, GALEN."
— ORSON KRENNIC TO GALEN ERSO

UNDER PRESSURE
The demands of the Imperial echelons place great pressure on Krennic. He is not of the principled Coruscanti classes, able to verbally parry and weave in debates and politics. Krennic's temper is far more volatile, a fact that makes some, like Grand Moff Tarkin, uncomfortable.

Custom-fitted macroscope

KRENNIC'S DT-29 HEAVY BLASTER PISTOL

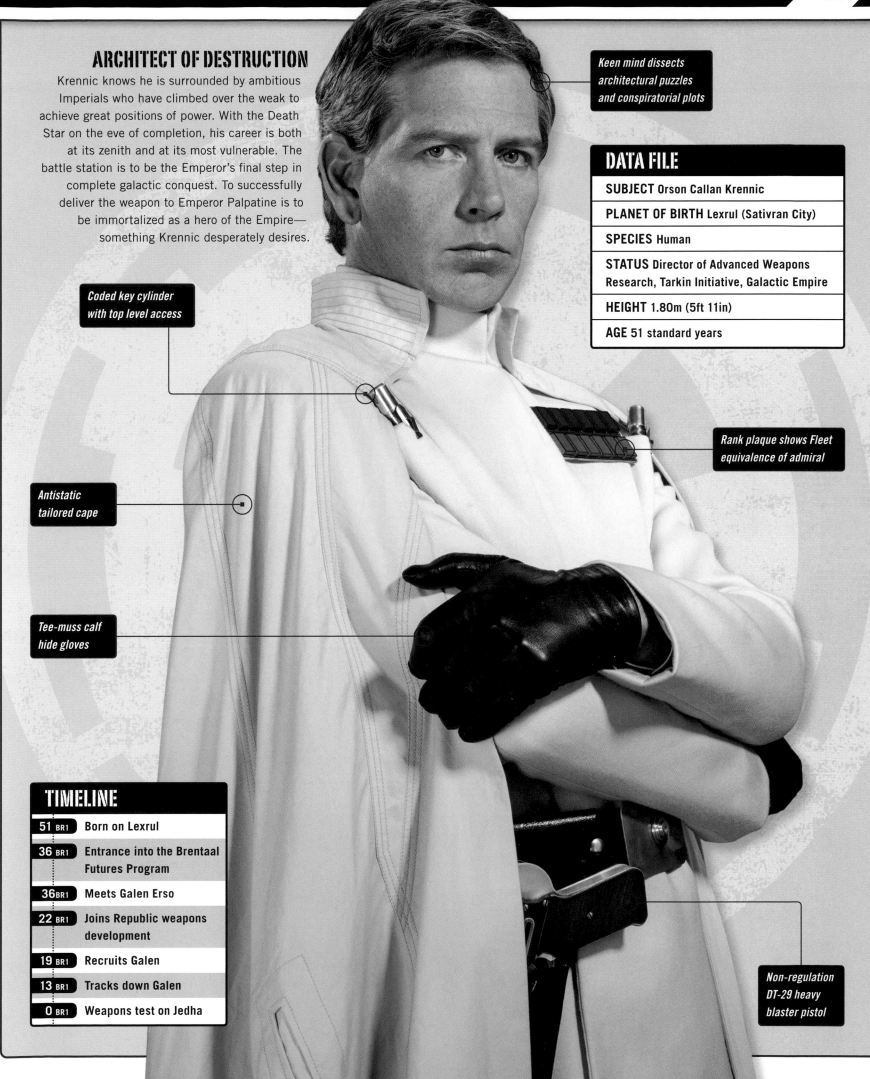

ARCHITECT OF DESTRUCTION

Krennic knows he is surrounded by ambitious Imperials who have climbed over the weak to achieve great positions of power. With the Death Star on the eve of completion, his career is both at its zenith and at its most vulnerable. The battle station is to be the Emperor's final step in complete galactic conquest. To successfully deliver the weapon to Emperor Palpatine is to be immortalized as a hero of the Empire—something Krennic desperately desires.

Keen mind dissects architectural puzzles and conspiratorial plots

Coded key cylinder with top level access

Antistatic tailored cape

Tee-muss calf hide gloves

Rank plaque shows Fleet equivalence of admiral

Non-regulation DT-29 heavy blaster pistol

DATA FILE

SUBJECT Orson Callan Krennic

PLANET OF BIRTH Lexrul (Sativran City)

SPECIES Human

STATUS Director of Advanced Weapons Research, Tarkin Initiative, Galactic Empire

HEIGHT 1.80m (5ft 11in)

AGE 51 standard years

TIMELINE

51 BR1	Born on Lexrul
36 BR1	Entrance into the Brentaal Futures Program
36 BR1	Meets Galen Erso
22 BR1	Joins Republic weapons development
19 BR1	Recruits Galen
13 BR1	Tracks down Galen
0 BR1	Weapons test on Jedha

DARTH VADER

THE FEARSOME, WRAITHLIKE presence that haunts the upper tiers of the Imperial military hierarchy, Vader has a peculiar yet necessary relationship with the Empire. He holds no formal rank and needs none, for he is the emissary of the distant and reclusive Emperor. When the Death Star project draws the express and personal interest of Palpatine, Vader is dispatched to keep vigil over the ambitious officers tasked with making it a reality.

In service to the Emperor, Vader is afforded command of many military resources, including the Star Destroyer *Devastator*.

On the volcanic world of Mustafar, the newly rechristened Darth Vader made an enemy of his former friend and mentor, Jedi General Obi-Wan Kenobi.

Vader is not a widely known public figure. His origins are even less so. Vader was once a hero of the Clone Wars, under his birth name: Anakin Skywalker. A powerful Jedi Knight, he carried out daring campaigns where he demonstrated an imaginative zeal for adventure and a willingness to push against the restraining doctrines of the Jedi Order.

When the Jedi Order refused to advance Skywalker to a position where he could make the most of his abilities, a way was paved for Supreme Chancellor Palpatine to be able to sway his loyalties. Palpatine, a secret practitioner of the Sith ways, promised the dark side of the Force was a pathway to greater power and the ability to reshape the galaxy to a strict and orderly ideal. Skywalker swore loyalty to the Sith, becoming Darth Vader.

Vader suffered mortal injuries duelling Obi-Wan on Mustafar. The elevated Emperor Palpatine saw to rebuild his prize pupil with cybernetic technology.

DARK LORD REBORN

Transformed into a mechanized tyrant, the man that was Anakin has been forever buried beneath an armored shell. Most of his physical body has been replaced or impregnated with cybernetics to keep him alive. In this state, he is rarely far from elaborate medical facilities that allow for maintenance and upgrades to his cybernetic systems.

"THE ABILITY TO DESTROY A PLANET IS INSIGNIFICANT NEXT TO THE POWER OF THE FORCE."

— DARTH VADER

DARK MONOLITH

Vader's personal abode is an obsidian tower on an inhospitable world. It is by the Emperor's design that Vader lives in such an unforgiving environment. Vader's attendant, Vaneé, visits Vader as he meditates within a rejuvenation chamber. The stark, modern structure is built over an ancient castle full of dark secrets.

DARTH VADER'S SITH LIGHTSABER

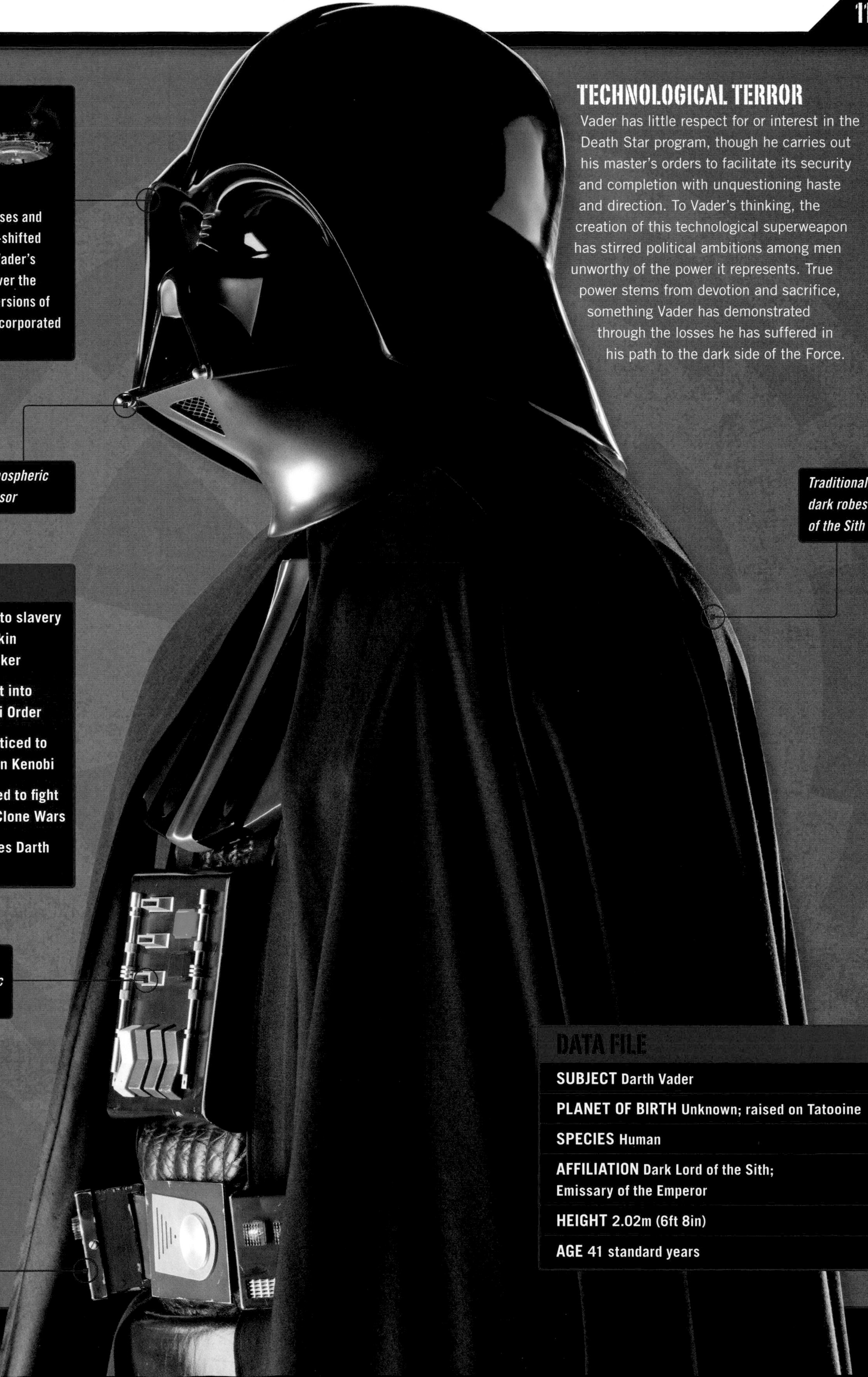

TECHNOLOGICAL TERROR

Vader has little respect for or interest in the Death Star program, though he carries out his master's orders to facilitate its security and completion with unquestioning haste and direction. To Vader's thinking, the creation of this technological superweapon has stirred political ambitions among men unworthy of the power it represents. True power stems from devotion and sacrifice, something Vader has demonstrated through the losses he has suffered in his path to the dark side of the Force.

RED EYES
Photoreceptor lenses and displays are color-shifted to accommodate Vader's weakened eyes. Over the years, different versions of his helmet have incorporated different optics.

Atmospheric sensor

Traditional dark robes of the Sith

TIMELINE

41 BRI	Born into slavery as Anakin Skywalker
32 BRI	Brought into the Jedi Order
32 BRI	Apprenticed to Obi-Wan Kenobi
22 BRI	Knighted to fight in the Clone Wars
19 BRI	Becomes Darth Vader

Respiratory systems diagnostic data-slot

Regulatory function box

DATA FILE

SUBJECT Darth Vader

PLANET OF BIRTH Unknown; raised on Tatooine

SPECIES Human

AFFILIATION Dark Lord of the Sith; Emissary of the Emperor

HEIGHT 2.02m (6ft 8in)

AGE 41 standard years

DATA FILE

REGION Mobile

DIAMETER 160 km (100 miles)

TERRAIN Layered decks surrounding power plant and propulsion systems; surface crust of city "sprawls" divided into functional sectors; equatorial and meridian service trenches; superlaser eye

MOONS Not applicable

POPULATION Mission dependent, service roster ranges from 1,186,295 to 1,206,293

Superlaser focus lens

Equatorial trench

Refinery levels

THAT'S NO MOON

THE DEATH STAR

THE CULMINATION of more than two decades of research, construction, and testing, the DS-1 Orbital Battle Station, codenamed the Death Star, nears completion. The size of a small moon, it is a mobile, planet-killing superweapon, able to transform and focus the raw energy of hypermatter reactions at its heart into a world-shattering superlaser. This energy transformation, using Galen Erso's kyber crystal formulae, was the most difficult technical hurdle to overcome. But now, at long last, the weapon is ready to deploy.

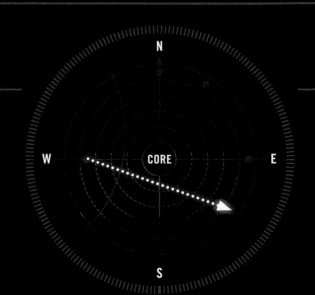

IMPERIAL BATTLE STATION

DEATH STAR DIRECTOR
Orson Krennic is tasked with making the Death Star a reality. He is on the eve of his greatest triumph, and is impatient for it to be realized.

CAREFUL OBSERVATION
The Death Star houses the greatest artificial concentration of power ever conceived. Monitoring its systems is essential.

DEMONSTRATION OF DESTRUCTION
Krennic longs to demonstrate the station's power to the Emperor, but he cannot gain an audience due to intervention from Grand Moff Tarkin.

SUPERLASER
After a long wait, a stable, operational superlaser assembly is guided into the Death Star superstructure and connected to the hypermatter reactor.

STANDING BY

The Death Star superlaser focuses eight tributary laser streams into an amplification nexus to create a blast magnified through kyber crystal field dynamics. Correct timing and balance of the streams is essential, as any error could upset the reaction with catastrophic consequences. Each of the eight firing stations has its own team of well-trained gunners and technicians, who all follow a carefully orchestrated firing sequence.

DS-1 EVOLUTION

THE DEATH STAR'S PATH TO COMPLETION is a long, circuitous one full of setbacks, intrigue, and breakthroughs. The galaxy at large remains unaware that Emperor Palpatine engineered the Clone Wars. The Death Star began under the auspices of the Separatists—the enemy faction that he secretly controlled. They had the technical know-how to plan out the massive battle station, and the triumphant Empire had the resources and political will to make it a reality.

Sublight ion
engines in recessed
equatorial band

OVER JEDHA

At Grand Moff Wilhuff Tarkin's behest, Director Orson Krennic makes ready a test of the Death Star's prime weapon. It is only a fractional test: a small portion of its total reactor yield is siphoned into a superlaser blast targeted at Jedha City. The results are unmistakably devastating, and a humbling preview of the power a full-powered test could produce. Krennic's pride soon evaporates as Tarkin claims control of the station upon seeing proof of its potency.

Jedha's ancient
tablelands

BIRTH OF AN ABOMINATION

HIVE MIND ORIGINS
Tasked by Count Dooku (Sith Lord Darth Tyranus), the Stalgasin hive of Geonosians forms plans for a deep-space battle station with a kyber crystal-based weapon.

POGGLE'S DIVULGENCE
Captured by Anakin Skywalker, Poggle the Lesser divulges the nature of the Separatists' master weapon. He insists that it only exists in theory.

TARKIN'S AMBITIONS
Upon learning of the weapon, Wilhuff Tarkin champions its construction. He believes its mere presence would be capable of ending wars.

A DEATH STAR BEGINS
Using captured Geonosian plans procured by Palpatine, construction of the Death Star is secretly started over Geonosis, under supervision of Tarkin and Krennic.

CONSTRUCTION OVER GEONOSIS
Enormous orbital construction domes begin transforming the rocky rings of Geonosis into raw construction materials. A spherical shape begins to emerge.

SAW'S OBSESSION
Obsessively following leads concering a secret Imperial superweapon, Saw Gerrera comes close enough to finding the Death Star to prompt the Empire to move it.

THE STERILIZATION
To keep the Death Star a secret, the Imperial military sterilizes Geonosis, killing its populace of billions. This genocide goes undetected for years.

KYBER TRANSFORMATION
The lack of a functional superlaser slows down the Death Star operation. It is not until Galen Erso is coerced to research kyber dynamics that progress is made.

FINAL FITTING
The final functional superlaser—created on Eadu—is transported to the Death Star where it is fitted into the superstructure. The Death Star is finally operational.

Superlaser
readies for only
single reactor
ignition

IMPERIAL-CLASS

STAR DESTROYER

TO MEET INTERSTELLAR DEFENSE NEEDS, the great shipyards of the galaxy were fired up during the Clone Wars, and those forges have stayed lit in the years since. Enormous construction facilities at Kuat, Corellia, Ringo Vinda, Fondor, and elsewhere have been converted from civilian graving docks to churn out massive *Imperial*-class Star Destroyers—the unmistakable warships of the Imperial Navy. Larger and more powerful than the Jedi cruiser of old, the Imperial Star Destroyer is the current standard, and a harbinger of even larger warships yet to come.

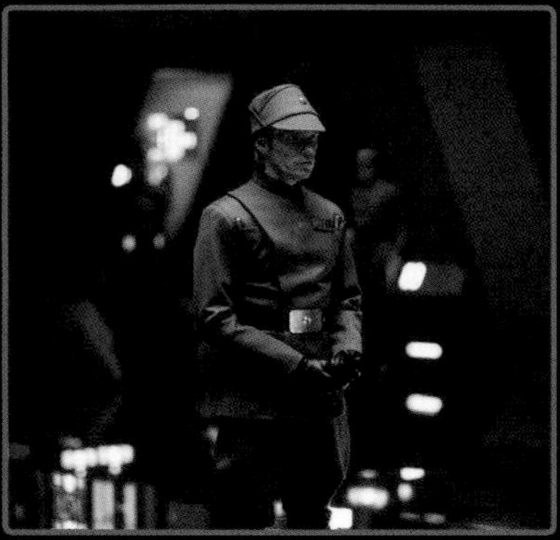

AT THE DARK LORD'S COMMAND The competent and fiercely focused Imperial Navy officer Captain Shaef Corssin is the commander of the Star Destroyer *Devastator*, the warship that serves as Darth Vader's personal flagship.

DATA FILE

MANUFACTURER Kuat Drive Yards

MODEL *Imperial I*-class Star Destroyer

AFFILIATION Galactic Empire

LENGTH 1,600m (5,249ft 3in)

CREW 9,235 (officers); 27,850 (enlisted); 9,700 (troopers)

ATMOSPHERIC SPEED 975kph (606mph)

WEAPONS 60 heavy turbolaser cannons, 60 ion cannons, 6 dual heavy turbolaser turrets, 2 dual heavy ion cannon turrets, 2 quad heavy turbolasers, 3 triple medium turbolasers, 2 medium turbolasers, 10 tractor beam projectors

EXECUTRIX

The Star Destroyer *Executrix* emerges from the shadow of the Death Star as the battle station's final superlaser is fitted. Under the command of Captain Hindane Darcc, the *Executrix* is the flagship of Grand Moff Tarkin, governor of the Outer Rim Territories. As Tarkin looks out from his command bridge he can see his dream project nearing completion. Director Krennic stands with Tarkin, eager to unveil this weapon to the Emperor himself, should Tarkin allow it.

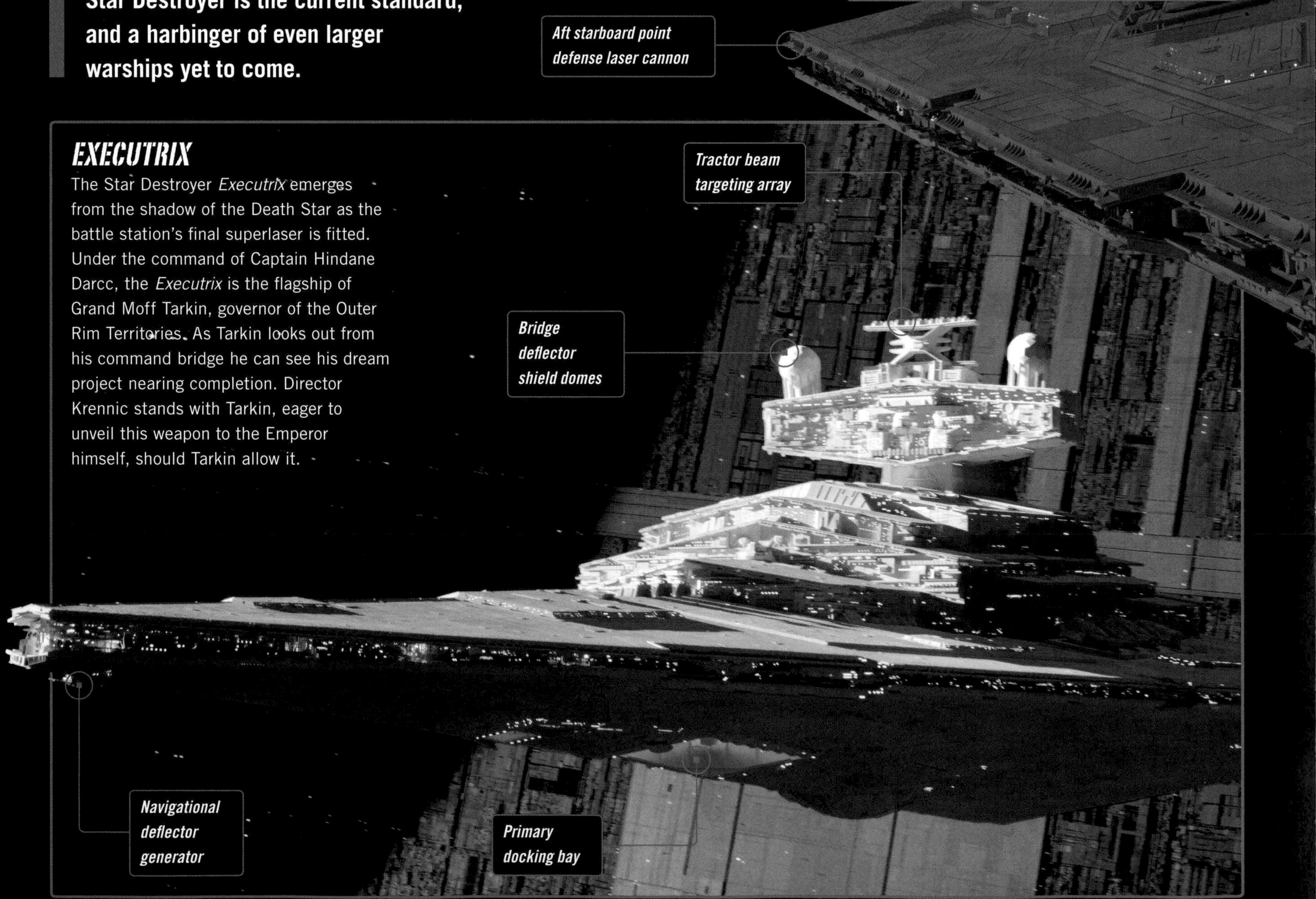

Aft starboard point defense laser cannon
Tractor beam targeting array
Bridge deflector shield domes
Navigational deflector generator
Primary docking bay

DAUNTLESS

The Star Destroyer *Dauntless* hovers like a dark cloud over the Holy City of Jedha. It offers protection for the many shuttlecraft extracting kyber deposits, and its presence offers an undeniable sign of Imperial power.

Crew decks and gunnery crew quarters

Port heavy turbolaser battery

Port lateral umbilical restocking vestibule

Fore starboard active sensor array pallet

Forward pursuit tractor beam array

DEVASTATOR

The last of the *Imperial I*-class Star Destroyers to lumber out of the Kuat Drive Yards before the facility began producing the *Imperial II*-class, the *Devastator* is still a state-of-the-art warship. It meets the exacting specifications of Darth Vader, who exhibits an affinity for cutting-edge warship design. Like other ships in its class, the *Devastator* bristles with heavy weapons emplacements, enormous batteries of turbolasers, and heavy ion cannons that line the ventral superstructure flanking the command tower.

POWER STRUGGLE

AS THE DEATH STAR nears operational readiness, it becomes a large and potent playing piece in the ongoing game of wits and ambition between Grand Moff Tarkin and Director Krennic. The cagey Tarkin has both taken and deflected credit for the project as it has fallen into and out of Imperial court favor over the years, but now its full power is undeniable. Krennic has stayed true to his vision, even when it appeared the station would never see completion.

TEST FIRING

Much to Krennic's frustration, Tarkin controls access to the
Emperor. The director feels he has much to offer Palpatine,
if he could only get an audience with him. When Tarkin
pressures Krennic for a demonstration of the station's power,
Krennic is dismayed that the Emperor is not present to witness
the Death Star in action. A precaution, says Tarkin, given past
failures of the weapon's primary weapon. The Death Star's
superlaser proves just as potent as expected, perhaps more so,
given that this initial blast is but a fraction of its full potential.

IMPERIAL COMMAND

THE LINE BETWEEN the Imperial political machine and the Imperial war machine has blurred. The Galactic Empire was formed from a Republic recovering from war. It transformed into stratocracy—a government headed by military chiefs—so gradually that many in the galaxy took no notice. The citizens simply believed that the Imperial Senate and powers in charge represented their best interests.

The upper echelons of the Empire include those whose influential families afforded them preferred treatment and advancement.

Ultimately, the Senate proved disposable in the Emperor's long-term plans, and authority ceded to the military command before funneling up to Palpatine. To ensure that this transformation would be accomplished to his very exacting demands, prestigious academies across the galaxy raised ambitious men and women who would perfectly echo the Imperial mantra of control through authority.

The culmination of the Empire's complete transition to a military state hinged on command of their fleet, the Death Star, and military nerve centers such as the base on Scarif. It is from Scarif that the most promising and ruthless Imperials arise, waiting for the call to completely and finally subjugate the galaxy.

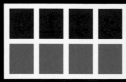

IMPERIAL INSIGNIA
A plaque with an arrangement of colored rectangles denotes rank. Sector-specific design schema creates a hodgepodge of non-uniform markings.

LIEUTENANT NILES GAVLA
Carida academy graduate Gavla is based on Scarif, where he serves as the planet-side administrative support liaison for the defenses officer based on the Death Star.

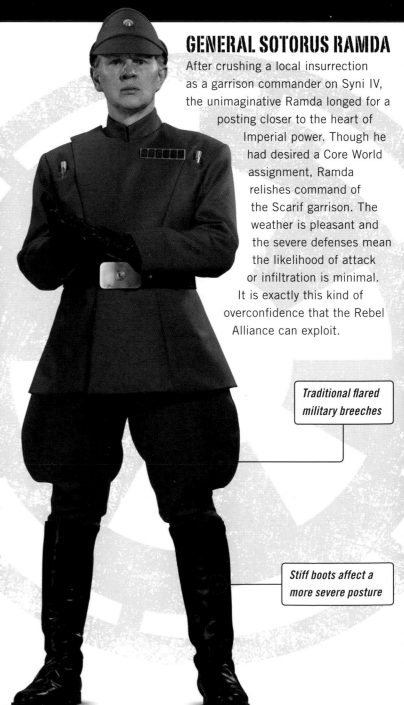

GENERAL SOTORUS RAMDA
After crushing a local insurrection as a garrison commander on Syni IV, the unimaginative Ramda longed for a posting closer to the heart of Imperial power. Though he had desired a Core World assignment, Ramda relishes command of the Scarif garrison. The weather is pleasant and the severe defenses mean the likelihood of attack or infiltration is minimal. It is exactly this kind of overconfidence that the Rebel Alliance can exploit.

Traditional flared military breeches

Stiff boots affect a more severe posture

Lieutenant Adema stands within a beehive of activity in the Scarif Citadel command center. It is to him that anomalous reports trickle in about rebels arriving on Scarif.

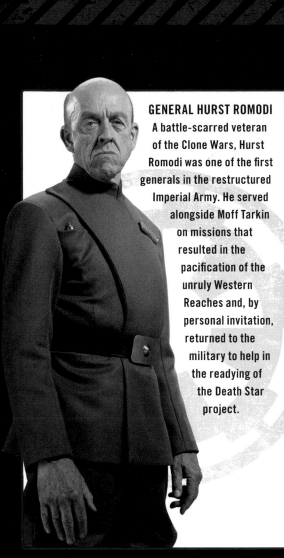

GENERAL HURST ROMODI
A battle-scarred veteran of the Clone Wars, Hurst Romodi was one of the first generals in the restructured Imperial Army. He served alongside Moff Tarkin on missions that resulted in the pacification of the unruly Western Reaches and, by personal invitation, returned to the military to help in the readying of the Death Star project.

LIEUTENANT (JUNIOR GRADE) TOBIX CHASSER
Operations personnel Chasser oversees the Death Star's allocation of staff. Those that are aware of the Death Star's near operational readiness vie for onboard assignment.

LIEUTENANT CRIDEN VALDAS
A readiness officer at the Scarif Citadel, Lt. Valdas reports up to General Ramda on matters of military technology management and contingency planning.

LIEUTENANT MYTUS ADEMA
A purposeful young officer more ambitious than most, Mytus Adema finds General Ramda's command of the Scarif Citadel distasteful. While Ramda believes the Death Star to be a waste of time and money, Adema thinks it a potent symbol of Imperial might to be respected. He watches Ramda's actions closely in the hopes that he will someday be able to present a damning account of the senior officer to Director Krennic.

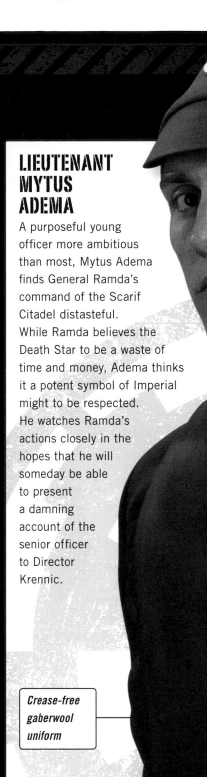

Officer's gaberwool cap

Coded rank cylinder

Crease-free gaberwool uniform

Private datapad contained in shockproof case

IMPERIAL SUPPORT

FILLING THE GULF between infantry troopers and the upper levels of the Imperial military are countless support personnel—men, women, and droids—keeping the war machine running. They span multiple branches of service and are every bit as loyal to the Empire as those on the frontlines. Whether stationed at ground installations, aboard Star Destroyers, or within the vast interior of the Death Star, they carry out the will of the Emperor.

A Death Star gunner monitors the precision energy-balancing required to safely operate the Death Star's superlaser.

Droids are on the lowest rung of the Imperial service ladder. Unlike the droids in the Rebel Alliance, those in the Empire are rarely afforded any privileges, respect, or acknowledgments. Similarly, service technicians are low down the Imperial hierarchy and are routinely ignored by those in command. Gray-uniformed technicians deal with the most menial of duties, while those in black coveralls are higher in station. Navy troopers, gunners, and ground crew are military roles that may not see combat, but play a vital role in day-to-day operations.

The Death Star project has great need of such personnel. The Service and Technical Sectors of the battle station's personnel number in the hundreds of thousands.

Without the work of Imperial service personnel, the Empire would be unable to deal with the growing rebel threat.

BlasTech SE-14 blaster pistol

CORPORAL ANSIN THOBEL

Navy troopers are a ubiquitous presence in Imperial operations. They are so numerous aboard the Death Star that they've earned the name of Death Star trooper. These marines are trained in shipboard combat, repulsing boarders, and pacifying escaped prisoners. Most are cross-trained in some operational duty, as Corporal Thobel is. When not on his sentry duty shift at the Death Star's command sector, Thobel mans a sensor suite station in the general sector.

4D6-J-A7

An RA-7 protocol droid based at the Scarif Citadel, 4D6-J-A7 is an administrative assistant to the Imperial Intelligence and Security Bureau offices there. She is routinely exposed to classified information. As such, the droid's databanks are protected from intrusion by electronic or other means. Such efforts have given her a conceited attitude. She is insufferably arrogant to droids beneath her station. So far, this has not affected her performance.

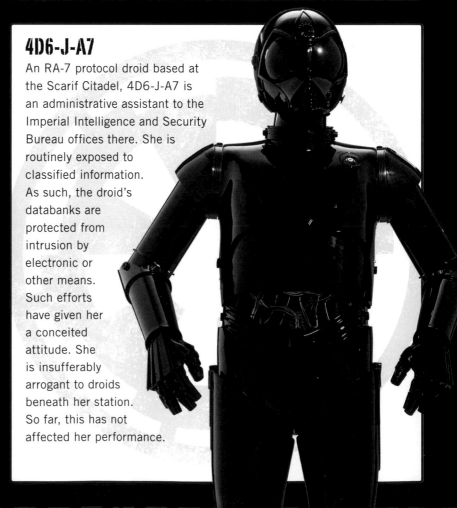

ENSIGN YORT CAVWOL

Fastidious duty officer Cavwol gives Lieutenant Adema and General Ramda reports on routine operations at the Scarif headquarters. Reports are tailored to their specific preferences.

CREWMAN TODES HALVAX

Computer technician Halvax is the systems administrator at the Scarif command room. He keeps the Citadel running to Krennic's exacting specifications and stands ready to tackle any technical issues that may arise.

LIEUTENANT DANBIT BRUN

A shield relay systems operator, Brun monitors the power systems on the orbital shield gate station above Scarif. He carefully monitors field dynamics to prevent dangerous buildup from stellar wind aurorae.

C2-B5

Within the vault of the Scarif Citadel, astromech C2-B5 patrols for maintenance needs and sweeps the computer network to probe for any electronic discrepancies. C2-B5 is routinely memory wiped and lacks any sort of distinctive personality.

2ND LIEUTENANT FROBB

From landing pad nine on Scarif's beach, deck officer Frobb catalogs shuttle landings and takeoffs. He ensures ships have enough fuel, life support, and victuals, and orders inspections should anything appear out of the ordinary.

MSE-6 DROID

A common sight at Imperial installations, Rebaxan Colmuni MSE-6 droids (nicknamed "mouse droids") zip along underfoot, relaying messages that are to be kept off-network, or couriering small items.

Wraparound helmet with removable faceplate

TECHNICIAN KENT DEEZLING

Busy Imperial surface ports benefit from dedicated crewmembers who help direct traffic where automated systems cannot typically make decisions fast enough on a rapidly changing landing field. The deck technicians are plugged into air traffic control via their headsets, but seem to prefer analog solutions. They wave ships in with luminous wands and eyeball distances without sensors. These techs wear piloting gear, as they are authorized to commandeer certain vessels in order to steer them into proper positions on a landing deck.

Spare power pack for suit systems

ILLUMINATED TRAFFIC WANDS

Tarkin Initiative
laboratory

DATA FILE

REGION Outer Rim Territories

DIAMETER 14,121 km (8,774 miles)

TERRAIN Mountain terrain

MOONS 1

POPULATION 2.5 million (estimated native population)

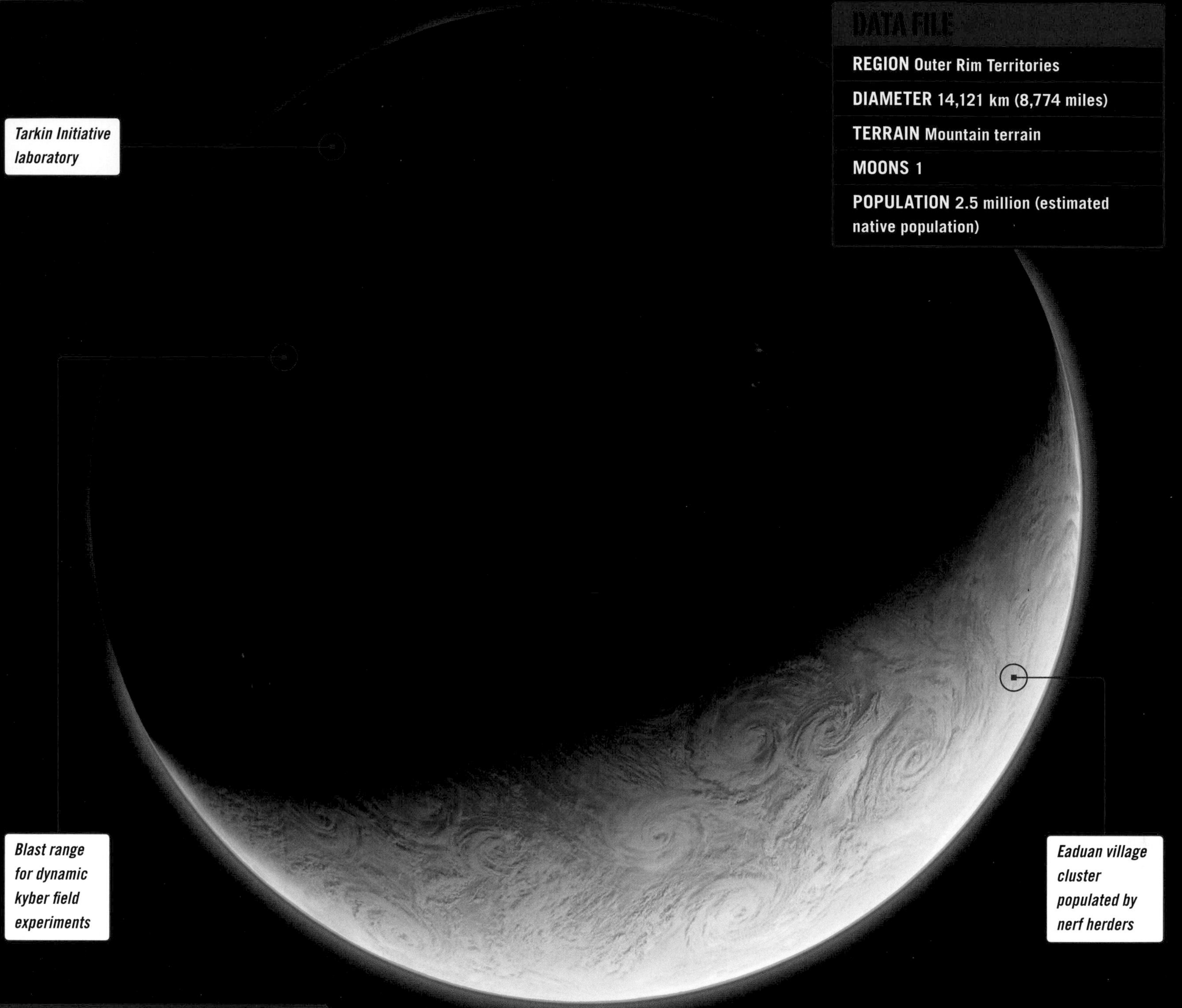

Blast range
for dynamic
kyber field
experiments

Eaduan village
cluster
populated by
nerf herders

SECRET LABORATORY

EADU

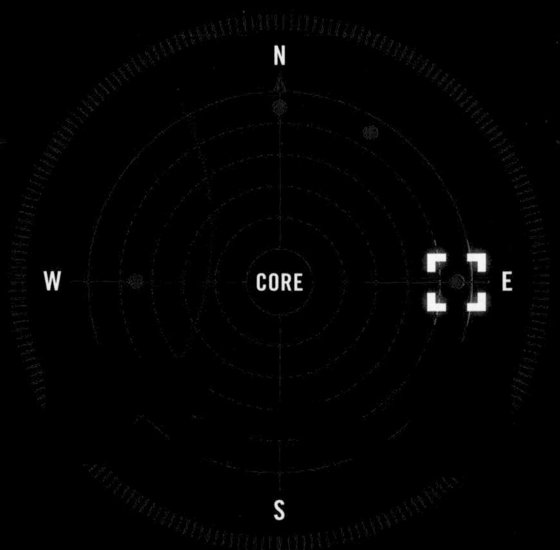

SAFETY AND SECURITY dictated that the most volatile
elements of the Death Star research took place far from the
construction of the main battle station itself. The mountains
of Eadu, a world owned by Grand Moff Tarkin and ceded to
his eponymous Tarkin Initiative, came to house a top-secret,
high energy conversion laboratory created by Director
Orson Krennic. It was here that Galen Erso led a team of
brilliant minds to unlock the secrets of kyber crystals.

N

W — CORE — E

S

LIFE UNDER WATCH

SURPRISE INSPECTION
Though the Empire conducts regular inspections on the science team, the surprise arrival of death troopers heralds an ominous change in fate.

THE DIRECTOR
Having evidence of a traitor on Eadu, Director Orson Krennic orders the entire contingent of scientists to be brought out before him.

VANTAGE POINT
From high above the windswept, rain-drenched mountains, rebel infiltrators can watch the standoff between Imperials and scientists.

GALEN'S REBELLION
To spare the lives of his scientists, Galen Erso admits to Krennic that he and he alone has compromised the secrecy of the Death Star project.

Stormtrooper squadron, armed with T-21 light repeating blaster rifles

Imperial ground crew

Kyber crystal shipping container

HEAVY DEFENSES
The remote location of the planet and the difficult terrain provide natural defenses for Eadu. However, a garrison of stormtroopers stands ready to secure the installation against any attack, as do a battery of heavy anti-aircraft turbolasers and a squadron of ready-to-launch TIE fighters.

GALEN ERSO

ONE OF THE GALAXY'S most renowned polymaths, Galen Erso is a gifted theoretician, mathematician, and experimental physicist. Born to hardworking parents locked in a life of poverty, Galen applied his genius to solving the problem of want. Observing that resources were scattered unevenly across the galaxy, Galen sought to examine the very structures of existence to see if he could unlock unlimited energy and even out the divide between those who have and those who have not.

Galen would always ask, "what if?", teasing out hitherto unimagined possibilities. At a young age, he mastered music and chemistry, and voraciously consumed knowledge through databooks and the HoloNet. Upon earning entry into the Futures Program on Brentaal, he met a gifted architect named Orson Krennic. The two worked well together. Though Galen was a few years older, the timid man shrank in the shadow of Orson's outsized personality and charisma.

After graduation, Galen spent much of his twenties in advanced studies, research internships, and teaching positions. Krennic assisted in getting Galen a visiting professorship at the Institute of Applied Science on Coruscant, at which time Galen focused his studies on kyber crystal research.

Galen's single-minded tenacity often caused him to neglect those around him. On Lah'mu, he made up for lost time with his daughter Jyn.

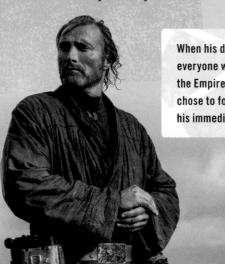

When his dreams of helping everyone were co-opted by the Empire, Galen instead chose to focus on helping his immediate loved ones.

"WE CALL IT THE DEATH STAR... THERE IS NO BETTER NAME."

— GALEN ERSO

Research division rank plaque

Imperial development project uniform

TWISTED PERCEPTION
Krennic believes he has been helping Galen reach his true potential. He cannot fathom that Galen would not be grateful.

ACCOMPLICE TO THE EMPIRE

It was Krennic who coerced Galen into joining a top-secret research project meant to help the galaxy recover from the Clone Wars. Project Celestial Power relied upon Galen's knowledge of energy enrichment and enhancement through kyber crystals to deliver previously unthinkable yields of power. While Galen worked to maximize the yields, he was unaware that Krennic planned to weaponize his work in the Death Star superweapon.

MOMENTS OF REBELLION
Upon learning the horrific nature of the Death Star project, Galen fled to Lah'mu with his family, only to be tracked down by Krennic a few years later. Forced to work alongside other similarly captured scientists at a secluded facility on Eadu, Galen begins to quietly rebel against Krennic and the Empire by allowing word of the Death Star to slip out.

DATA FILE

SUBJECT Galen Walton Erso

PLANET OF BIRTH Grange

SPECIES Human

AFFILIATION Formerly Project Celestial Power; currently Tarkin Initiative

HEIGHT 1.83m (6ft)

AGE 55 standard years

Hair dampened by exposure to incessant rain on Eadu

IN NEW FOCUS

During a six-month field expedition to Espinar, Galen met and fell in love with a guide named Lyra. The two married on Coruscant and had a child, Jyn, born during the first few months of the Clone Wars. That galactic conflict trapped the Erso family on Vallt—a world siding with the Separatists—until the intervention of Orson Krennic freed the Ersos, but led to a different kind of captivity as Galen became ensnared in Krennic's growing Imperial ambitions.

CRYSTALLINE SYMBOL
This faceted kyber crystal becomes the logo of the think tank known as the Tarkin Initiative.

Coded rank cylinder allows limited data access

Project lead uniform

TIMELINE

56 BR1	Born on Grange
40 BR1	Entrance into the Brentaal Futures Program
36 BR1	Meets Orson Krennic
25 BR1	Marries Lyra
22 BR1	Jyn Erso born on Vallt
17 BR1	Flees Coruscant
13 BR1	Captured by Krennic

Standard Imperial dress belt

ACADEMIC ACHIEVEMENTS

Grange subadult science and engineering fair scholarship

Top honors, Brentaal Futures Program materials competition

The Kuat Systems Engineering Medal

The Ashgad Prize

The Roche Foundation Prize

DEATH STAR SCIENTISTS

THE DEATH STAR has been developed in secret in scattered scientific research laboratories for over two decades, beginning as a detailed set of theoretical schematics envisioned by the Stalgasin hive of Geonosians. Though Geonosian engineering solved many of the construction challenges, the heart of the station's power proved elusive. The Geonosians simply could not translate the yields of kyber crystal energy bombardment into a safe, scalable output.

To the Empire, cracking the mysteries of kyber crystals and completing the Death Star became of paramount importance. However, kyber crystals were extremely rare, especially of the size required for maximum energy output. Smaller fragments were of limited use. Additionally, the energy shed through crystalline amplification was extremely dangerous—too dangerous to be tested within the battle station itself. So while the main superstructure neared completion, superlaser development research continued far away from the station construction sites, secreted in the remote mountaintops of rainswept Eadu.

Under the direction of Galen Erso, a team of scientific geniuses undertook two interconnected projects: the fusing of crystal shards into larger forms, and the creation and redirection of a controlled chain reaction. In total, the kyber crystal research team, a division within the Tarkin Initiative, has been kept secluded for nearly 20 years.

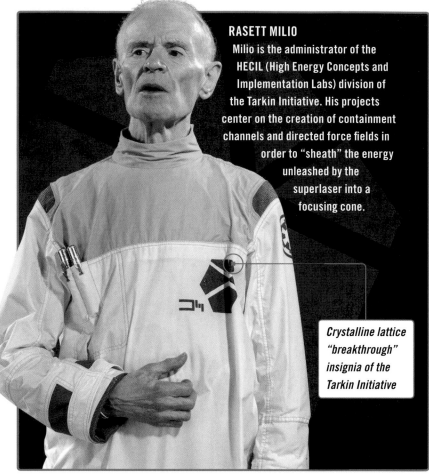

RASETT MILIO

Milio is the administrator of the HECIL (High Energy Concepts and Implementation Labs) division of the Tarkin Initiative. His projects center on the creation of containment channels and directed force fields in order to "sheath" the energy unleashed by the superlaser into a focusing cone.

Crystalline lattice "breakthrough" insignia of the Tarkin Initiative

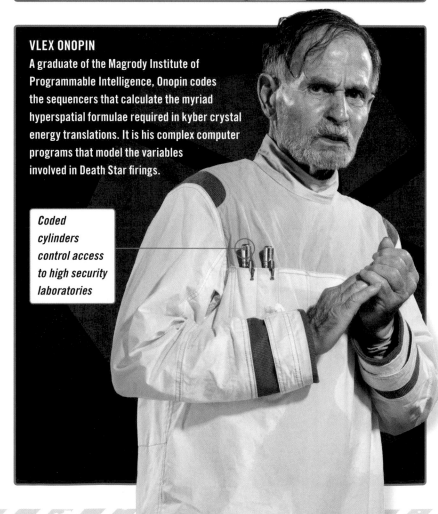

VLEX ONOPIN

A graduate of the Magrody Institute of Programmable Intelligence, Onopin codes the sequencers that calculate the myriad hyperspatial formulae required in kyber crystal energy translations. It is his complex computer programs that model the variables involved in Death Star firings.

Coded cylinders control access to high security laboratories

Suspicious of a rebel sympathizer within the scientific ranks, Director Krennic assembles the team for interrogation.

AMES URAVAN

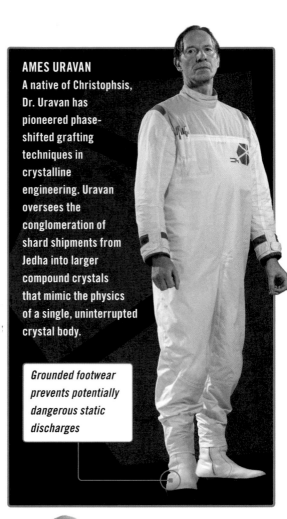

A native of Christophsis, Dr. Uravan has pioneered phase-shifted grafting techniques in crystalline engineering. Uravan oversees the conglomeration of shard shipments from Jedha into larger compound crystals that mimic the physics of a single, uninterrupted crystal body.

Grounded footwear prevents potentially dangerous static discharges

SIRRO ARGONNE

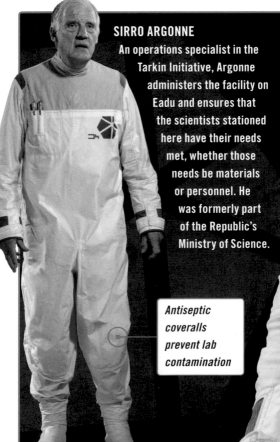

An operations specialist in the Tarkin Initiative, Argonne administers the facility on Eadu and ensures that the scientists stationed here have their needs met, whether those needs be materials or personnel. He was formerly part of the Republic's Ministry of Science.

Antiseptic coveralls prevent lab contamination

FEYN VANN

Once a leading researcher at Nordoxicon Unlimited, Vann's principal area of study is shield technology. He has created a series of deflector arrays that direct hypermatter streams from the Death Star's main reactor up to the crystalline firing array.

Tunic top alters color in the presence of dangerous radiation

Imperial cog symbol

STORMTROOPERS

THE STORMTROOPERS of the Empire are an evolution of the clone troopers that defended the Republic in its twilight. Rather than relying on Kaminoan cloning technology, the Empire recruits its soldiers from its population and instills in them a fierce loyalty and patriotism. By replacing genetic cloning with dehumanizing military doctrine, Imperials have ironically achieved greater uniformity and eliminated individuality among the ranks.

The Imperial occupation of Jedha turns the once-peaceful world into a powder keg of insurrection. Stormtroopers scramble to quell outbursts of rebellion.

Stormtroopers are increasingly common on worlds that pique Imperial interest with strategic value or seditious unrest.

After the Clone Wars, the emergent Empire began retiring its clone trooper ranks. Clone soldiers featured built-in age acceleration to force them into fighting shape in a fraction of the time required by untouched human biology, but this also made them age out faster. In the early years of the Empire clone trooper veterans were heralded as heroes, but in time the populace came to forget about these soldiers. Consequently it became hard for many clone troopers to find a place in the rapidly changing galaxy. The rising new face of the Empire became the stormtrooper—produced by a quickly expanding network of Imperial Academies across the galaxy.

FIGHTING FORCES

Some Imperial Academies begin training cadets as young as 13 standard years of age, molding young minds to become subservient to the Empire. This proves to be startlingly easy, especially on impoverished Outer Rim worlds or war-torn planets where the Empire is embraced as a savior. After years of mental and physical conditioning, a cadet emerges as an anonymous soldier with a number for a name.

"HALT, CITIZEN. LET'S SEE SOME SCANDOCS"
— IMPERIAL STORMTROOPER

Targeting macroscope

Blaster gas cylinder cap

E-11 BLASTER RIFLE

During the Clone Wars, customization of armor was common. This was done away with by the more stringent protocols of the Imperial military.

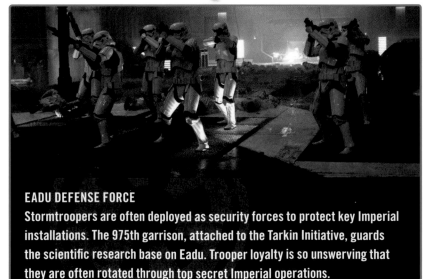

EADU DEFENSE FORCE
Stormtroopers are often deployed as security forces to protect key Imperial installations. The 975th garrison, attached to the Tarkin Initiative, guards the scientific research base on Eadu. Trooper loyalty is so unswerving that they are often rotated through top secret Imperial operations.

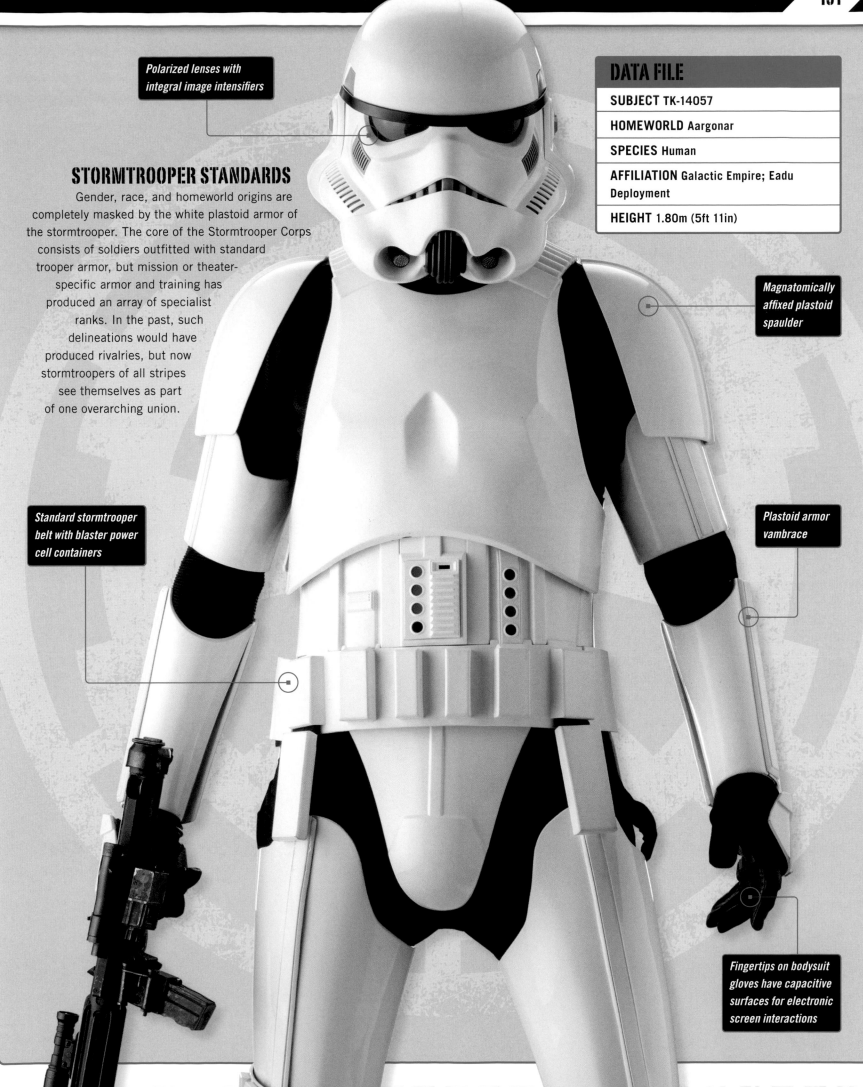

Polarized lenses with integral image intensifiers

STORMTROOPER STANDARDS

Gender, race, and homeworld origins are completely masked by the white plastoid armor of the stormtrooper. The core of the Stormtrooper Corps consists of soldiers outfitted with standard trooper armor, but mission or theater-specific armor and training has produced an array of specialist ranks. In the past, such delineations would have produced rivalries, but now stormtroopers of all stripes see themselves as part of one overarching union.

Standard stormtrooper belt with blaster power cell containers

DATA FILE

SUBJECT TK-14057

HOMEWORLD Aargonar

SPECIES Human

AFFILIATION Galactic Empire; Eadu Deployment

HEIGHT 1.80m (5ft 11in)

Magnatomically affixed plastoid spaulder

Plastoid armor vambrace

Fingertips on bodysuit gloves have capacitive surfaces for electronic screen interactions

TROOPERS ON ALERT

In addition to ground combat, stormtroopers of varied divisions serve as on-site security for starships and ground installations. They operate on escalating strata of responsiveness depending on their Defstat (defense status) level. Suspected rebel incursions send troopers scattering to battle stations.

STORMTROOPER EQUIPMENT

THE EMPIRE KEEPS ITS TROOPS equipped with modern technology, ensuring they stay a step ahead of armed insurrectionists. As has become apparent, however, rapid mass production has left shortcomings in Imperial equipment that rebels can exploit. Stormtrooper armor, while capable of intimidating subjugated populations, can be breached by well-placed blaster shots. While more advanced armor has been developed for elite units, the standard rank and file soldier has to make do with this vulnerable kit. Operating in large numbers helps make up for such deficits.

SANDTROOPER PATROL
On Jedha, troopers wearing variant armor are known as sandtroopers. Filtration systems prevent dust contamination that would clog standard armor breathing ports over time. The cooling units employed on hot desert worlds are not needed on the cold moon.

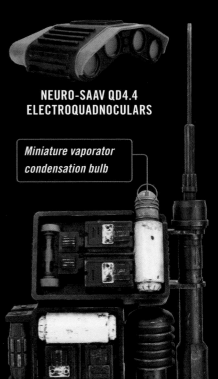

NEURO-SAAV QD4.4 ELECTROQUADNOCULARS

Miniature vaporator condensation bulb

LONG-RANGE TRANSMITTER ANTENNA

SANDTROOPER TYPE 4 FIELD PACK

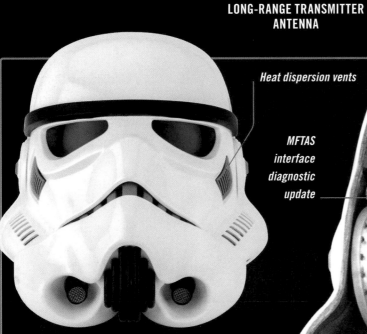

STORMTROOPER HELMET
The stormtrooper helmet (known colloquially as a "bucket"—affectionately when used by Imperials, derisively by rebels) is packed with electronics that filter the real world into focused military lenses. The multi-frequency targeting and acquisition system (MFTAS) creates an in-lens display for a trooper. Though the helmet can be hermetically sealed, it does not have a contained air supply. Scrubbers filter out smoke and the most common particulates, but for complete environmental purity, a stormtrooper must attach an external atmospheric tank.

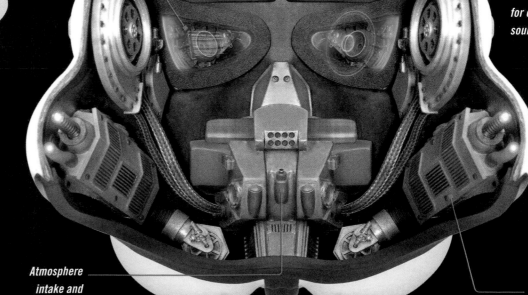

Heat dispersion vents

MFTAS interface diagnostic update

Shock padding

Comtech Series IV speaker uses three-phase sonic filtering for clear sound

Atmosphere intake and processing unit

Power cell

CRYSTAL PATROL DUTY

While specialist branches of the Stormtrooper Corps such as snowtroopers, scout troopers, and shoretroopers use customized armor and equipment, the standard stormtrooper can increase his versatility with field-specific kit. In addition to carrying out police actions in the occupied Holy City, these stormtrooper patrols are tasked with confiscating any kyber crystals from citizens, regardless of size or quality, for eventual delivery to Eadu for processing. To better preserve the crystals, stormtroopers seal collected fragments in vac-sealed, armored canisters carried in a well-secured backpack.

NEURO-SAAV MODEL TD2.3 ELECTROBINOCULARS

Weather shroud covers shock-resistant cargo carrier

Pauldron denotes rank or mission specialization

Datapad for cataloging crystal captures kept in weatherproof pouch

MULTI-FREQUENCY SPOTLIGHT GLOW ROD

DLT-19 heavy blaster rifle

ARMOR ACCESSORY CUBE LOCKER

EADU EXTRACTION

THE MISSION TO EADU turns tragic when conflicting orders collide. Alliance Intelligence, fearful of the knowledge that Galen Erso holds, calls in an airstrike to level the Tarkin Initiative installation, not realizing that Cassian Andor, Jyn Erso, Baze Malbus, Chirrut Îmwe, Bodhi Rook, and K-2SO are in the firing range. Caught in a blast, Jyn and Galen Erso have but brief moments of reunion. Galen looks upon his daughter—his beloved "Stardust"—for the first time in years.

VENGEANCE FIRE

From cover afforded by the rainy gloom, Baze Malbus opens fire upon the Eadu complex landing platform, blasting rows of stormtroopers as they emerge from their armored bunker. Chirrut Îmwe uses his keen hearing to target incoming TIE fighters with his lightbow.

DRAVEN'S FALLBACK

General Draven had charged Cassian Andor with the instruction to assassinate Galen Erso, rather than rescuing him, fearing he knew too much. However, he also organized a backup plan involving a squadron of X- and Y-wings, which at his orders swoops down on Eadu with deadly deposits of bombs and limpet charges.

CHAPTER 5

GOING ROGUE

Having witnessed a fraction of the destructive potential of the Death Star, Jyn Erso will not sit idly by while the rebel leadership deadlocks on their next course of action. She musters a team of rule-breaking rebels to depart on their own unsanctioned mission, deep behind Imperial lines. Their objective: to steal the plans of the Death Star battle station, no matter what the risk.

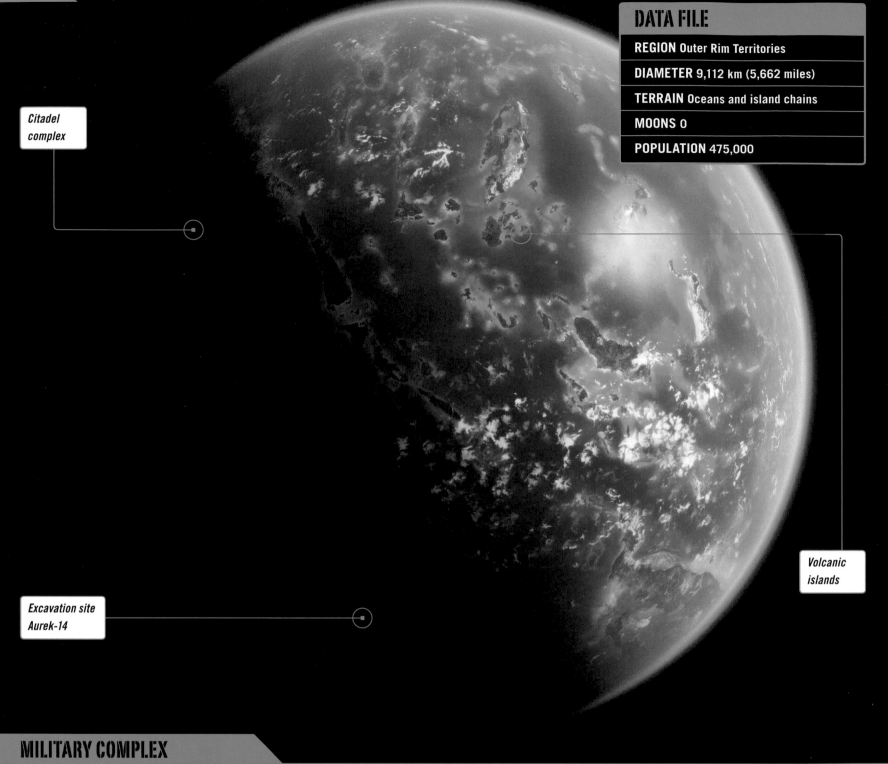

Citadel
complex

DATA FILE

REGION	Outer Rim Territories
DIAMETER	9,112 km (5,662 miles)
TERRAIN	Oceans and island chains
MOONS	0
POPULATION	475,000

Volcanic
islands

Excavation site
Aurek-14

MILITARY COMPLEX

SCARIF

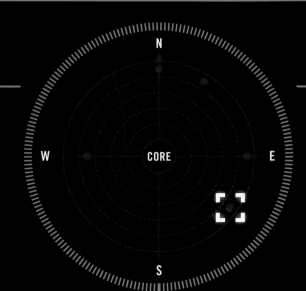

A SMALL WORLD of tropical islands rising from clear, shallow oceans, Scarif has a mantle that is filled with dense metals valuable in starship construction. Its placement deep in the Outer Rim makes supplying the shipyards of the Core too costly, but allows for development of projects too sensitive to be located within inspection distance of the Senate. These factors combined to turn Scarif into an incubator for Imperial military research, with a stronghold known as the Citadel below the sand.

IMPERIAL OPERATIONS

CRYSTAL DELIVERY
The research on the planet Eadu consumes the bulk of Imperial kyber shipments, but some are taken to Scarif for specific experiments.

BUNKER NETWORK
Scattered landing pads surround the Scarif Citadel, with barracks leading to a repulsor rail system that connects them all together.

COMMAND TOWER
The Citadel is capped with an immense tower that affords a commanding view of the beach and is the center of operations.

SHORE DEFENSES
When infiltrators do the unthinkable and breach Scarif defenses, the base is placed on high alert. Stormtroopers take to the beaches.

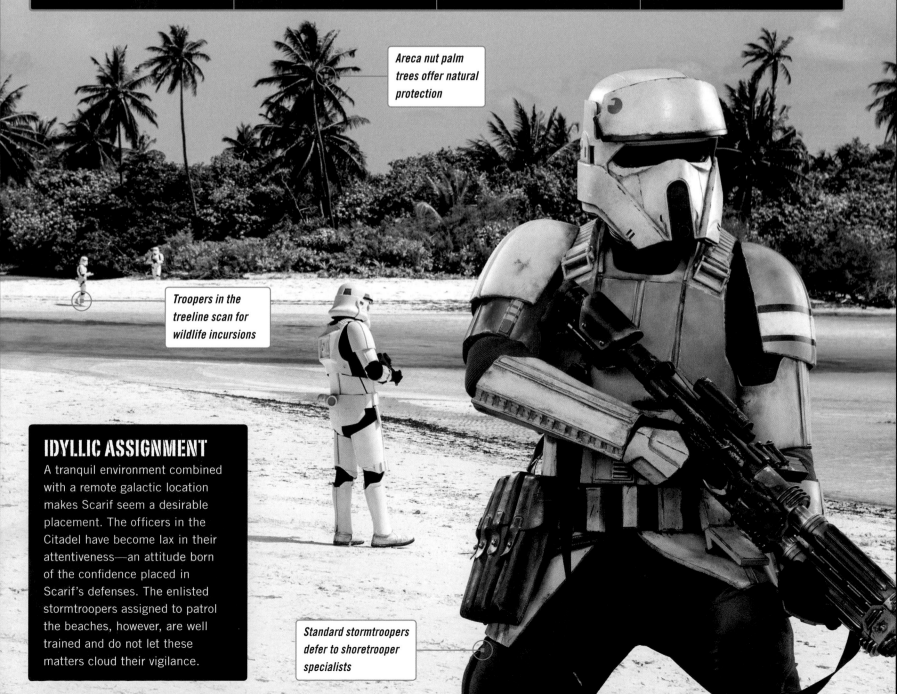

Areca nut palm trees offer natural protection

Troopers in the treeline scan for wildlife incursions

IDYLLIC ASSIGNMENT
A tranquil environment combined with a remote galactic location makes Scarif seem a desirable placement. The officers in the Citadel have become lax in their attentiveness—an attitude born of the confidence placed in Scarif's defenses. The enlisted stormtroopers assigned to patrol the beaches, however, are well trained and do not let these matters cloud their vigilance.

Standard stormtroopers defer to shoretrooper specialists

CARGO SHUTTLE

THE TELGORN CORPORATION and Sienar Fleet Systems pooled resources to create the *Zeta*-class shuttle, one of the most versatile transport craft employed by the Empire. Pressed into both military and civilian government service, the Zeta is built around a modular pod that can accommodate varied cargo needs. As the Death Star operation nears completion, and components from scattered hidden laboratories need to be ferried to the battle station, Zeta shuttles are in constant use. Pilots routinely fly cryptically labeled cargo loads, unaware of what the goods in their holds are contributing to.

One of four synchronized articulated stabilizer foils

Sienar Fleet Systems sublight drive system

INCREASED DEMAND
Work on the Death Star sees steady flows of cargo shuttle traffic connecting various worlds. From Jedha, kyber crystals are flown to Eadu. From Eadu, refined agglomerated crystals are returned either to the Death Star or to Scarif for further analysis. Scarif also sees deliveries of turbolaser, shielding, and other technical componentry for eventual fitting onto the battle station.

MODULAR CARGO

The *Zeta*-class shuttle's ventral cargo pod uses standardized umbilicals and docking sleeves for firm purchase into the spaceframe. These pods draw power from the Zeta's reactor plant, providing energy for specific cargo needs such as refrigeration or life support. Seasoned pilots can drop off and pick up without having to commit to a full landing, should expediency require it. Larger *Eta*-class supply barges can hold multiple pods aloft on a dorsal cargo bed.

Integrated main entry ramp leads to holding bay and cargo pod's nested airlock

Modular cargo pod finished in faded "interstellar orange" paint

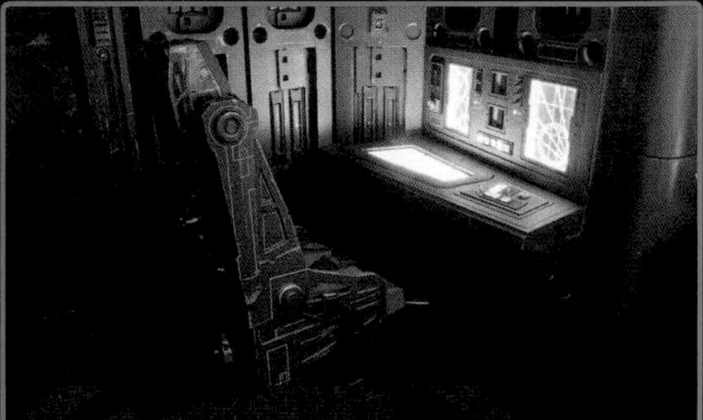

Wings contain
robust repulsorlifts
to counter weight
of carried mass

TECH STATION
Once a cargo pod is secured, it relays diagnostics
information directly to the main tech station in the
shuttle. Depending on the security clearance of the
crew, this may or may not include a full detailed
sensor readout of the carried load.

Deflector shield
projector plane

DATA FILE

MANUFACTURER Telgorn Corporation

MODEL *Zeta*-class cargo shuttle

AFFILIATION Galactic Empire

HEIGHT 28.74m (94ft 4in) with wings upright

LENGTH 35.50m (116ft 5in)

CREW 2; passenger load variable—
depending on cargo requirements

ATMOSPHERIC SPEED 700kph (435mph)

WEAPONS 2 wing-mounted paired heavy
laser cannons, 3 hull-mounted paired laser
cannons

Rigid bracing
hull structure
for stability

Pivoting heavy
double laser cannons
deter pirates

THE COMMAND DECK

Safe operation of a *Zeta*-class
shuttle requires a pilot and copilot
bearing accredited operator licenses
from the Imperial Space Ministry. The
urgent need for cargo fliers in the Empire
means that even rookie pilots with minimal security
clearances are pressed into service. However,
access to Imperial ports is very restricted and most
pilots are not permitted to exit their ships at all.

Hull-mounted Taim & Bak KX7
laser cannons pair with wing-
mounted Taim & Bak KV22
heavy laser cannons

SHUTTLE SW-0608

DURING THEIR HASTY DEPARTURE from Eadu, the Operation Fracture team commandeers Imperial shuttle SW-0608. After a brief visit to Yavin 4, where Jyn Erso entreaties the Rebel Alliance for official support, the shuttle becomes a key part of the Scarif infiltration. Pilot Bodhi Rook feigns that he has departure clearance and improvises a name for the shuttle and its mission: "Rogue One." The Imperial vessel disappears into hyperspace, Scarif-bound, and loaded with rebel commandos.

Outbound shuttle SW-4415 with deflector shield matrix circuitry

Self-diagnostic sensor node

Laser cannon positioning servo cap

Bodhi Rook and Corporal Tonc sit in the cockpit

Tech station

Replaceable laser cannon barrel tip

Forward viewpoint

Avionics bay and control interfaces

Primary active sensor bay

FLYING CASUAL

Bodhi has a working familiarity with the Scarif approach—he's flown it over a dozen times before. However, his paltry security clearance means he has never set foot beyond a landing pad, several kilometers distant from the team's ultimate objective: the Scarif Citadel. One obstacle at a time is the only way to succeed in this foolhardy mission against overwhelming odds. Bodhi's clearance codes get the shuttle past its first obstacle—an otherwise impenetrable shield barrier that envelops the entire planet, save for a high-altitude gate station.

Cassian Andor (disguised as Lieutenant Colin Hakelia)

Jyn Erso (disguised as Technician Kent Deezling)

Hydraulic ramp actuator

K-2SO

Deployed entry ramp

Auxiliary communications terminal and patch bay

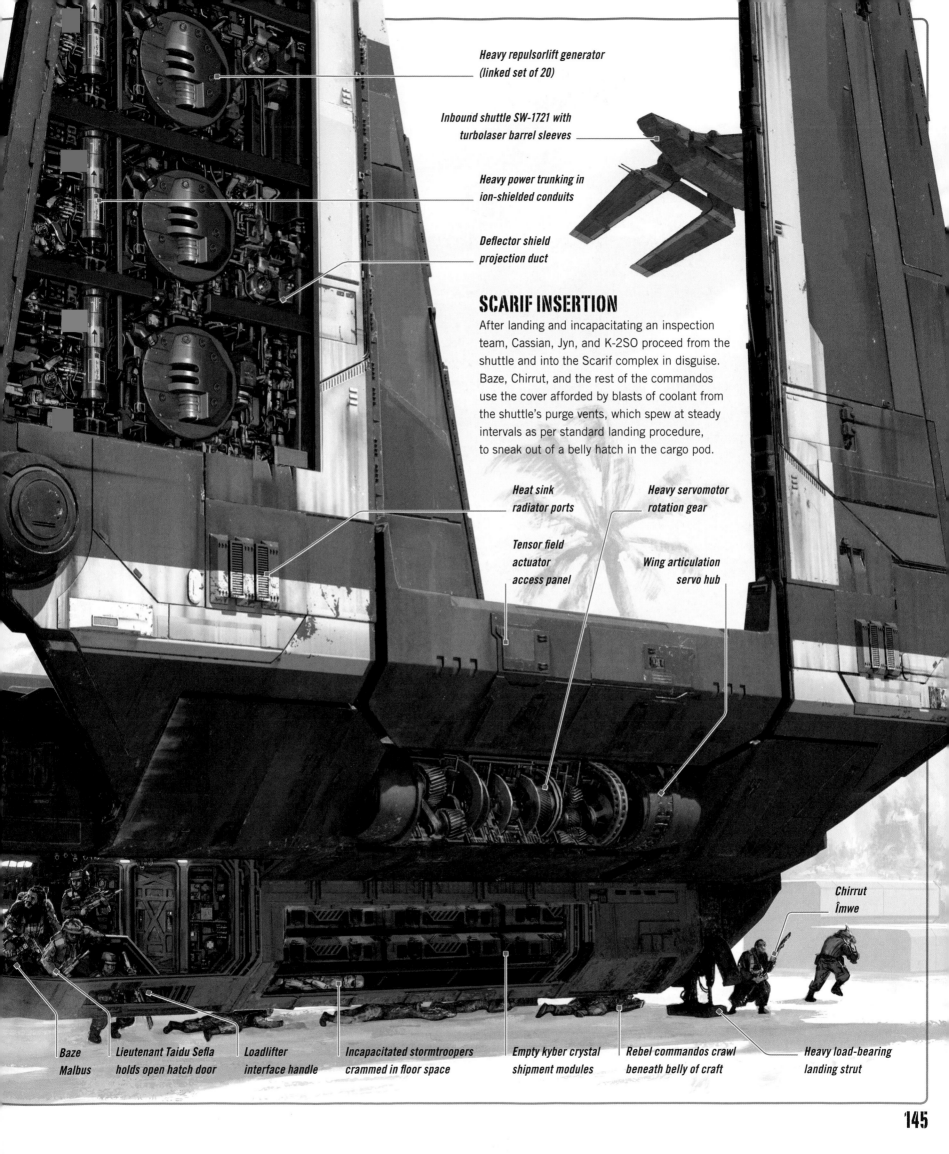

Heavy repulsorlift generator
(linked set of 20)

Inbound shuttle SW-1721 with
turbolaser barrel sleeves

Heavy power trunking in
ion-shielded conduits

Deflector shield
projection duct

SCARIF INSERTION

After landing and incapacitating an inspection
team, Cassian, Jyn, and K-2SO proceed from the
shuttle and into the Scarif complex in disguise.
Baze, Chirrut, and the rest of the commandos
use the cover afforded by blasts of coolant from
the shuttle's purge vents, which spew at steady
intervals as per standard landing procedure,
to sneak out of a belly hatch in the cargo pod.

Heat sink
radiator ports

Heavy servomotor
rotation gear

Tensor field
actuator
access panel

Wing articulation
servo hub

Chirrut
Îmwe

Baze
Malbus

Lieutenant Taidu Sefla
holds open hatch door

Loadlifter
interface handle

Incapacitated stormtroopers
crammed in floor space

Empty kyber crystal
shipment modules

Rebel commandos crawl
beneath belly of craft

Heavy load-bearing
landing strut

*TK-40121
stands on
guard duty*

*Quadanium-tungsten
composite vault door*

HEART OF THE CITADEL

SCARIF VAULT

AT THE VERY CORE of the Citadel complex is a multi-tier data
vault that houses the deepest technological secrets of the
Empire. The enormous library of datatapes is "cold" stored,
whereby cartridges are kept disconnected from any network
to prevent unauthorized electronic access. Security guards
surround the inner vault, as do heavy security doors and
sophisticated electronic scanners meant to restrict computer
systems from reaching too close to the library itself.

SCREENING TUNNEL
The defenses of the inner vault are geared toward preventing
electronic theft. The entryway is lined with cyclic degaussers
capable of disabling droids or computer equipment. Actual physical
theft of the datatapes is considered beyond the bounds of probability

EMERGENCY ACCESS

In case emergency access to the locked-down vault is required, personnel with Director-level approval can access molecular torches—extremely powerful plasma cutters that use a high energy quantum-kerf ray—to slice into key points in the compound armor.

BORALLIS M&M Q-1041 PLASMA CUTTER

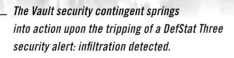

The Vault security contingent springs into action upon the tripping of a DefStat Three security alert: infiltration detected.

INSPECTOR GENERAL BOZEDEN JEEMS

Weapons development falls under the arm of Imperial Intelligence, and looks to its sister agency, the Imperial Security Bureau, to defend its secrets. Inspector Jeems is an up-and-coming ISB officer who is eyeing the position of Deputy Director. The disastrous breach of the Empire's most valuable military data vault causes his dreams of advancement to dissipate. Jeems scrambles troops in a vain effort to salvage his career first, and Imperial secrets second.

LIEUTENANT MILTON PUTNA

A librarian-turned-security officer, Putna is well versed with the layout of the datatape library tree. Access into the main vault door is keyed to his palm print.

DATATAPE SELECTOR

Once inside the vault control hub, authorized personnel can use remote manipulator arms to temporarily remove datatapes from the climate-controlled library tree. Tapes such as the one containing the Death Star plans are organized by Imperial weapons development protocols.

GOING UNDERCOVER

For the Rogue One mission, Jyn dons the all-concealing uniform of an Imperial deck crewmember. With the help of K-2SO, Cassian and Jyn penetrate the heart of the vault. When Imperial security surrounds the vault, K-2SO takes the only course of action and locks his partners inside.

DEATH STAR PLANS

COMPRESSED AND ENCODED in a nondescript, high-density datatape cartridge is the salvation of the Rebel Alliance. Galen Erso's modifications to the Death Star superlaser design resulted in a top-to-bottom reassessment of the Death Star's reactor system. Unbeknownst to the Empire, a weakness sits in the connection point between the primary power amplifier and the hypermatter reactor—which can be exploited by a high energy rupture into the reactor system. The unthinkable superweapon now has a nearly undetectable, yet insurmountable, flaw.

High density shockproof polyplast casing

Monomolecular-switching binary tape with 512-million exanode capacity

Electromagnetic shielding sink

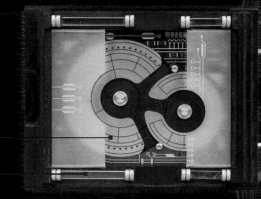

DATATAPE CARTRIDGE

Slotted into the Scarif vault's Structural Engineering node in its datatree is a cartridge nearly identical to all others. It contains the design history of the Death Star, from earliest explorations to final approved schematics. In the rebels' infiltration of the vault, Jyn is able to remove the cartridge from its storage slot and abscond with the plans.

Equatorial trench features major docking arrangements

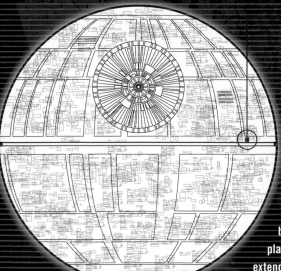

DEATH STAR EXTERIOR
The Death Star makes judicious use of replicable construction segments. The surface consists of a repeating variety of quadanium-based prefabricated sprawl segments plasma-bonded onto a latticework extending from the interior decks.

IMPERIAL DS-1 PLANS
0412.481.545GE
REVISIONS_V631

SUPERLASER LENS

An array of artificially conglomerated crystals creates an amplification field that unites the tributary laser streams into the cumulative planet-shattering blast.

FATAL FLAW

The hypermatter reactions at the heart of the Death Star create superheated gases that must be shunted away from the superlaser array to prevent overheating. A network of exchangers closer to the core attempts to repurpose this heat energy, but some works its way out through dedicated ports. One particularly vulnerable port lies along a meridian trench.

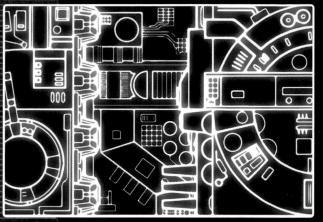

Trenches such as these allow for recessed cooling elements not directly exposed to stellar or hyperspatial radiation.

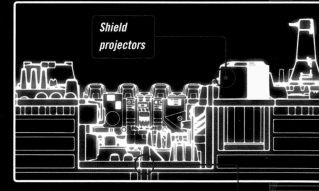

Shield projectors

Located beneath a main port, the exhaust port is at the end of a trench that terminates with an array of defensive turbolaser batteries.

1 Ion-drive reactor
2 Atmosphere-processing unit
3 Sector computer cluster
4 Turbolift shaft
5 Emergency radiation discharge
6 Secondary power converters
7 Central power column
8 Tractor-beam power coupling
9 Main power generator
10 Hypermatter reactor
11 Power cell
12 Central computer core
13 Power-processing networks
14 Superlaser power cell
15 Primary power amplifier
16 Atmosphere-processing unit
17 Sector computer cluster
18 Hyperdrive
19 Tributary superlaser beam shaft
20 Magnetic shielding
21 Primary beam focusing magnet
22 Targeting field generator

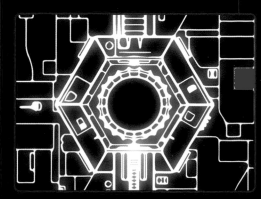

A scant two meters wide, this particular hexagonal port's placement allows for a straight, unobstructed line into a section of the vulnerable reactor system.

SHORETROOPERS

SPECIALIST ELITE STORMTROOPERS assigned to the once-beautiful world of Scarif, these soldiers lead security patrols, scout the beaches, and man the barracks of the Imperial military installation on the planet. While their armor affords them greater mobility in the seaside terrain, at their core they are standard stormtroopers elevated by military necessity. Most shoretroopers operate at an effective sergeant rank, allowing them to command squads of stormtrooper infantry.

When brazen infiltrators somehow breach the Scarif perimeter, shoretroopers lead the charge to defend their posts.

Due to the environmentally specific nature of their postings, shoretroopers—formally known as coastal defender stormtroopers—are a rare sight in the galaxy. The troopers assigned to Scarif wear armor specific to their location, meaning shoretroopers encountered elsewhere may not necessarily look the same. Being a shoretrooper is a rotational role that stormtroopers adopt when their orders demand it, and their rank and training qualifies them for it. Scarif's isolation, and the heavy defenses that surround it, mean that shoretroopers do not expect to see combat operations. However, grueling drills and live-fire exercises keep them in peak readiness, a disposition that—unfortunately for the Empire—is not shared at all levels of command on Scarif.

Shoretroopers are concentrated on the outer landing platforms, which see a steady stream of traffic as cargo transports deliver supplies.

Reciprocating double barrels

E-22 BLASTER RIFLE

PLATFORM CONFRONTATION
As chaos erupts during the rebel infiltration of Scarif, a squad of troopers determines that the invasion origin point is landing pad nine. Shoretroopers lead stormtroopers into a fierce firefight and target the turncoat Imperial pilot Bodhi Rook, who has ferried the rebels to Scarif.

"REBEL INFILTRATORS AT PAD TWO! REPEAT, INFILTRATORS AT PAD TWO! MOVE OUT!"
— TK-32028

SECURITY FORCE
Scarif's heavy defenses lead many confident Imperial officers stationed in the Citadel tower to view the beachside security as an extravagant adornment. Such talk does nothing to faze the shoretroopers, who take to their duty with utmost solemnity. Should an infiltrator find a way to penetrate the orbital screens, they are the last line of defense.

TROOP SCRAMBLE
Alarms within the enormous Citadel complex indicate the unthinkable has happened. A series of explosions on the beachside indicates invasion.

Plastoid greave with expandable plates

DATA FILE

SUBJECT TK-32028

HOMEWORLD Carida

SPECIES Human

AFFILIATION Galactic Empire; Scarif Deployment

HEIGHT 1.80m (5ft 11in)

Helmet crown includes built-in cooling fans

Covered airfilters prevent sand buildup

Plastoid-coated armor prevents salt corrosion

Blaster gas cartridge magazine holder

Lengthened armor combined with colored chestplate pieces indicate rank of captain

DEADLY BEACHWEAR

Like the standard stormtrooper armor, the plastoid shoretrooper armor is magnatomically fitted onto a form-fitting, temperature-controlled and sealed bodysuit. Similar to that of the stormtrooper scout, sandtrooper armor has fewer plates allowing for a more flexible and lightweight fit. Shoretrooper captains are distinguished from enlisted ranks by the larger blue-gray colored area on the chestplate and a set of plastoid faulds instead of a fabric kama around the hips.

Plastoid plackart torso piece with control systems interface

Blaster power cell cartridge belt

REBEL TROOPS

ENTRUSTED WITH defense and missions vital to Alliance High Command, Special Forces (SpecForces) are the handpicked best of the rebel ground soldiers. Of these elite infantry, the Pathfinders stand apart as some of the most hardened, brave, and exceptional warriors in the Rebellion. On Scarif they are tasked with covert infiltration into enemy territory, establishing a beachhead, and holding ground until the arrival of the main military force.

As Imperials counterattack, the Pathfinders scramble to create as much destruction and confusion as they can to draw the Empire away from the infiltrators.

With operations spanning some of the most remote worlds of the Outer Rim, the SpecForces have been witness to the worst of Imperial brutality. Hit and fade missions have accomplished small objectives, but the Empire still enjoys political and military dominance.

When Jyn Erso proposes to the rebel council a strike at the heart of the Imperial military, these soldiers take notice. While those in the council debate their next course of action, it is clear that Jyn is willing to risk all in a daring mission that will prove what the Rebel Alliance is capable of. Drawn to action, many Pathfinders volunteer to join her.

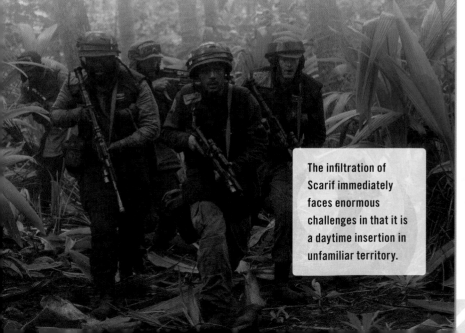

The infiltration of Scarif immediately faces enormous challenges in that it is a daytime insertion in unfamiliar territory.

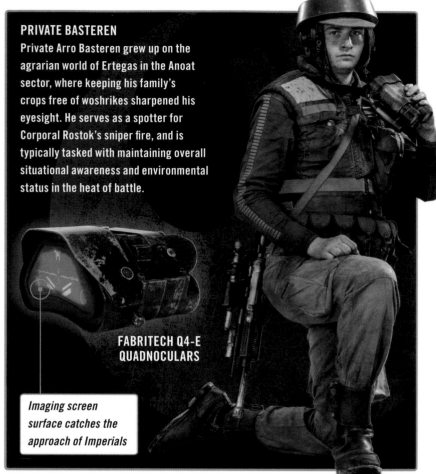

PRIVATE BASTEREN
Private Arro Basteren grew up on the agrarian world of Ertegas in the Anoat sector, where keeping his family's crops free of woshrikes sharpened his eyesight. He serves as a spotter for Corporal Rostok's sniper fire, and is typically tasked with maintaining overall situational awareness and environmental status in the heat of battle.

FABRITECH Q4-E QUADNOCULARS

Imaging screen surface catches the approach of Imperials

PRIVATE KAPPEHL
Forward observer Farsin Kappehl specializes in recon and assisting indirect fire teams to zero in on targets with his rifle-mounted lasing scope. This mission places Kappehl deeper into frontline action than he's ever experienced. The brave soldier welcomes the change of pace.

BlasTech DH-17 with extended magazine and spotting laser

CORPORAL TIMKER

Combat engineer Walea Timker arrives on Scarif as part of reinforcements delivered by Blue Squadron. She specializes in finding, improvising, and constructing temporary fortifications across a battlefield. Given how much wreckage the Pathfinders kick up in their initial incursion, she has lots of smoldering structures to choose from.

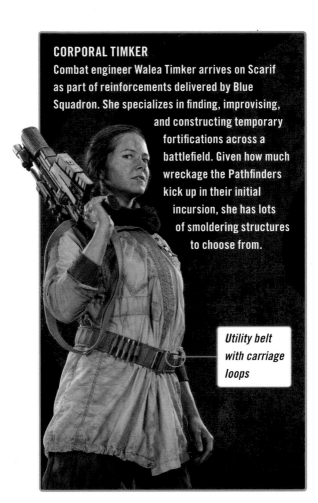

Utility belt with carriage loops

CORPORAL MEFRAN

A wilderness fighter specialist from the 4th SpecForce Regiment, Jav Mefran masks his misgivings about the Scarif mission by focusing on the beautiful environment. Mefran helped clear out the jungle brush surrounding the Great Temple on Yavin 4 when the rebels relocated there from Dantooine, and he has an affinity for rain forest surroundings.

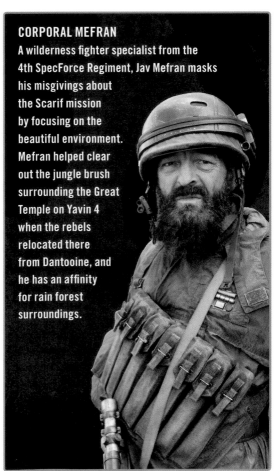

Reinforced Czerka ACH-14 advanced combat helmet

CORPORAL TONC

A regular infantry soldier who recently joined the Yavin rebels following an uprising on Qemia 7, Stordan "Stordie" Tonc had aspired to one day join the SpecForces, but now finds that path shortened by necessity. Once landed on Scarif, Tonc stays with the shuttle on landing pad nine along with several Pathfinders and Bodhi Rook while the rest of the team fans out into the surrounding jungle. Alongside Bodhi, Tonc is able to create confusion among the rapidly dispersing Imperial defenders by creating false accounts of rebel incursions on landing pads not currently under assault. When the Imperials finally arrive at pad nine to investigate, Tonc and his fellow troops file out from the shuttle to defend their vessel.

BlasTech A-300 blaster rifle

REBEL TROOPS

SERGEANT MELSHI

At Captain Andor's orders, SpecForces Infiltrator Sergeant Ruescott Melshi is placed in command of the Pathfinders that infiltrate the Imperial compound on Scarif. This requires several breaks from formal command structure as Melshi is not the highest-ranking soldier on the ground. However, Andor knows Melshi personally and trusts him to carry out the hard task of making his small fighting force feel like a much bigger unit in the eyes of the Empire. Melshi leads by example. If he decides that an objective is attainable, or worth risking everything for, then his troops will follow him into battle unquestioningly.

Headset comlink repeater and earpiece

Collapsed barrel A-300 blaster rifle

Long-range communications booster

CORPORAL ESKRO CASRICH

SpecForces commando and thrill seeker Casrich has rappelled the peaks of Scipio, spelunked the sinkholes of Utapau, and sand-sailed the dunes of Ingo, Casrich sees the Rogue One mission as yet another adrenaline trip. Were it not for his skill in combat, his squadmates would tire of his recklessness.

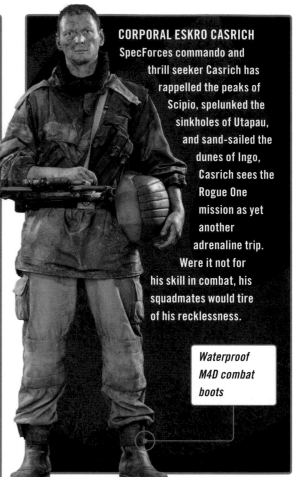

Waterproof M4D combat boots

PRIVATE CALFOR

A demolitions specialist from Mykapo, Private Yosh Calfor can be relied upon to handle the most dangerous explosives in combat operations without breaking a sweat. He prides himself on having at least three grenades within reach. Calfor's electrocochlear implant helps offset hearing loss sustained from working with thermal detonators.

CORPORAL MADDEL

An intelligence agent recruited by Cassian Andor, Rodma Maddel is an advanced scout for urban combat units. Upon learning that Cassian is part of the Rogue One operation, she does not hesitate to join Blue Squadron's ground reinforcements.

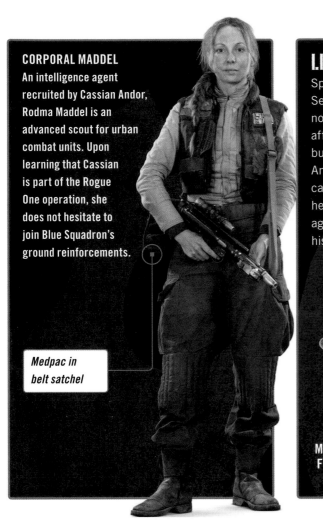

Medpac in belt satchel

LIEUTENANT SEFLA

SpecForces officer Taidu Sefla officially outranks Sergeant Melshi and Jyn Erso (who holds no formal rank, so Sefla gives her an affectionate brevet rank of sergeant), but respectfully defers to Captain Andor's unit formation. A strong, capable soldier, Sefla has a lot of heart that he brings to the fight against the Empire, and he gives his all in every mission.

Neuro-Saav NT-43.3 electroscope

Field ration and survival kit

MERR-SONN C-35 FRAGMENTATION GRENADE

CORPORAL ROSTOK

A qualified sharpshooter specialist when part of a SpecForces commando squad, Serchill Rostok works with Private Basteren as his spotter, lining up long-distance targets from under cover to strike swiftly with maximum surprise. Rostok is exceptional at camouflage and stealth. He is able to hold his breath for over 15 standard minutes and sit rock solid—earning the nickname Rostok the Rock. A superstitious type, he relies on a specific "lucky" electroscope with a pronounced drift for which he mentally compensates.

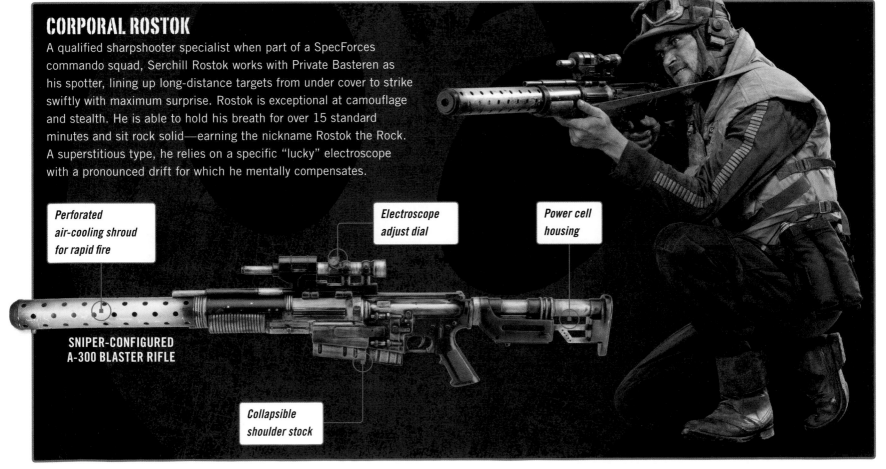

Perforated air-cooling shroud for rapid fire

Electroscope adjust dial

Power cell housing

SNIPER-CONFIGURED A-300 BLASTER RIFLE

Collapsible shoulder stock

PAO

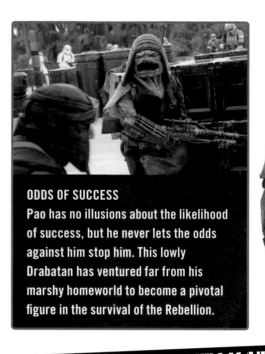

THE EMPIRE'S EXPANSION has displaced many civilizations as the war machine gobbles up material to fuel the growth of Imperial military forces. This has affected native populations on many far-flung worlds, including the amphibious Drabatans of Pipada. One such Drabatan—the fierce rebel commando Pao—particularly hates the Empire. He charges into battle shouting a full-throated war cry of "Sa'kalla!" as is his custom.

ODDS OF SUCCESS
Pao has no illusions about the likelihood of success, but he never lets the odds against him stop him. This lowly Drabatan has ventured far from his marshy homeworld to become a pivotal figure in the survival of the Rebellion.

Transmitter antenna with mounted glowrod

PAO'S BACKPACK

After sneaking onto Scarif in an Imperial shuttle, Pao and his fellow SpecForce commandos hide in the jungle canopy.

Pao is most often heard muttering oaths and curses in his native tongue. His full name is Paodok'Draba'Takat, and although his understanding of Basic is solid, his gaping maw has a hard time forming the shapes required to pronounce it effortlessly. Given Pao's seasoned combat skills, his squadmates are fine with him speaking in his native Drabatese, since most of the time he's not relaying mission-specific instructions.

Pao's large lungs and strong diaphragm muscles contribute to his booming voice and also grant him the ability to hold his breath for long periods of time. A freshwater amphibiod, he doesn't find the saltwater of Imperial stronghold Scarif particularly comforting, despite being surrounded by aquatic environments.

"PAODOK'DRABA'TAKAT SAP'DE'REKTI NIK'LINEK'TI KI'VEF'NIK' NE SEVEF'LI'KEK."
– PAO'S RESPONSE WHEN ASKED HIS FULL NAME

BEACHFRONT STANDOFF
Pao is a key part of the commando mission to sow confusion around the Citadel complex. The Empire is caught off guard of the incursion.

SAPPER SKILLS
Pao is trained in explosives, and his amphibious nature makes him particularly well suited for underwater demolitions. If the Empire had not interfered in his life, Pao would have become an engineer. Study in structural dynamics aids him in knowing where to best place charges to bring down Imperial structures.

Pao charges into battle at an Imperial landing pad, goading his squadmates to give it their all.

DATA FILE

SUBJECT Paodok'Draba'Takat

PLANET OF BIRTH Pipada

SPECIES Drabatan

STATUS Corporal, Rebel Alliance SpecForces

HEIGHT 1.72m (5ft 8in)

AGE 31 standard years

Folded reed armor from homeworld

Replacement galven barrels

Transmission antenna in armored sheath

WORDS OF WAR

Drabatese is a complex language that strings discrete syllables into unwieldy words that encompass multilayered ideas. Context, tense, and other grammatical pieces of information are determined by volume—Drabatese is a singularly loud language. When circumstances require more hushed tones, Drabatans switch to a secondary form of communication, passing air through a vocal pouch that produces a softer, croaking sound that they can vary in pitch. Drabatese love songs are said to require no translation due to their haunting beauty.

TIBANNA-JACKED BLASTER RIFLE

Pao wields a black-market blaster rifle with an external tibanna gas chamber that amps up its destructive power output. Such a modification burns through galven barrels quickly, requiring constant upkeep.

Water-shedding fatigues

BISTAN

THE REBELLION HAS DRAWN WARRIORS from across the galaxy—soldiers fighting to liberate their homes and free their people from the oppression of the Empire. Though Bistan wants to ensure the freedom of his fellow Iakaru, the truth is that he'd fight no matter what. He relishes the thrill of action and is driven by adrenaline, feeling most alive when the repetitive recoil of his heavy ion rifle thumps his flank, and his ears ring with the roar of combat.

Despite having only recently left his homeworld, Bistan is quick to master modern technology.

Iakaru are an uncommon sight in the galaxy, as they have not developed hyperdrive technology. Their homeworld, Iakar, has been visited by interstellar trade for nearly a century, with pharmaceutical corporations drawing valuable organic compounds from the lush rain forests girdling the planet. During the Clone Wars, companies such as Chiewab, Merisee Prime, and Fabreth Medical set up major research installations on Iakar, driving the Iakaru deeper into the jungle and straining the tentative trading relationship the natives had established with the offworlders. With the rise of the Empire and its military expansion, demand for medical supplies escalated, bringing a full-scale seizure and occupation of Iakar.

Bistan's unending, gregarious energy makes him popular among fellow rebels, though his personnel file lists multiple incidents of insubordination.

COVER FIRE SPECIALIST
Bistan's specialty is maintaining directed cover fire from the main entry hatch of a U-wing fighter during flight and landing operations. He pours out streams of deadly antipersonnel fire support with his overpowered repeating blaster, to protect troops racing in or out of the U-wing.

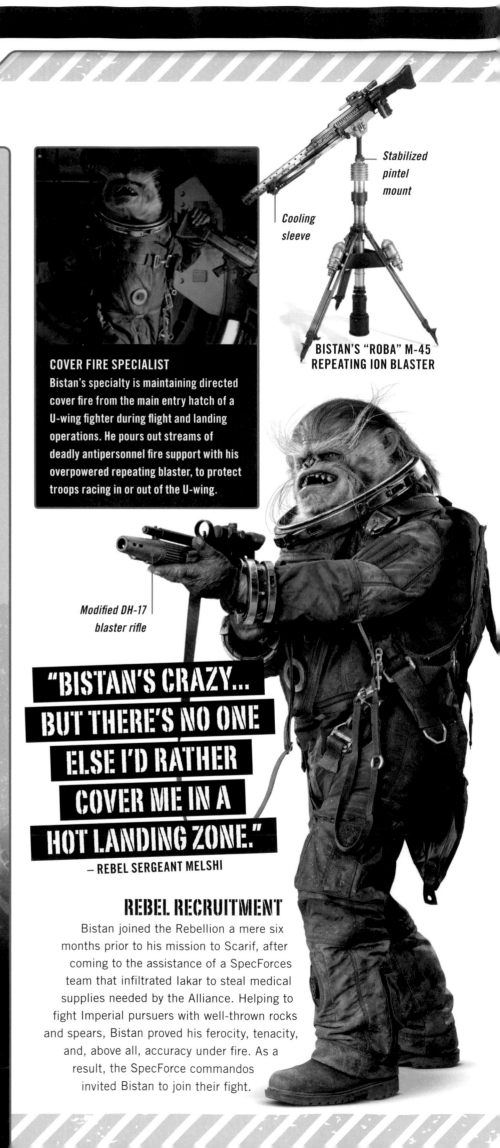

Stabilized pintel mount

Cooling sleeve

BISTAN'S "ROBA" M-45 REPEATING ION BLASTER

Modified DH-17 blaster rifle

"BISTAN'S CRAZY... BUT THERE'S NO ONE ELSE I'D RATHER COVER ME IN A HOT LANDING ZONE."
— REBEL SERGEANT MELSHI

REBEL RECRUITMENT
Bistan joined the Rebellion a mere six months prior to his mission to Scarif, after coming to the assistance of a SpecForces team that infiltrated Iakar to steal medical supplies needed by the Alliance. Helping to fight Imperial pursuers with well-thrown rocks and spears, Bistan proved his ferocity, tenacity, and, above all, accuracy under fire. As a result, the SpecForce commandos invited Bistan to join their fight.

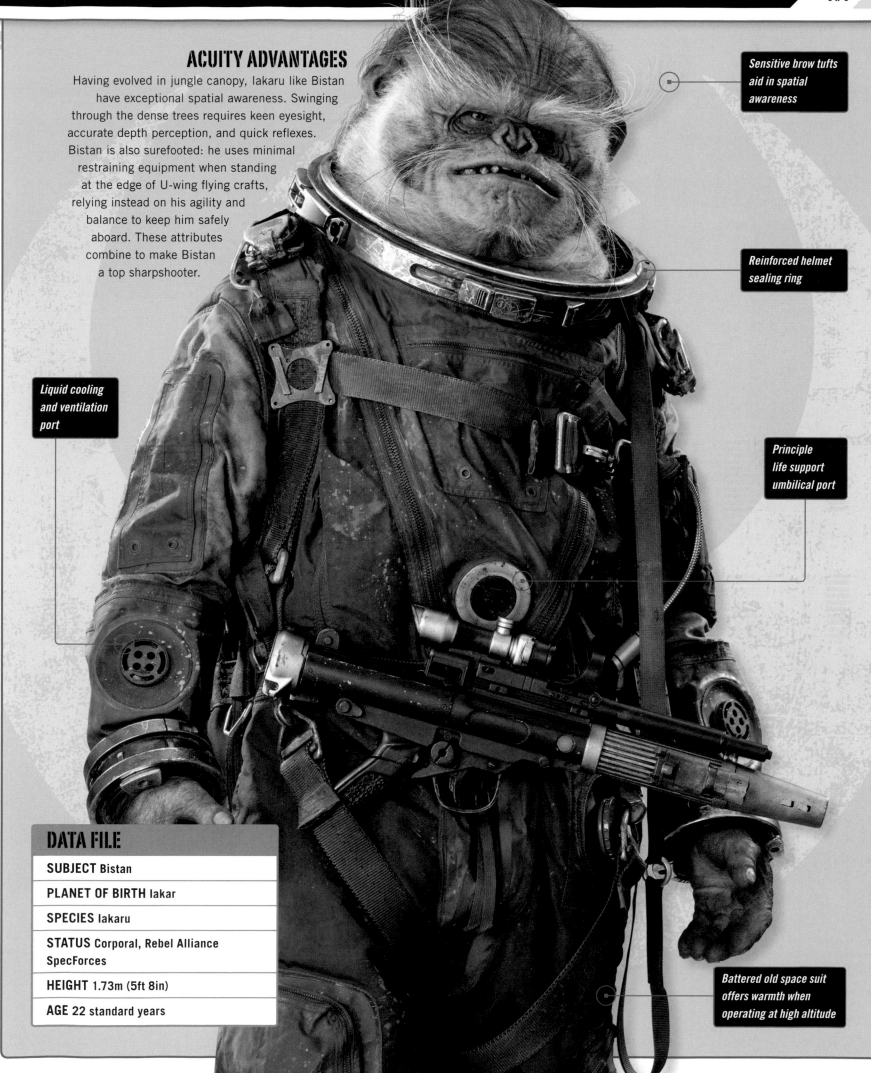

ACUITY ADVANTAGES

Having evolved in jungle canopy, Iakaru like Bistan
have exceptional spatial awareness. Swinging
through the dense trees requires keen eyesight,
accurate depth perception, and quick reflexes.
Bistan is also surefooted: he uses minimal
restraining equipment when standing
at the edge of U-wing flying crafts,
relying instead on his agility and
balance to keep him safely
aboard. These attributes
combine to make Bistan
a top sharpshooter.

*Sensitive brow tufts
aid in spatial
awareness*

*Reinforced helmet
sealing ring*

*Liquid cooling
and ventilation
port*

*Principle
life support
umbilical port*

DATA FILE

SUBJECT Bistan	
PLANET OF BIRTH Iakar	
SPECIES Iakaru	
STATUS Corporal, Rebel Alliance SpecForces	
HEIGHT 1.73m (5ft 8in)	
AGE 22 standard years	

*Battered old space suit
offers warmth when
operating at high altitude*

CANOPY COMBAT

The rebel Pathfinders who have infiltrated the grounds on Scarif quickly disappear into the jungle canopy. This is their element: wilderness fighting while camouflaged. They take to heart Captain Cassian Andor's orders to make ten men feel like a hundred.

AT-ACT

TOWERING ABOVE major Imperial construction projects are the plodding All Terrain Armored Cargo Transports, or AT-ACT walkers. A larger version of the standard All Terrain Armored Transport (AT-AT), the AT-ACT walker features a dedicated cargo bed for the transportation of heavy building materials or combat munitions. Although not built for combat, the AT-ACT can nonetheless pose a formidable obstacle to infantry, as is discovered by the commando forces of the Rogue One team.

HEAVY BURDEN

The cargo module housed within the AT-ACT's frame encompasses nearly 550 cubic meters of space and is capable of holding many thousands of metric tons of raw material. Loads are carefully managed by stevedore droids who divide up partial holds of ultradense materials into manageable trips. Powerful engines and tensor field-supported legs keep the massive AT-ACTs trampling forward, from mining sites to processing facilities, carrying cargo in situations where repulsorfields are unreliable or not suitable due to material incompatibilities.

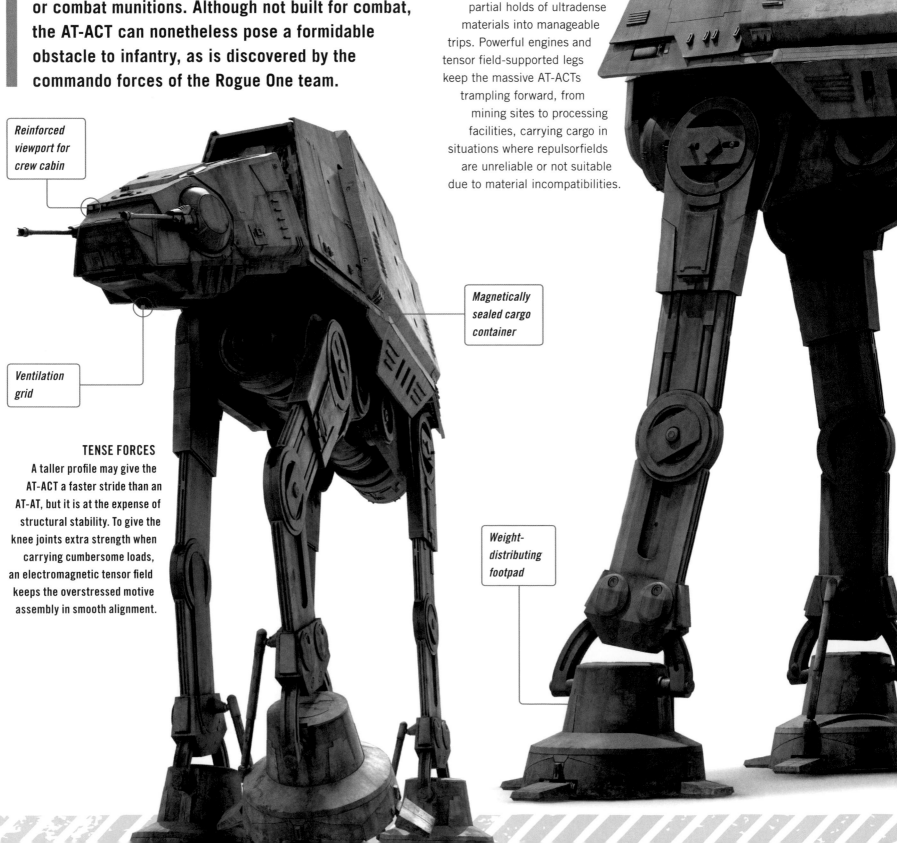

Reinforced viewport for crew cabin

Ventilation grid

Magnetically sealed cargo container

TENSE FORCES
A taller profile may give the AT-ACT a faster stride than an AT-AT, but it is at the expense of structural stability. To give the knee joints extra strength when carrying cumbersome loads, an electromagnetic tensor field keeps the overstressed motive assembly in smooth alignment.

Weight-distributing footpad

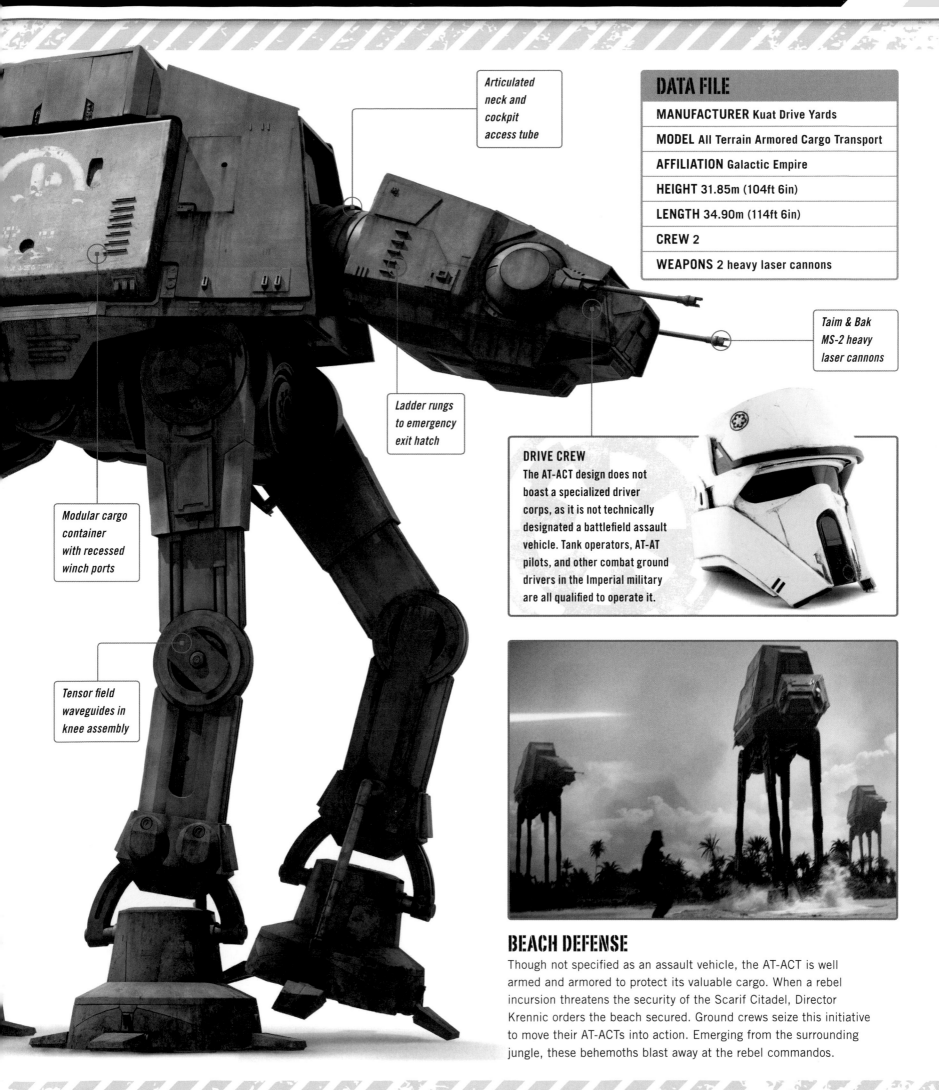

Articulated neck and cockpit access tube

DATA FILE

MANUFACTURER Kuat Drive Yards

MODEL All Terrain Armored Cargo Transport

AFFILIATION Galactic Empire

HEIGHT 31.85m (104ft 6in)

LENGTH 34.90m (114ft 6in)

CREW 2

WEAPONS 2 heavy laser cannons

Taim & Bak MS-2 heavy laser cannons

Ladder rungs to emergency exit hatch

Modular cargo container with recessed winch ports

Tensor field waveguides in knee assembly

DRIVE CREW

The AT-ACT design does not boast a specialized driver corps, as it is not technically designated a battlefield assault vehicle. Tank operators, AT-AT pilots, and other combat ground drivers in the Imperial military are all qualified to operate it.

BEACH DEFENSE

Though not specified as an assault vehicle, the AT-ACT is well armed and armored to protect its valuable cargo. When a rebel incursion threatens the security of the Scarif Citadel, Director Krennic orders the beach secured. Ground crews seize this initiative to move their AT-ACTs into action. Emerging from the surrounding jungle, these behemoths blast away at the rebel commandos.

BATTLE OF SCARIF

USING THE CARGO SHUTTLE stolen from the Empire's Eadu installation, Bodhi Rook ferries the Rogue One team past the otherwise impenetrable shield barrier that envelops Scarif. It's a run he's made over a dozen times before—but never with a hold full of rebel soldiers. During the battle that ensues, a shoretrooper lobs a thermal detonator into the shuttle, causing an explosion that means the team must look to find another way off the fortified world.

LANDING PAD STRIKE

As an infiltration team disguises itself as Imperial personnel, the commandos—accompanied by Baze Malbus and Chirrut Îmwe—sneak from inside the hold of the cargo shuttle onto the landing field. A network of landing pads connected by a railspeeder system spreads across the low-lying islands. The rebels disappear into the underbrush, setting themselves into strategic positions to launch a surprise attack on the unsuspecting Imperials.

BEACHFRONT BATTLE

The rebels are chased back into the jungle by Imperial forces on the defensive. At Krennic's furious orders, all available Imperial forces focus on stopping these intruders. TIE strikers unleash devastating fire from the skies, and enormous AT-ACTs join the fray. The rebels are forced onto the beaches where there is little cover. But hope never dies in the Rebel Alliance—reinforcements from Yavin 4 are on their way.

X-WING PILOTS

THE STARFIGHTER PILOTS of the Massassi outpost are a varied lot, unified by a love of freedom embodied in flight. Some learned their skills in rigid Academy training, and defected or otherwise escaped being drafted into the Imperial Starfleet. Others are commercial fliers who chafed at routine and sought a life of consequence and adventure. Some are civilian hobbyists while others are agrarian pilots. Such myriad origins paired with outsized daredevil egos leads to intense competition among all.

Downtime and shared experiences create an easy camaraderie between pilots.

The Massassi outpost has more pilots than battle-ready craft at any given moment—the result of supply difficulties and the scarcity of available combat vessels under Imperial rule. Fighter pilots train regularly within ground-based simulators, competing for a spot in Red, Blue, Green, or Gold Squadron. Once airborne, these pilots all work together because trust and reliance are necessary for survival in the blink-and-die reality of starfighter combat.

Landing a seat in a squadron is an honor, but a tempered one: it results from a vacancy created by another pilot's injury, fatigue, or worse. It is up to the next pilot to continue flying under an inherited call-sign.

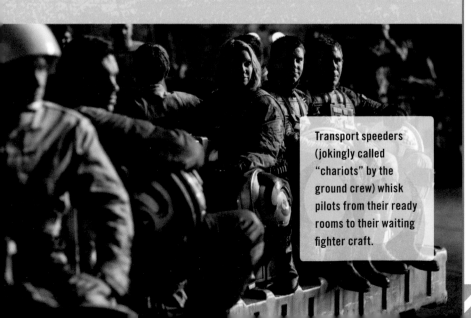

Transport speeders (jokingly called "chariots" by the ground crew) whisk pilots from their ready rooms to their waiting fighter craft.

CADET HARB BINLI (RED SEVEN)

As a relatively new addition to the Red Squadron roster, Harb Binli of Eriadu has barely worn through his first flight helmet. His talent and tenacity means he particularly excels at strafing runs against point defense cannons. Binli has already absorbed many lessons from his more seasoned wingmate, Pedrin Gaul.

Control conduit/ life support umbilical

LIEUTENANT ZAL DINNES (RED EIGHT)

When encroaching Imperial patrols forced the rebels to scuttle their Tierfon launch base, the defending Yellow Aces Squadron was broken apart and reallocated to other outposts. The largest contingent— four pilots—transferred to Yavin 4, with Zal Dinnes and her wingmate Jek Porkins (Red Six) assigned to Red Squadron.

Insignia of the Tierfon Yellow Aces

LIEUTENANT NOZZO NAYTAAN (RED NINE)

Nozzo Naytaan fled his job as a test pilot for the Corellian Engineering Corporation when Imperialization meant he would be building and testing TIE fighters.

CAPTAIN BROAN DANURS (GREEN TEN)

Formerly a Y-wing pilot who flew in Gold Squadron while stationed on Dantooine, Danur was transferred to fill an X-wing vacancy. He is a close friend to his mentor, Davish Krail, who flies as Gold Five.

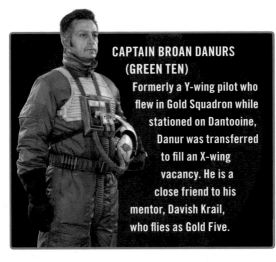

MAJOR RALO SURREL (RED ELEVEN)

A dashing stunt pilot who flew rickety antiques for the amusement of Outer Rim audiences, Ralo is now wingmate to Red Leader, Garven Dries.

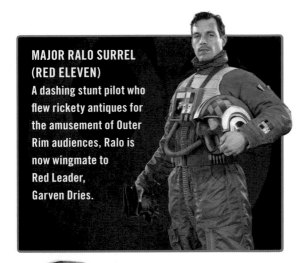

LIEUTENANT ATTICO WRED (GREEN FOUR)

Attico Wred was a TIE fighter pilot before defecting to the Rebellion after disobeying a direct order to fire on unarmed civilian craft. He has a boisterous rivalry with a fellow Corellian, Nozzo Naytaan.

LIEUTENANT WION DILLEMS (GREEN TWELVE)

Dillems grew up in the wilds of Yelsain among the rustic Tree Dweller tribes living in the dense forests. Unlike most of his compatriots, he was drawn to technology because it afforded him the ability to fly at unimaginable speeds. Ordinarily based on Raddus' *Profundity*, Dillems stepped in to fill the Green Twelve slot vacated by Puck Naeco, who broke an ankle in a rough landing.

G-Force indicator and warning klaxon

Wrist-mounted comlink/ beacon

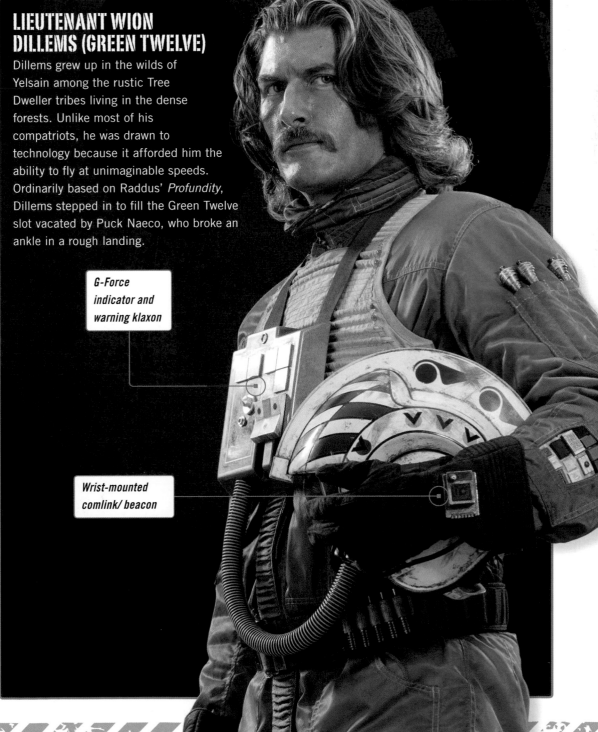

CADET PEDRIN GAUL (RED FIVE)

From Denon, Pedrin was a transport flier shuttling passengers and freight through the congested skylanes of his metropolitan homeworld. After assisting the exodus of fugitives wanted by the Empire, Gaul was branded a traitor and was forced to flee.

Signal flares in ankle belt

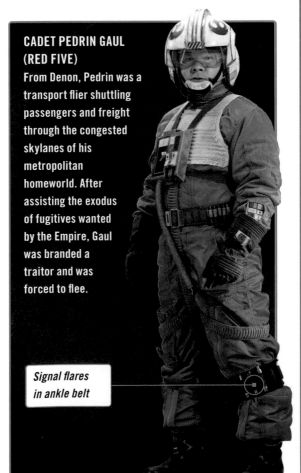

BLUE SQUADRON

GENERAL MERRICK'S PERSONAL COMMAND, Blue Squadron, is a unit expanded well beyond the usual 12 ships of the same design. It is a mix of T-65 X-wings, assigned to escort UT-60D U-wings into combat zones, and a small number of Y-wings reallocated from squadrons in neighboring sectors. The raid on Scarif is its first fully mobilized mission, with all wings scrambled for the all-out effort to assist Jyn Erso's unsanctioned Rogue One operation.

Jaldine Gerams (Blue Three) plunges her X-wing through the shield gate controlling access to the skies of Scarif.

As the fighters of Red, Green, and Gold Squadron engage the capital ship and starfighter forces in orbit above Scarif, it is Blue Squadron that is tasked with taking the battle down to the dirt. The team seizes advantage of an open shield gate that is in the midst of allowing transit to a cargo-laden transport shuttle, and streaks past the lumbering ship. Anti-starfighter point defense cannons track the fighters as they approach, but most of Blue Squadron survives this initial volley. The plan is for the U-wings that reach Scarif's Citadel beach to unload additional troops to assist the Rogue One team, while General Draven leads the X-wings in defending the infantry from incoming TIE strikers.

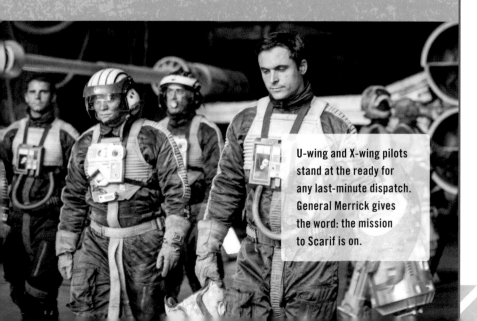

U-wing and X-wing pilots stand at the ready for any last-minute dispatch. General Merrick gives the word: the mission to Scarif is on.

HEFF TOBBER (BLUE EIGHT)

Lieutenant Heff Tobber had been stationed as a transport pilot at the rebels' Crait outpost prior to its abandonment. Upon transfer to Base One, he joined Blue Squadron, where he became one of the most popular U-wing pilots around for his sense of humor and booming voice. Unable to reach the Scarif shield gate before it closes, he peels off and joins Green Squadron in the battle above the planet. When circumstances require, Tobber also serves as an X-wing pilot.

Flight helmet with integral comlink and intercom link

PARIL RITTA (BLUE TWELVE)

Paril Ritta of Generis pilots one of four Y-wing fighters transferred from Atrivis sector to bolster the *Profundity's* starfighter forces. For the Scarif mission, he serves in Blue Squadron.

JALDINE GERAMS (BLUE THREE)

Computer specialist Gerams logged many hours in self-authored starfighter simulator programs and jumped at the opportunity to fly a real X-wing when the Alliance arrived on her homeworld of Fresia.

CALUM GRAM (BLUE NINE)
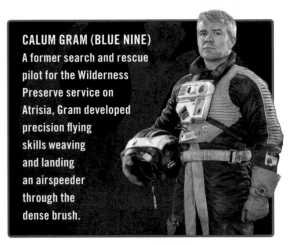
A former search and rescue pilot for the Wilderness Preserve service on Atrisia, Gram developed precision flying skills weaving and landing an airspeeder through the dense brush.

BARION RANER (BLUE FOUR)
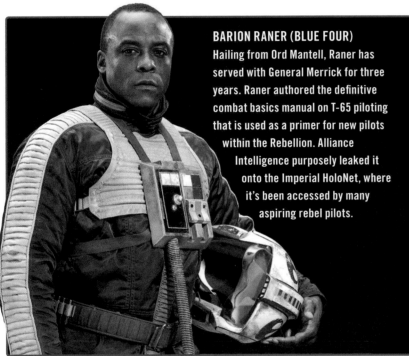
Hailing from Ord Mantell, Raner has served with General Merrick for three years. Raner authored the definitive combat basics manual on T-65 piloting that is used as a primer for new pilots within the Rebellion. Alliance Intelligence purposely leaked it onto the Imperial HoloNet, where it's been accessed by many aspiring rebel pilots.

LAREN JOMA (BLUE ELEVEN)

Warrant Officer Joma is Bistan's "delivery driver"—piloting the U-wing in which the Iakaru serves as a door gunner. Even-keeled Joma tolerates Bistan's exuberance because the "space monkey," as she jokingly nicknames him, is an unerring shot. Joma flies with a steady hand to help Bistan's aim remain true and keep everyone on board alive.

High-atmosphere specialist life support pack

FARNS MONSBEE (BLUE FIVE)
Though Monsbee works well within a squadron, he has logged more solo flying hours than the rest of his wingmates as he was the sole snubfighter pilot on the tiny, ill-supplied rebel outpost on Cassidode VI. At Yavin he often serves as a recon flier.

REBEL PILOT HELMETS

THE REBEL STARFIGHTER PILOTS assembled at Yavin 4 come from scattered cells now accumulated at the most well-supplied launch base in the growing Rebellion's history. The personalized iconography worn by pilots on their helmets occasionally identifies their unit origins, homeworlds, or beliefs. Such variation cannot be found within Imperial ranks.

Polarized plastex visor

WONA GOBAN (GOLD NINE)

ZAL DINNES (RED EIGHT)

ATTICO WRED (GREEN FOUR)

WION DILLEMS (GREEN TWELVE)

TORGE GOMMER (GREEN TWO)

CALUM GRAM (BLUE NINE)

BRACE MARKO (GOLD SIX)

Raised ridge conceals comlink antenna

ROBICH DUGGSIN (BLUE SEVEN)

PEDRIN GAUL (RED FIVE)

DATCHI CREEL (GOLD EIGHT)

BARION RANER (BLUE FOUR)

GAZDO WOOLCOB (GOLD SEVEN)

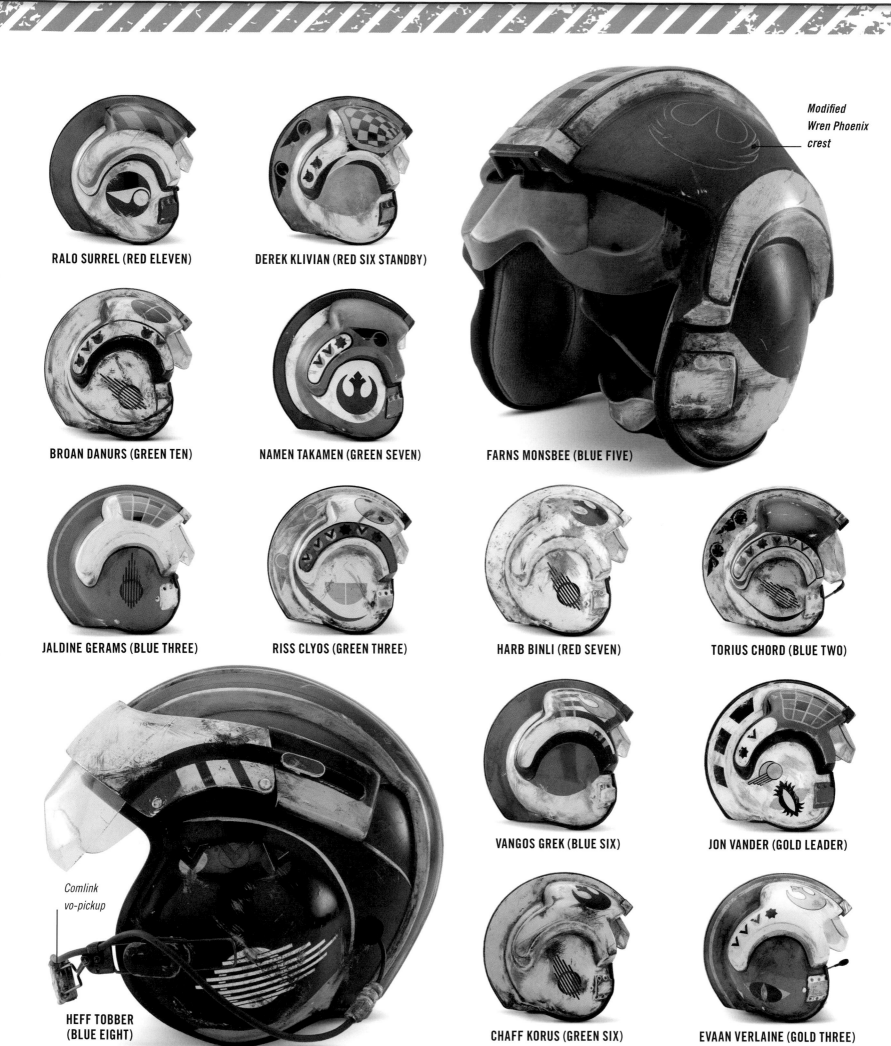

RALO SURREL (RED ELEVEN)

DEREK KLIVIAN (RED SIX STANDBY)

Modified Wren Phoenix crest

BROAN DANURS (GREEN TEN)

NAMEN TAKAMEN (GREEN SEVEN)

FARNS MONSBEE (BLUE FIVE)

JALDINE GERAMS (BLUE THREE)

RISS CLYOS (GREEN THREE)

HARB BINLI (RED SEVEN)

TORIUS CHORD (BLUE TWO)

VANGOS GREK (BLUE SIX)

JON VANDER (GOLD LEADER)

Comlink vo-pickup

HEFF TOBBER (BLUE EIGHT)

CHAFF KORUS (GREEN SIX)

EVAAN VERLAINE (GOLD THREE)

Y-WING FIGHTER

A BATTLE-TESTED DESIGN dating back to the Clone Wars, the Y-wing was one of the earliest vessels used by the fledgling Rebellion in its fight against the Empire. Their relative ease of access as outdated war surplus makes them popular with rebel forces, as do their reliable hyperdrive, sturdy construction, and powerful ordnance. The rebel group on Yavin 4 stocks its Gold Squadron entirely with Y-wing fighters, with additional units rotating into Green or Blue Squadron as needed.

Ring houses articulated vectrals that steer ion thrust for increased maneuverability

Baffled hyperdrive tachyonic exhaust port

Turbo-modified R200 starboard ion engine

Main coolant pump reservoir

Composite signal-transparent dome covers long-range targeting sensor array

DATA FILE

MANUFACTURER Koensayr Manufacturing

MODEL BTL-A4 Y-wing assault starfighter / bomber

AFFILIATION Rebel Alliance

HEIGHT 2.44m (8ft)

LENGTH 16.24m (53ft 3in)

CREW 1, plus astromech droid

ATMOSPHERIC SPEED 1,000 kph (621mph)

WEAPONS 2 laser cannons, 2 ion cannons, ordnance launcher (proton and ion torpedoes)

CLONE WARS VETERAN

Though the Y-wing boasted an excellent track record as a Clone Wars long-range bomber, the emphasis on capital ships as the backbone of the Imperial Starfleet meant the hyperdrive-equipped ship fell out of favor. Koensayr lost a major government contract, and was forced to sell its surplus to local planetary defense markets before the Empire intervened. Unsold stock and repossessed Y-wings were then destined for reclamation, where they would be scrapped for parts. The Rebellion was able to spare many Y-wings from this fate with raids that liberated the ships.

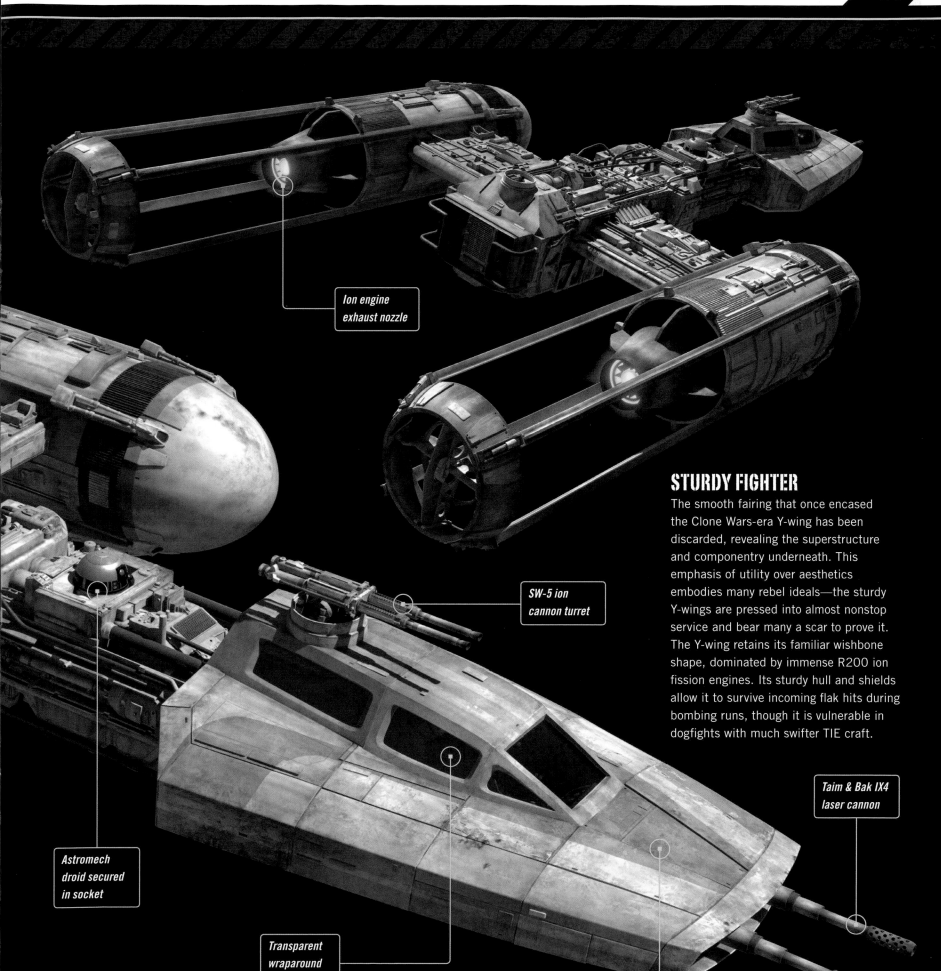

Ion engine
exhaust nozzle

SW-5 ion
cannon turret

Astromech
droid secured
in socket

Transparent
wraparound

Taim & Bak IX4
laser cannon

STURDY FIGHTER

The smooth fairing that once encased
the Clone Wars-era Y-wing has been
discarded, revealing the superstructure
and componentry underneath. This
emphasis of utility over aesthetics
embodies many rebel ideals—the sturdy
Y-wings are pressed into almost nonstop
service and bear many a scar to prove it.
The Y-wing retains its familiar wishbone
shape, dominated by immense R200 ion
fission engines. Its sturdy hull and shields
allow it to survive incoming flak hits during
bombing runs, though it is vulnerable in
dogfights with much swifter TIE craft.

TIE FIGHTER

WITH ITS RECOGNIZABLE SILHOUETTE, the TIE fighter has become the de facto symbol of Imperial space superiority. TIE fighters are inexpensive to produce, and the Empire churns them out in factories scattered across the galaxy. More than capable of enforcing Imperial law against unarmed or lightly defended civilian transports, the TIE fighter has recently begun facing a more formidable enemy in the starfighters of the Rebel Alliance.

SHORT-RANGE FIGHTERS

As capital ships are preferred for tactical discussion among the Imperial Starfleet, its starfighter units are not afforded the independence enjoyed by the equivalent rebel pilots. All but the most specialized TIE fighters lack hyperdrives, making them dependent on launch bases or carrier craft for deployment. The lack of a hyperdrive and resultant navigational systems alongside extended life support and fuel combine to cut down on the TIE's mass.

Solar gather panel energy collection hub

FIGHTER OF THE LINE
The TIE fighter's design lineage can trace roots to the Jedi interceptor flown in the late Clone Wars era, as well as the V-wing fighters that continued to fly during the early years of the Galactic Empire. The current model is designated the TIE/ln, or line edition.

Top hatch forms primary access point when not rack-mounted

DATA FILE

MANUFACTURER Sienar Fleet Systems

MODEL TIE/ln space superiority starfighter

AFFILIATION Galactic Empire

HEIGHT 8.82m (28ft 11in)

LENGTH 7.24m (23ft 9in)

CREW 1 pilot

ATMOSPHERIC SPEED 1,200kph (746mph)

WEAPONS Twin laser cannons

SHOWDOWN
At the stratostructure on top of the Scarif Citadel, Jyn Erso stares down a TIE/ln starfighter. The TIE has vertical takeoff and landing (VTOL) ability thanks to repulsorlift cyclers in its wing struts—reducing its already small mass to negligible weight—and micropositioning thrusts from the twin ion engines.

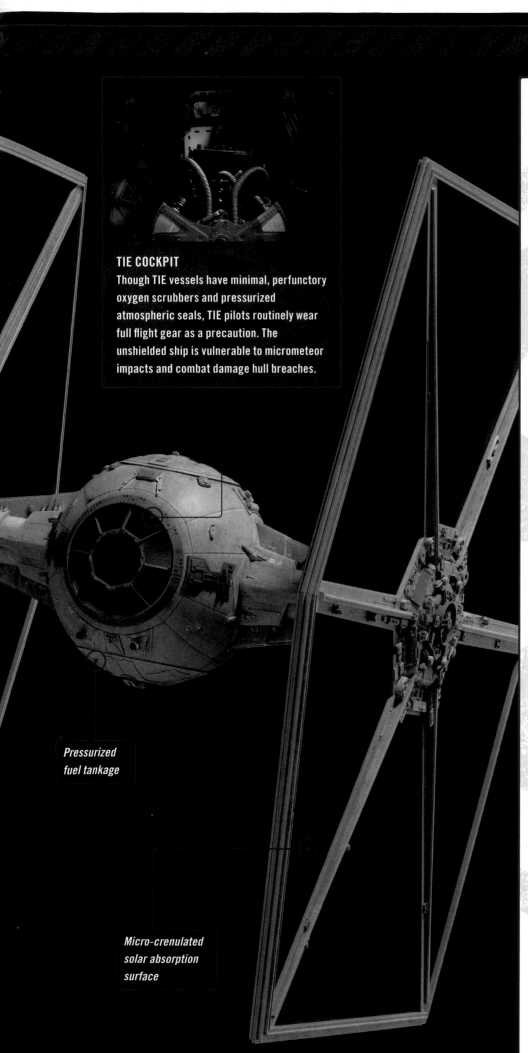

TIE COCKPIT
Though TIE vessels have minimal, perfunctory oxygen scrubbers and pressurized atmospheric seals, TIE pilots routinely wear full flight gear as a precaution. The unshielded ship is vulnerable to micrometeor impacts and combat damage hull breaches.

Pressurized fuel tankage

Micro-crenulated solar absorption surface

Reinforced helmet with gas transfer hoses

Emergency atmospheric unit

Comlink / transponder in shockproof belt case

Positive-gravity pressure boots

TIE FIGHTER PILOT
Graduates from prestigious flight academies across the galaxy undergo rigorous training and testing to become TIE pilots. The final phase of testing often occurs onboard a larger battleship, such as a Star Destroyer, in order to expose cadets to realistic and relevant surroundings. In the growing fight against the Rebellion, this means TIE cadets may undergo literal trials by fire, plunged into combat situations where to excel is to survive.

TIE/SK ATMOSPHERIC FIGHTER

TIE STRIKER

THE MILITARY DESIGN THINK TANK on Scarif is tasked with developing and testing next-generation designs, subjecting them to shakedown flights, monitoring their performance, and recommending whether or not they see more widespread deployment. The TIE striker is one such experimental design. A streamlined variant of the classic TIE fighter, the striker is specifically constructed for atmospheric patrols over Imperial ground-based installations. Though the TIE/sk is capable of suborbital flight, it is best deployed in low to high atmospheric defense capacity.

AERIAL COCKPIT
The TIE striker's enlarged cockpit houses a crew of two—the pilot and an optional bombardier/gunner. The larger hull allows for ordnance payload and increased acceleration compensator and emergency repulsor features. Though lacking a true ejection system, the striker has emergency repulsors designed to help soften crash landings.

Duplex solar gather surface / frictional heat convertors

Honeycombed titanium hull

TOP VIEW

SIDE VIEW

REPULSORLIFT FIGHTER
Though twin ion engines supply the striker with forward thrust, it has more advanced and specialized repulsorlifts for its atmospheric operations. These antigravity engines reduce the overall weight of the craft, giving the ion engines greater push.

UNUSUAL VERSATILITY
The Imperial starfleet generally frowns on versatility, believing instead that the Empire succeeds through its large number of specialized ships. The TIE striker is a bold departure from that philosophy, and is therefore unpopular among the higher ranks. Admiralty sees a distasteful indecision and wasteful expenditure in multiple design features such as the striker's atmospheric streamline, ground support cannons, tactical bombing suite, and pressurized life support. Pilots, conversely, are immediately enamored by such novelty.

Ventral bomb port (closed)

*Rigid
quadanium
steel foil brace*

*SFS L-s9.3 laser
cannon*

DATA FILE

MANUFACTURER Sienar Fleet Systems

MODEL TIE/sk x1 experimental air superiority fighter

AFFILIATION Galactic Empire

HEIGHT 2.95m (9ft 8in) **LENGTH** 17.18m (56ft 4in)

CREW 2

SPEED 1,500kph (932mph)

WEAPONS 4 fire-linked laser cannons, 2 heavy
laser cannons, proton bomb chute

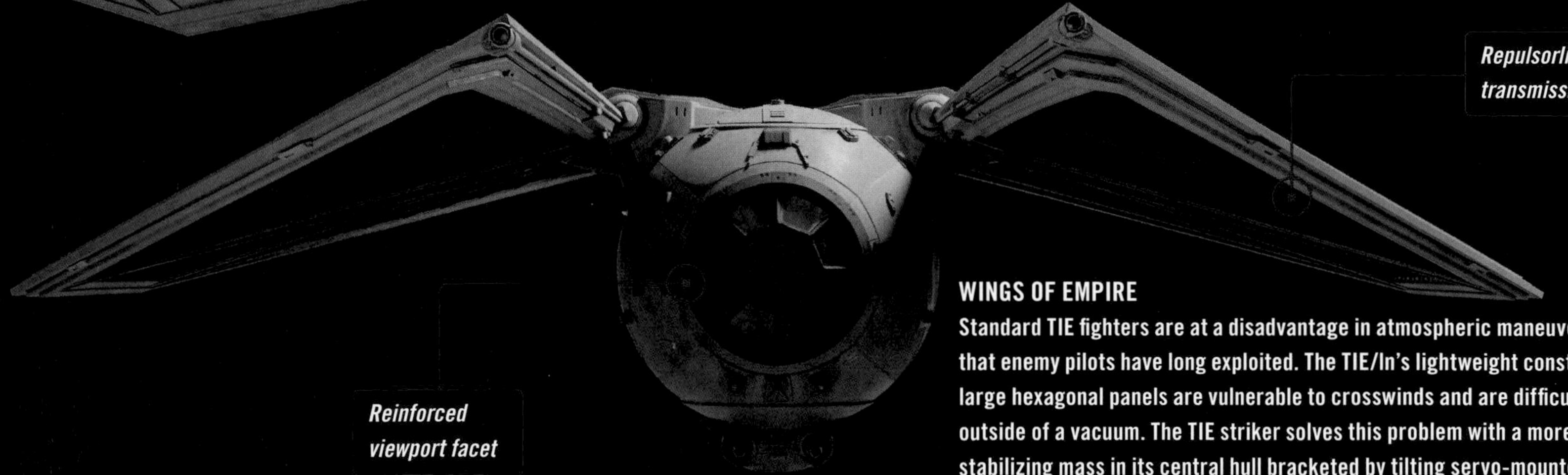

*Repulsorlift field
transmission plane*

*Reinforced
viewport facet*

WINGS OF EMPIRE

Standard TIE fighters are at a disadvantage in atmospheric maneuvers, a fact
that enemy pilots have long exploited. The TIE/ln's lightweight construction and
large hexagonal panels are vulnerable to crosswinds and are difficult to steer
outside of a vacuum. The TIE striker solves this problem with a more solid
stabilizing mass in its central hull bracketed by tilting servo-mounted wings.

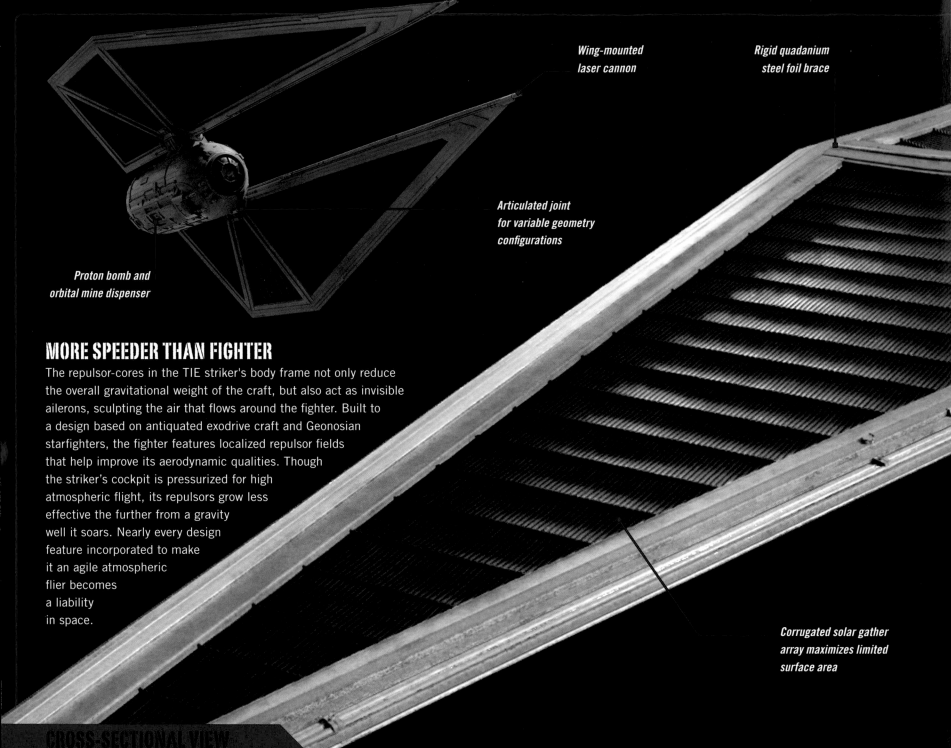

Wing-mounted laser cannon

Rigid quadanium steel foil brace

Articulated joint for variable geometry configurations

Proton bomb and orbital mine dispenser

MORE SPEEDER THAN FIGHTER

The repulsor-cores in the TIE striker's body frame not only reduce the overall gravitational weight of the craft, but also act as invisible ailerons, sculpting the air that flows around the fighter. Built to a design based on antiquated exodrive craft and Geonosian starfighters, the fighter features localized repulsor fields that help improve its aerodynamic qualities. Though the striker's cockpit is pressurized for high atmospheric flight, its repulsors grow less effective the further from a gravity well it soars. Nearly every design feature incorporated to make it an agile atmospheric flier becomes a liability in space.

Corrugated solar gather array maximizes limited surface area

CROSS-SECTIONAL VIEW

TIE/SK FIGHTER

STARFIGHTER PILOTS refer to atmospheres as "goo"—a derisive reference to the drag experienced in suborbital flight. Although it is a different discipline, in-air combat draws upon the same core strengths of tenacity, reflexes, and daring as space combat. TIE pilot culture has pitted atmospheric fliers against space-based pilots in a never-ending contest of dominance. Striker pilots tend to call fighter pilots "vac-heads," while fighter pilots retaliate with "ground hogs."

ATTACK MODE

Unusual for a TIE-series craft, the striker's solar panel is articulated. The upward configuration is meant to maximize VTOL (vertical takeoff and landing) capability, increasing lift for rapid ascent or descent. The horizontal configuration is built for linear velocity, transforming the TIE striker into a blazingly fast dart exceeding speeds of 1,500 kilometers per hour. The fighter is remarkably well armed, with a pair of fixed heavier cannons to provide ground support and anti-armor fire. The wingtip mounted cannons are rapid-fire and well designed for aerial combat.

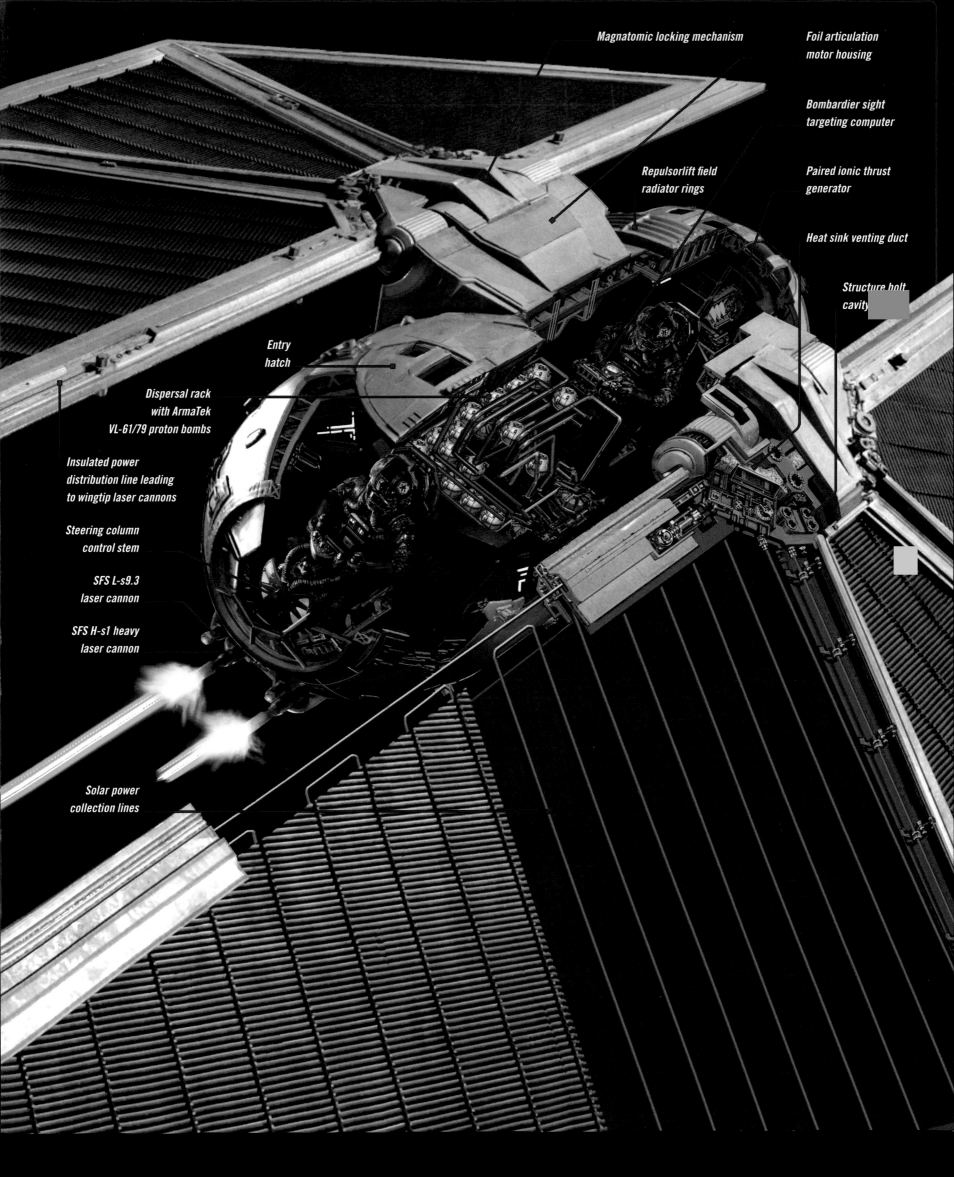

Magnatomic locking mechanism

Foil articulation
motor housing

Bombardier sight
targeting computer

Paired ionic thrust
generator

Repulsorlift field
radiator rings

Heat sink venting duct

Structure bolt
cavity

Entry
hatch

Dispersal rack
with ArmaTek
VL-61/79 proton bombs

Insulated power
distribution line leading
to wingtip laser cannons

Steering column
control stem

SFS L-s9.3
laser cannon

SFS H-s1 heavy
laser cannon

Solar power
collection lines

THE *PROFUNDITY*

THE PEACEFUL MON CALAMARI learned harsh and costly lessons during the Clone Wars. So when the Empire brought them more subjugation, the aquatic race was ready. A launch of spaceworthy structures that the Empire mistook to be city buildings heralded a mass exodus from the watery world to safer shoals in the depths of space. The Mon Calamari took to converting these transports and passenger liners into capital ships, with Admiral Raddus' *Profundity* one of the first ready for battle.

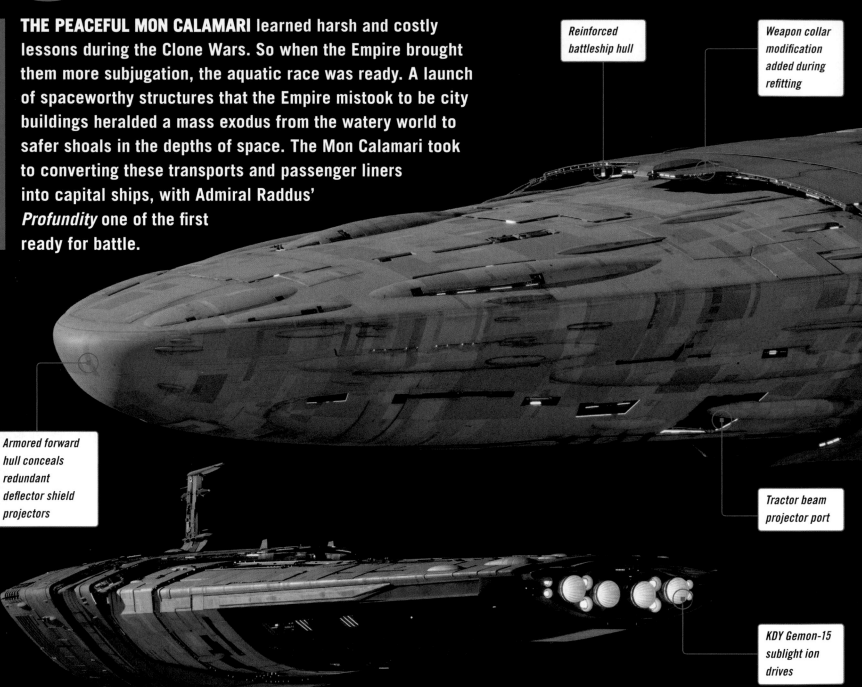

Reinforced battleship hull

Weapon collar modification added during refitting

Armored forward hull conceals redundant deflector shield projectors

Tractor beam projector port

KDY Gemon-15 sublight ion drives

SUBLIGHT DRIVES
12 repurposed Kuat Drive Yards sublight thrusters propel the massive warship *Profundity* through realspace, giving it the cruising speed required to stay apace with its escorting swarm of starfighters.

Armored outrigger fin holds bridge pod

THE MON CALAMARI
Pre-war, the *Profundity* was the civic governance tower of Nystullum—an underwater city beneath the northern ice floes of the planet. Much of the crew consists of the city's defense staff, led by its former mayor—and now fleet commander—Admiral Raddus.

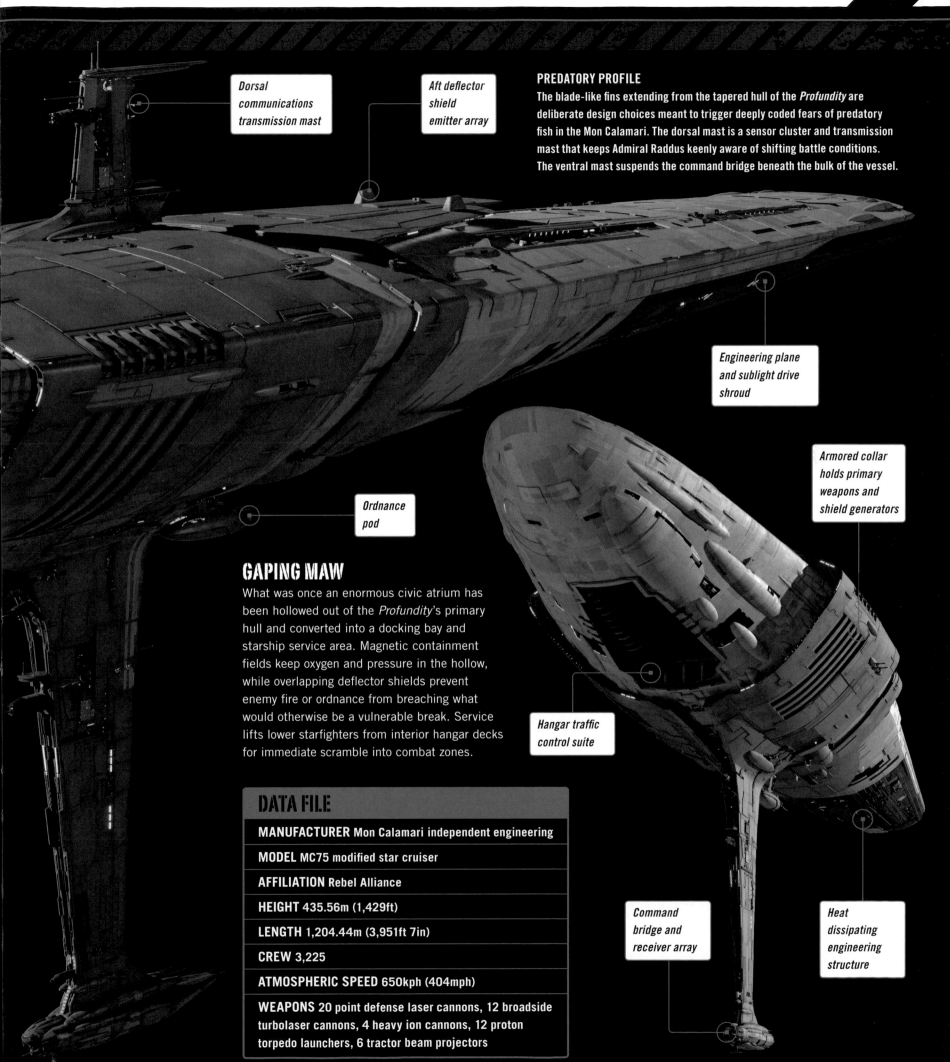

Dorsal communications transmission mast

Aft deflector shield emitter array

PREDATORY PROFILE

The blade-like fins extending from the tapered hull of the *Profundity* are deliberate design choices meant to trigger deeply coded fears of predatory fish in the Mon Calamari. The dorsal mast is a sensor cluster and transmission mast that keeps Admiral Raddus keenly aware of shifting battle conditions. The ventral mast suspends the command bridge beneath the bulk of the vessel.

Engineering plane and sublight drive shroud

Armored collar holds primary weapons and shield generators

Ordnance pod

GAPING MAW

What was once an enormous civic atrium has been hollowed out of the *Profundity*'s primary hull and converted into a docking bay and starship service area. Magnetic containment fields keep oxygen and pressure in the hollow, while overlapping deflector shields prevent enemy fire or ordnance from breaching what would otherwise be a vulnerable break. Service lifts lower starfighters from interior hangar decks for immediate scramble into combat zones.

Hangar traffic control suite

DATA FILE

MANUFACTURER Mon Calamari independent engineering

MODEL MC75 modified star cruiser

AFFILIATION Rebel Alliance

HEIGHT 435.56m (1,429ft)

LENGTH 1,204.44m (3,951ft 7in)

CREW 3,225

ATMOSPHERIC SPEED 650kph (404mph)

WEAPONS 20 point defense laser cannons, 12 broadside turbolaser cannons, 4 heavy ion cannons, 12 proton torpedo launchers, 6 tractor beam projectors

Command bridge and receiver array

Heat dissipating engineering structure

SIZE COMPARISON

COMBAT VESSELS ARE CATEGORIZED in scales, with labels depending on specific schools of thought and battle tactics. Until the birth of the Death Star, "capital" scale ships were the largest unit-type to be factored into combat strategies. This class of warship grew throughout the Clone Wars, with the Imperial ships of the line stretching to over a kilometer long. Though capital ship vessels are, according to Imperial military doctrine, only threatened by vessels of the same class, the Rebel Alliance is seeing increasing success with surgical strikes launched from their starfighters. Whether or not similar success can be had against something as gargantuan as a Death Star remains to be seen.

1 The *Profundity* Length: 1,204.44m (3,951ft 7in)
2 Imperial Star Destroyer Length: 1,600m (5,280ft)
3 Imperial cargo shuttle Length: 35.50m (116ft 5in)
4 Imperial TIE fighter Height: 8.82m (29ft)
5 Imperial *Delta*-class shuttle Height: 32.23m (105ft 8in)
6 Rebel X-wing starfighter Length: 13.40m (44ft)
7 Imperial combat assault tank Length: 7.30m (24ft)
8 Rebel Y-wing starfighter Length: 16.24m (53ft 3in)
9 Rebel U-wing gunship/transport Length: 24.98m (82ft)
10 Imperial TIE striker Length: 17.18m (56ft 4in)
11 Imperial AT-ACT walker Height: 34.90m (114ft 6in)
12 Imperial AT-ST walker Height: 9.04m (29ft 8in)

UNTHINKABLE SCALE
Even the massive Imperial Star Destroyers are mere specks when compared to the enormous size of the Death Star. Warships clear the way for the battle station's prime weapon to be fitted.

0m 2m 4m 6m 8m 10m

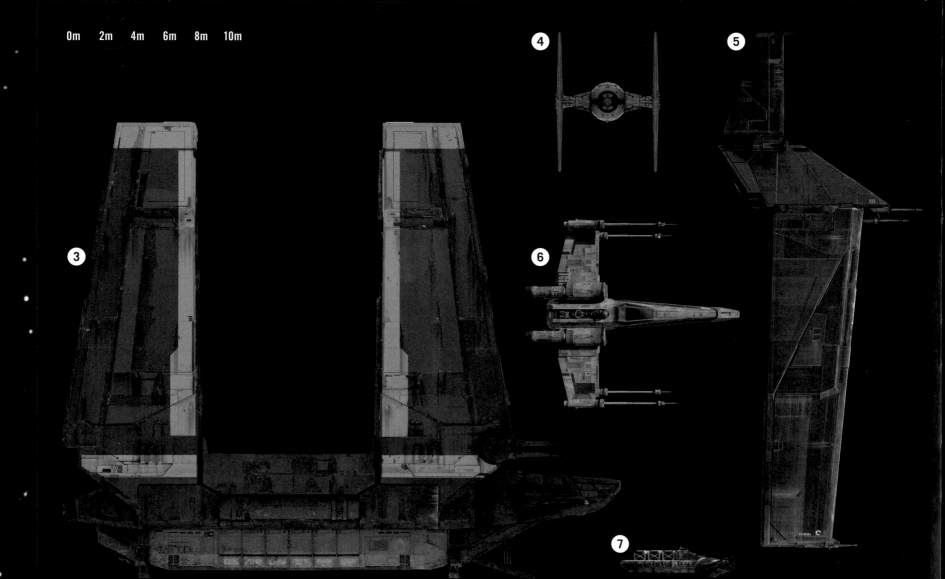

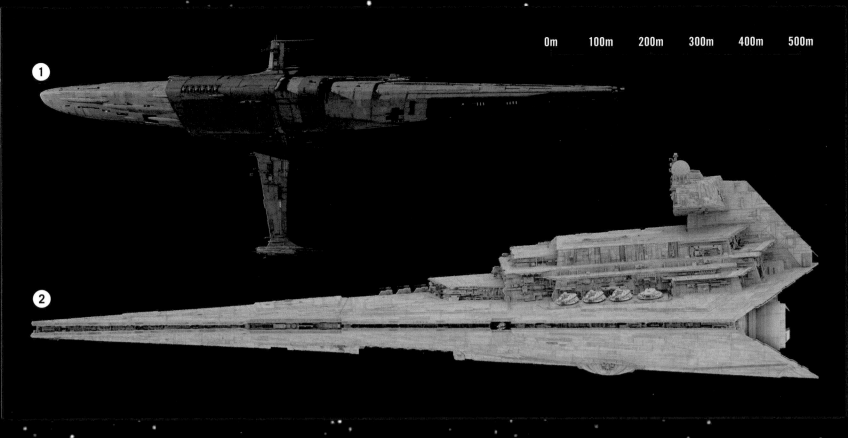

0m   100m   200m   300m   400m   500m

1

2

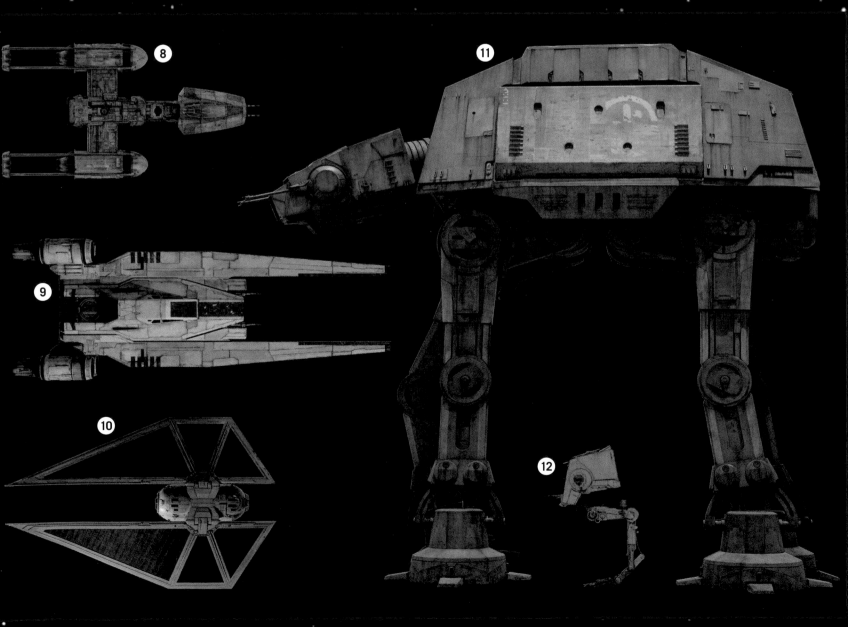

8

9

10

11

12

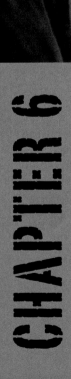

CHAPTER 6

A STAR WARS STORY

With *Rogue One: A Star Wars Story*, Lucasfilm Ltd. embarked on an unprecedented new format for big screen *Star Wars* storytelling. From the start, the idea was irresistible when condensed to its most basic form: "the story of the rebels who stole the Death Star plans." Constructing that story for the screen required relying on the best of Lucasfilm traditions as well as a bold new vision.

CONCEPT ART

BY TRADITION, long before a *Star Wars* tale is finalized, the director unleashes a team of concept artists to imagine possibilities without restraint. It is here that a steady stream of ideas—some feasible, some decidedly less so—emerge to help shape and steer the storyline. Production designers Doug Chiang and Neil Lamont led teams on either side of the Atlantic Ocean, in San Francisco and at Pinewood Studios respectively, to imagine heroes, villains, aliens, technology, and settings that would, after a lengthy process of winnowing, make their way into *Rogue One: A Star Wars Story*.

MISSION TO EADU
An earlier iteration of the story set Eadu as the first mission undertaken by the team. In this incarnation, "Sergeant Jyn Erso" was a seasoned rebel agent—hence the hashmarks on her helmet in this artwork by John McCoy. The illustration features Jyn on a multi-prong U-wing insertion into the occluded world of Eadu.

SPACE MONKEY
Costume concept artist Adam Brockbank produced this early incarnation of the primate door gunner, affectionately known in preproduction as "Space Monkey" (later named Bistan). From the start, this character was to exude a primitive, primal energy.

ENSEMBLE TEAM
The *Rogue One* story was always intended to revolve around an ensemble crew undertaking a heist-focused military mission. This art, by Jon McCoy, envisions most of the team—Baze, Chirrut, K-2, Jyn, and Cassian—in the stark landscape of Jedha.

HOLY CITY
Matt Allsopp's exploration of the mesa-top Holy City of Jedha used Middle Eastern architecture as a starting point for design. The location would come to represent the ideals of a Jedi in a film devoid of their presence.

TANK PATROL
Kevin Jenkins' illustration shows an Imperial patrol, complete with armored hovercraft. When realized in production, this armored vehicle retained its caterpillar tracks, losing the adjective "hover" from its description.

IN PRODUCTION

PINEWOOD STUDIOS became the hub for the production of *Rogue One: A Star Wars Story*. Located 32 kilometers (20 miles) outside central London, Pinewood is a storied film studio, made famous as the place where the legendary James Bond lived out most of his larger-than-life adventures. Lucasfilm secured a lengthy agreement to make Pinewood the production base for future *Star Wars* projects and, as *Rogue One* underwent production, *The Force Awakens* was wrapping up, and *Star Wars: Episode VIII* was beginning preproduction. The community of *Star Wars* filmmaking creatives grew with each passing month.

TIES IN ACTION
Many of the code names for *Rogue One* were inspired by the historical Cold War. As such, the Empire was given "communist" nomenclature, with TIE fighters described as "MiGs," named after Soviet aircraft. Here, a digital camera captures the cramped confines of a TIE cockpit.

SPACE MONKEY TESTS
Director Gareth Edwards closely examined each new creation to emerge from the creature shop of Neal Scanlan, to gauge each alien's star potential. "Space Monkey"—known for months by its production code indicator of "G007"—was an early standout. Using a slip-on mask filled with servo-driven articulation, Space Monkey became an ensemble performance from Nick Kellington (the man under the mask) and the remote control operators driving his expressions.

DROID AUDITION
The cryptic code names adopted for the production labeled the various *Rogue One* droid characters as "senators," and this homestead droid—code-named "S001"— was one of the earliest creations. It was realized as a practical rod puppet shot on location in Iceland, with its performers digitally removed from the final shot.

GEARING UP

The prop department manufactured an arsenal of rebel and Imperial small-arms. Many were built around Airsoft guns to produce realistic recoil and interaction cues for the performers carrying them.

STANDING BY

With the mantra to capture original trilogy elements "how you remember it," fighter pilots wore polished flightsuits, rather than the dyed boiler suits seen in the original 1977 *Star Wars* movie.

TRADITIONAL PLAYER

A veteran of three *Star Wars* movies, Warwick Davis returned for *Rogue One*, once again playing a character whose name starts with "W"—Weeteef Cyu-Bee.

CAPTURING MOROFF

Hairy Moroff (played by Ian Whyte) started out as a rebel character named Senna before ending up as a background character in Saw's militia. Here, the creature character (coded GO3O) stands before an array of photogrammic analysis cameras that capture every possible angle for future effects and product use.

THE SHOOT

CAMERAS ON *ROGUE ONE: A STAR WARS STORY* began rolling in the summer of 2015. Director Gareth Edwards favored a dynamic shooting style, with many sequences being "caught" by handheld cameras as if in the thick of spontaneous action. To best facilitate this seemingly wild, yet methodical, approach, the production used digital cameras for maximum flexibility and shooting time. Crewmembers would in some cases dress as extras, so that takes that might accidentally capture a stagehand or gaffer could still be used.

LED HYPERSPACE

To best capture the cinema verité documentary style that Edwards favored, many of the effects-heavy sequences benefited from large-scale LEDs. These projected pre-rendered visuals of postproduction effects work—lending the production authentic performance and lighting cues.

BEACHFRONT ACTION

The tropical landscape of Scarif was created in the decidedly non-tropical Bovingdon, north of London. Sand and imported palm trees helped frame the landing field where the *Rogue One* team would infiltrate Imperial headquarters, but the full landscape would be realized by digital set extensions created by Industrial Light & Magic (ILM).

THE REAL DEAL

Intense battlefield action captured on location in the Maldives filled out the Scarif sequences. Rebels and Imperials faced off in the shallow seawater surrounding the spectacular reefs.

CAPTURING K-2SO

Throughout production, actor Alan Tudyk wore a specially printed motion-capture suit to translate his movements into what would drive the computer-generated character of K-2SO. To bring Alan up to K-2's two-meter (seven-foot) height, he played most of his scenes wearing stilts.

PINEWOOD BACKLOT

The Pinewood backlot became the Holy City of Jedha after an extensive set build. Street blocks and intersections filled most of the frame, with set extensions painstakingly created by ILM to fully realize the ancient city.

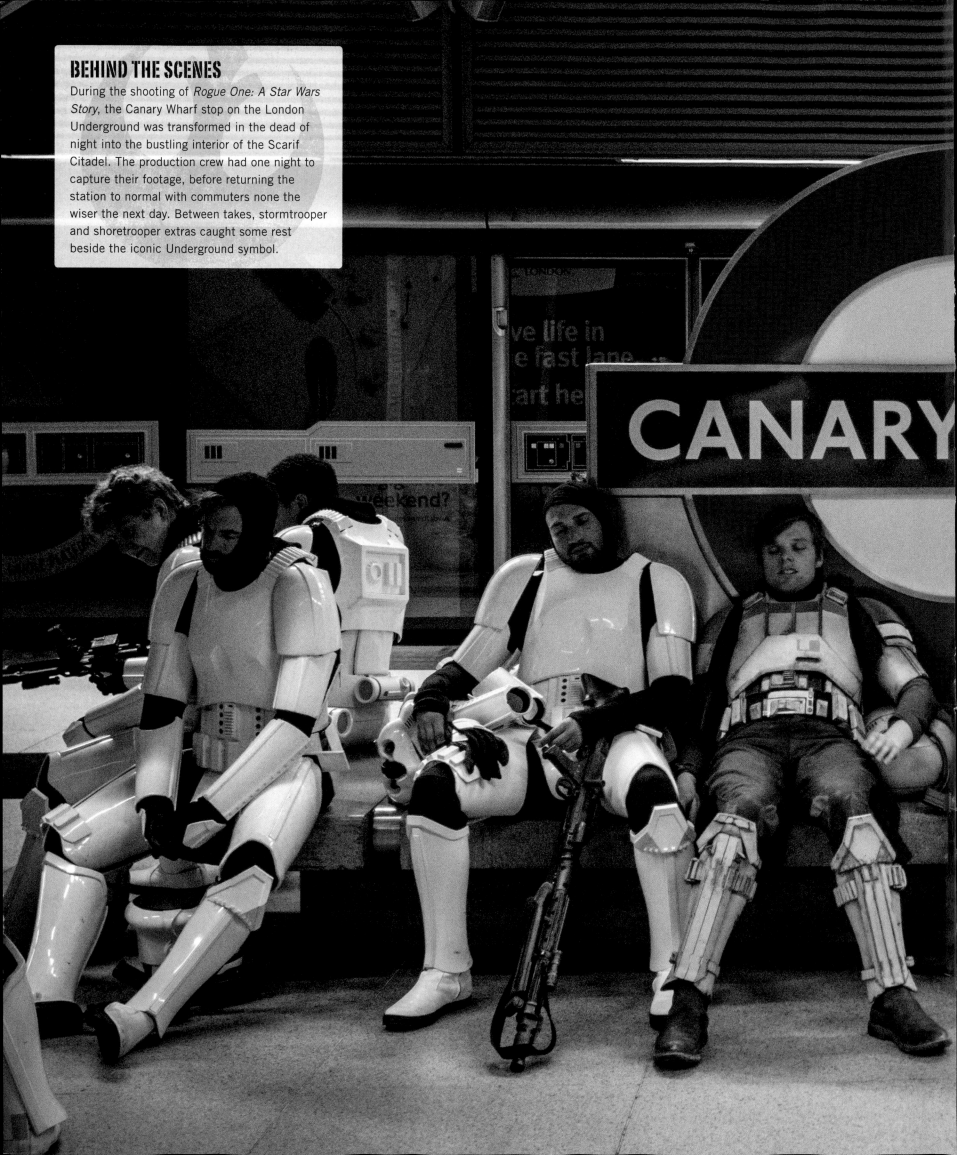

BEHIND THE SCENES

During the shooting of *Rogue One: A Star Wars Story*, the Canary Wharf stop on the London Underground was transformed in the dead of night into the bustling interior of the Scarif Citadel. The production crew had one night to capture their footage, before returning the station to normal with commuters none the wiser the next day. Between takes, stormtrooper and shoretrooper extras caught some rest beside the iconic Underground symbol.

CANARY

Jubilee line
Westbound
platform 1

INDEX

Main entries are in **bold**

Penguin Random House

Senior Editor Emma Grange
Senior Designer Owen Bennett
Creative Technical Support Tom Morse, Andy Bishop
Pre-production Producer Marc Staples
Senior Producer Mary Slater
Managing Editor Sadie Smith
Managing Art Editor Ron Stobbart
Art Director Lisa Lanzarini
Publisher Julie Ferris
Publishing Director Simon Beecroft

For Lucasfilm
Editor Samantha Holland
Senior Editor Frank Parisi
Image Unit Newell Todd, Gabrielle Levenson,
Erik Sanchez, Bryce Pinkos, and Tim Mapp
Associate Technical Director Cameron Beck
Story Group Leland Chee, Pablo Hidalgo, and Matt Martin
Creative Director of Publishing Michael Siglain

First American Edition, 2016
Published in the United States by DK Publishing
345 Hudson Street, New York, NY 10014

ACKNOWLEDGMENTS

Pablo Hidalgo: For keeping me in the loop during all steps of *Rogue One's* production, thanks to John Swartz. My gratitude to Simon Emanuel and Allison Shearmur for extending warm invitations to the set to get a close look, and to Vanessa Davies for showing me around. For a seat at the table during development, thank you to Gareth Edwards, Gary Whitta, Chris Weitz, and Tony Gilroy. I have to thank John Knoll for starting this Death Star-sized ball rolling, and thanks to Hal Hickel, Vick Schutz, and the many talented artists at ILM for their work. Thanks to DK, the Lucasfilm Story Group, and the image teams at LFL for making this book possible, with special thanks to Sammy Holland. And, as always, thank you, Kristen.

Kemp Remillard: I'd like to thank Owen Bennett, Cameron Beck, Pablo Hidalgo, Samantha Holland, Chris Medley-Pole, Frank Parisi, Emma Grange, Simon Beecroft, Sadie Smith, Ron Stobbart, Claire Morrison, and all the fine people at DK Publishing and Lucasfilm that made this book possible. Also a galaxy-sized thank you to my family and friends for all the support.

DK Publishing: We would like to thank Kathleen Kennedy, John Swartz, John Knoll, Brian Miller, and Natalie Kocekian at Lucasfilm for their assistance with the creation of this book—with special thanks to Frank Parisi and Samantha Holland. Additional thanks to Rob Perry and Chris Gould for design work, David Fentiman for editorial help, and Julia March for proofreading and for the index.

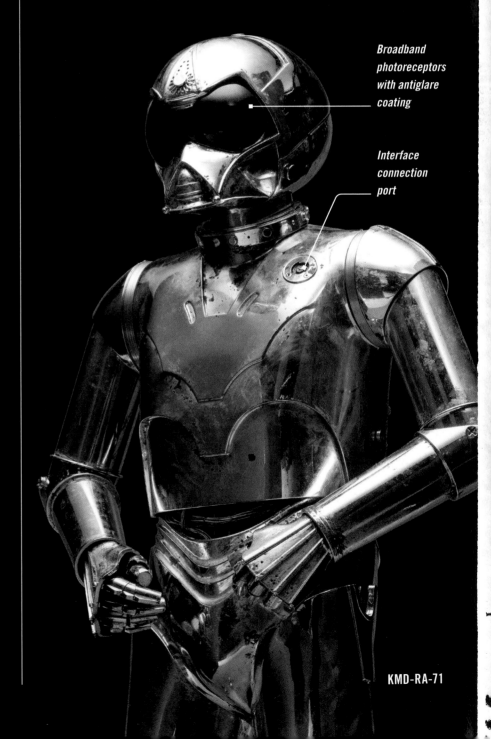

Broadband photoreceptors with antiglare coating

Interface connection port

KMD-RA-71